TWENTIETH CENTURY VIEWS

The aim of this series is to present the best in contemporary critical opinion on major authors, providing a twentieth century perspective on their changing status in an era of profound revaluation.

Maynard Mack, *Series Editor*
Yale University

L O R C A

A COLLECTION OF CRITICAL ESSAYS

Edited by

Manuel Duran

A SPECTRUM BOOK

Prentice-Hall, Inc., *Englewood Cliffs, N.J.*

Permission to use and to translate Lorca's poems has graciously been granted by New Directions for the Estate of Federico García Lorca.

Third printing ...... August, 1965

© 1962 BY PRENTICE-HALL, INC.

ENGLEWOOD CLIFFS, N.J.

LIBRARY OF CONGRESS CATALOG CARD NO.: 62-13724

Printed in the United States of America

54063-C

To My Wife

Table of Contents

INTRODUCTION—*Manuel Duran*   1

FEDERICO GARCÍA LORCA—*William Carlos Williams*   18

LORCA—*J. B. Trend*   27

LORCA AND THE EXPRESSION OF THE SPANISH ESSENCE—
Dámaso Alonso   50

A POET CRAZY ABOUT COLOR—*Louis Parrot*   57

THE EARLY POEMS—*Roy Campbell*   65

TRIUMPH OF SENSUAL REALITY—MATURE VERSE—*Edwin
Honig*   80

LORCA AND THE POETRY OF DEATH—*Pedro Salinas*   100

THE RITUAL SACRIFICE IN LORCA'S *POET IN NEW YORK*—
Richard Saez   108

LYRICAL PRIMITIVISM: GARCÍA LORCA'S *ROMANCERO GI-
TANO*—*Juan López-Morillas*   130

LORCA'S THEATER—*Angel del Rio*   140

HUMOR IN THE PLAYS OF FEDERICO GARCÍA LORCA—*Susan
Smith Blackburn*   155

DON PERLIMPLÍN: LORCA'S THEATER-POETRY—*Francis
Fergusson*   167

Chronology of Important Dates   177

Notes on the Editor and Authors   178

Selected Bibliography   180

Introduction

by Manuel Duran

It is curious and significant that we find it still difficult to "see" Lorca clearly, to analyze in detail his personality and the meaning of his creative work. (Even the photographs that remain of him have a certain fuzzy quality.) Symbol of Spain and of all things Spanish, compared to Lope de Vega by Dámaso Alonso because of his direct and profound understanding of the popular idiom, acclaimed outside Spain and in his own country as the embodiment of the Spanish spirit, he nevertheless could state a few days before his death that he was "a brother of all men" and that he detested the Spaniard who was only a Spaniard. The very Lorca who was said to be "the perfect Spaniard" and who deemed it impossible to live outside the borders of his country stated in his magazine, *Gallo*, that his group acknowledged the influence of "Picasso, Gris, Ozenfant, Chirico, Joan Miró, Lipchitz, Brancusi, Arp, Le Corbusier, Reverdy, Tristan Tzara, Paul Eluard, Aragon, Robert Desnos, Jean Cocteau, Stravinsky, Maritain, Raynal, Zervos, André Breton, etc., etc." This manifesto was signed by Dalí, Montanya and Gasch, but Lorca approved it; either he was well aware of international artistic trends or he "felt" them intuitively and by and large accepted them.

We know of course that Lorca, like all—or almost all—poets, loved both liberty and mystery. Liberty helped him avoid being classified too narrowly; mystery enabled him to escape from indiscreet eyes. Both helped him to delve into things. The friend and ally of the "daimon," enchanted by "dark sounds" and the wavering lines of his own sketches, he could exasperate any professional pigeonholer by proclaiming that he was simultaneously a "Catholic, communist, anarchist, liberal, conservative, and monarchist." Even the most definite circumstances of his life and the details of his assassination (despite the research of Gerald Brenan, the more or less fantastic reconstruction of Claude Couffon, and the interpretation of Jean-Louis Schonberg with its disagreeable insistence on the theme of a "vengeance among homosexuals") remain nebulous, uncertain, *of necessity* incomplete.[1] "I am of the kingdom of Granada," Lorca once asserted to an offensive fellow who was quizzing him on his background in a café of Barcelona. Not of the province, but of the "kingdom"—an historic, fabulous, mythical region. And in one of his most famous poems, "Reyerta," in the *Gypsy Ballads*, he describes a struggle in an Andalusian field of today in words that transcend the present, that take us to a past time outside the bounds of history, immobilizing the fury of men in a "no man's land" that is timeless and forever buried in the inner recesses of an unapproachable fastness:

> Gentlemen, village police,
> nothing unusual is happening here.
> Four Romans have died
> and five Carthaginians.

In like manner, he shows his intuitive grasp of the barren complexities of the modern world, of the inarticulate existence of the "lonely crowds" in New York. Many poets of his generation, and of his group, left Spain, but in no other is the understanding of a foreign and "exotic" culture (as that of New York was for Lorca) so penetrating and so complete. England left its trace in the poetry of Cernuda, and Mexico in his prose. Juan Ramón Jiménez has recorded his impressions of Florida in the *Ballads of Coral Gables*. In Pedro Salinas we find the imprint of New England (*El desnudo impecable* [*The Impeccable Nude*]), of New York ("Civitas Dei" in *El contemplado*), and of Puerto Rico. But these are echoes, mere echoes. In none of these works can we find the amorphous masses of the great modern metropolis—altogether alien to the mystic, serious, and familiar Granada of Lorca's youth and also to the busy and gay city of Madrid that he knew later in life—portrayed so completely as in Lorca's interpretation of New York. Anchored to the village, to tradition, to the provinces, Lorca was, nevertheless, wholly and authentically antiprovincial. His goal was to rise above Granada, above gypsy folklore, Andalusia, Madrid, even Spain, to go from one extreme to the other, faithful in his own way, betraying no one (including himself) and nothing around him. Lorca was a bridge suspended between two distant shores, between, let us say, the obscure, traditional myths of his province and the international dream worlds of French Surrealism. His work touches now one shore, now another, and the abyss between them trembles in the feverish lines of his poetry.

[1] On Lorca's death, see J.-L. Schonberg, *Garcia Lorca. L'Homme—l'oeuvre* (Paris: Plon ed., 1956), chap. vi, "Viznar."

See also Gerald Brenan, *The Face of Spain* (New York: Farrar, Straus, and Cudahy, Inc., 1951), pp. 127-147; Claude Couffon, "Ce que fut la mort de Federico García Lorca," *Le Figaro littéraire* (Paris), August 18, 1951; Cipriano Rivas Cherif, "Poesía y drama del Gran Federico," *Excelsior* (Mexico), January 7, 1957, p. 7; F. Vázquez Ocaña, *Garcia Lorca: vida, cántico y muerte* (Mexico: Atlante, 1957); Hugh Thomas, *The Spanish Civil War* (New York: Harper & Brothers, 1961), pp. 169, 170 fn., 608.

Born in 1898 at Fuente Vaqueros, a small village west of Granada, he studied first at Almería, a nearby seaport, and later at the University of Granada, where he studied law and began a course in "Philosophy and Letters," which in 1920 he continued at the University of Madrid. His father was a successful farmer, quite wealthy by local standards; his mother had been a schoolteacher. The family manor boasted a library. Yet it was music that first interested Lorca: the great composer De Falla became his respected friend and adviser, almost his idol. Lorca was a precocious child, and in spite of a disease that seems to have affected his walk and speech during his early years he developed into a gifted pianist, a talkative and vivacious adolescent, a mimic intent upon satirizing friends and acquaintances, a voracious if undisciplined reader. At Granada he had met and impressed Fernando de los Rios, professor at the University and important political figure who was to become his mentor. Following de los Rios' advice, he left for Madrid in 1919. Within a short time he had acquired a reputation as a poet, a gifted conversationalist, a musician of talent, and even a painter. He lived at the *Residencia de Estudiantes,* a Spanish version of an Oxford college where the atmosphere was serious, learned, cosmopolitan. Some of the most distinguished lecturers from other countries, such as Paul Valéry and Sir Arthur Eddington, came to talk there. His new friends included Gerardo Diego, the poet, Luis Buñuel, who was to become a great film director, Salvador Dalí. Lorca and his group often met at cafés, taverns, and night clubs. But Lorca also found time to work. In 1921 he published his *Libro de poemas*; in 1927 he scored a dramatic success for the first time with *Mariana Pineda* and held a show of colored drawings in Barcelona; in 1928 he published the first edition of the *Gypsy Ballads*, which made him famous overnight. In this same year he founded and edited an avant-garde magazine, *Gallo*, published in Granada, which unfortunately went out of business after only two issues. In 1929 and 1930 he traveled through the United States and Cuba. He was in the throes of an emotional crisis, the nature of which has never been fully revealed, and his friend and adviser, Fernando de los Rios, arranged his stay at Columbia University. He came back to a Spain on the verge of a political change: in 1931 the King fled, the Republic was proclaimed. He plunged feverishly into his work, turning his attention to the stage, founding a theater group, traveling overseas again in 1933 and 1934, to Buenos Aires and Montevideo, where he produced mainly classical Spanish plays. Upon his return he settled in Madrid and devoted himself to writing plays.

Several biographers have left us portraits or sketches of Lorca as he was in those days of maturity that preceded his death. Schonberg writes:

Federico was ugly, with an ugliness much more beautiful than a banal beauty; his appearance was that of an Andalusian peasant of average height, large, massive, with eyes of night, quick, splendid, and radiating intelligence. His complexion was sallow and his expression changing. The hair was raven-black, the forehead too heavy, the cheekbones prominent. He radiated sympathy and exuberant gaiety. When he sang at the piano, emotion transfigured his rough-hewn face.[2]

Neruda exclaims: "He was a physical flash of lightning, a force in perpetual motion, a jubilation, a splendor, a wholly superhuman charm. His being was magical and golden; happiness poured out of him." [3] And Sebastián Gasch: "What sincere laughter: luminous, cordial, half naive, half picaresque; what a fiery temperament, spontaneous and even savage; what a way to talk and talk till dawn. Each sentence was an idea, each word a verse." [4]

The main impression he created was undoubtedly expressed in one single word: charm. But it is too simple a word, and we should at least try to analyze some of the ingredients of Lorca's charm. He was certainly warmhearted and generous, witty and talkative. He could improvise a song about almost any subject. He could also communicate through music: an excellent pianist, he would play and sing for hours. Painting was a favorite pastime with him, or rather drawing. He could do it anywhere: on a café table, on the back of a menu, in a letter. He had become thoroughly familiar with certain subjects, such as Spanish folklore, art, and literature, and could talk about them for hours, but, being both intelligent and sensitive, he ordinarily took care not to monopolize the conversation. Herschel Brickell, who knew him well, speaks of his youthful enthusiasm combined with a curious childishness, deep understanding of the Spanish soul, and avant-garde sophistication: Lorca was for him an "ageless Merlin," a charmer, a sorcerer who had delved into the abysses of evil and flown over heavenly spaces.

In July 1936 Lorca left Madrid for Granada. The political situation was extremely tense in the Spanish capital after the murder of the Rightist politician Calvo Sotelo; a military coup seemed imminent. The province seemed calmer. Moreover, Lorca wanted to celebrate his saint's day, San Federico, with his family. The revolt against the Republic began on July 17 in Spanish Morocco, then spread rapidly over many parts of Spain. Lorca took refuge with the Rosales family. He was a good friend of the poet Luis Rosales, whose house was the headquarters of the Falangist movement in Granada. To no avail: a few days later (August 18) a squad arrested him there. He was shot on the dawn of the following day. His body lies in an unmarked grave, probably at Viznar, in the mountains, a few miles from Granada. Lorca's murder created a wave of shocked indignation around the world. In a century hardened by crime and violence his death is still unforgotten. His fame

[2] Schonberg, *op. cit.*, p. 25.
[3] In the magazine *Hora de España* (Valencia), II, 1937, p. 65.
[4] F. García Lorca, *Cartas a sus amigos,* with a preface by Sebastián Gasch (Barcelona: Cobalt, 1950).

grew rapidly. He was first a name, then a symbol. When the readers discovered the poet and the dramatist behind the symbol, his lasting influence became assured.

Lorca began his poetic career as a post-romantic, a sensitive and melancholy disciple of Juan Ramón Jiménez, the great Andalusian Symbolist whose intimate style and refined sensitivity was to mark a generation. He ended his career as a dramatist increasingly conscious of the need to rid his work of the lyrical ballast that slowed the rhythm of his first plays and delayed the development of plot. About halfway in the evolution of his work come the *Gypsy Ballads* and *Poet in New York*. *Gypsy Ballads* no longer shows the influence of Juan Ramón Jiménez; the lyrical elements of folklore, tradition, myth, are transformed by dramatic situations and reworked in a new, bold style often inspired by avant-garde images and subconscious associations. *Poet in New York* is the product of a critical period, spent in America, an interval of solitude during which Lorca was to find the key to his stage career, the formula for his plays. These two books, *Poet in New York* and *Gypsy Ballads*, are quite dissimilar. They differ in subject and in style. Yet in both the result is attained by the fusion of "something old and something new." In the *Gypsy Ballads*, it is the fusion of legend and folklore on the one hand, daring experimental imagery on the other. In *Poet in New York*, an age-old feeling, the feeling of revulsion that overpowers a man from a provincial culture when confronted by the vast city, is expressed in a new style, derived from Surrealism, in which symbols keep coming to the surface like bubbles in a pool. We are reminded that another great Spanish writer, Azorin, said that every renaissance has at its roots a foreign influence. The renaissance in Spanish lyrical poetry during the generation of Lorca—a renaissance that has at times been compared to a new Golden Age, and which was produced not only by Lorca but also by Jorge Guillén, Pedro Salinas, Rafael Alberti, Gerardo Diego, and several other great poets—is clearly indebted to outside influences. Cubism, Surrealism, and the experimental styles of the Twenties enriched the Symbolism that, since Rubén Darío, had renewed Spanish poetry. The task was to assimilate these movements without destroying the Spanish tradition, or rather to assimilate them in a way that would allow this tradition to make itself felt again, to acquire a new vitality. This is precisely what Lorca and his group did.

The poetic ideas of the mature Lorca seem to have crystallized shortly before his trip to the United States. In 1928 he wrote to his friend Jorge Zalamea,

Fortunately we are almost at fall, which inspires me again. I have also gone through a very bad period. One has to have the reserves of joy God has given me, in order not to break down before the number of conflicts which have rent me recently. But I am working. After working out my *Odes* that I have such hopes for I am going to put a period to this poetic cycle, in order to begin something else. Now I am going to create a poetry that will flow like blood when you cut your wrists, a poetry that has taken leave of reality and is written with a feeling that reflects all my love for things and my amusement at things. The love of death and the joking with death.

A little before in his lecture on Góngora he had declared,

The poet should carry a map of the places that he is going to visit, and he should be calm when faced with the thousand beauties and the thousand uglinesses disguised as beauties which must pass before his eyes. He should blindfold himself like Ulysses before the sirens, and he should shoot his arrows at the living metaphors and not at the contrived and false ones which surround him. The poet must never surrender himself, because if he does it just once, he will never rescue his work again.

In other words: the poet should come to grips with things, but he must come to them with a plan of action—and of vision—previously decided upon. There is no contradiction between this stand and the idea of a poetry that will flow like blood from cut wrists and escape reality. Rather, there is an evolution.

For the reader who likes neat divisions and clear-cut periods, it is possible to offer a tentative classification of Lorca's poetic output in four sections:

1) Early books, up to—but not including—the *Poem of the Cante Jondo*: a subdued, nostalgic style, inspired partly by Juan Ramón Jiménez. The subjects are mostly connected with adolescent longing and disappointment. This period includes the *Book of Poems* (1921), the *First Songs*, the *Book of Songs* (1922, 1921-24). The style is drier, more whimsical, more "unexpected" than that of Juan Ramón Jiménez and his Spanish Symbolist followers.

2) The *Poem of the Cante Jondo*, the *Gypsy Ballads*, the *Odes*: Lorca reaches a personal style, based upon a fusion of traditional and dramatic subjects and new metaphors. Although the *Poem of the Cante Jondo* was written in 1921 it already has many stylistic traits that the *Gypsy Ballads* are to develop fully. Lorca falls in love with images. It was perhaps inevitable. The cult of the image was in the air. Amy Lowell and the Imagists were moving in this direction in the North American world; Apollinaire, Max Jacob, Pierre Reverdy, and the early Surrealists were producing an outpouring of new images abroad. In Spain Gerardo Diego and Ramón Gómez de la Serna had placed the image at the core of their style. Gómez de la Serna was somewhat older than Lorca, having been born in 1891; he began to publish his images, in the form of short poetic and whimsical sentences, in 1910. His style has been called facile and

flippant: it can also be tender and mysterious. Here are some of his images: "The black umbrellas are widowers in mourning for the departed sunshades." "The seagulls were born from the handkerchiefs waving good-bye in ports." "Streets are longer at night than in daytime." "From this star, as from a lit window, comes the sound of a violin." "That star, full, exuberant, was not thus a while ago. That star is pregnant." "Stale bread is like a newly born fossil." "They put prisoners in striped pajamas in the hope that they will not be able to escape if dressed in bars." "On the telegraph wires hang, when it is raining, the tears making the telegrams sad." If we read Lorca's *Gypsy Ballads* we will occasionally find expressions reminding us of Gómez de la Serna's paradoxical images:

> Tres golpes de sangre tuvo
> y se murió de perfil.
> Viva moneda que nunca
> se volverá a repetir.
>
> (He had three leakages of blood
> and then, in profile, there he died,
> long-lived gold coin whose like
> can never be again supplied).

Or:

> Noche de torsos yacientes
> y estrellas de nariz rota
> aguarda grietas del alba
> para derrumbarse toda
>
> (A night of scattered torsos
> and stars with broken noses
> awaits cracks in the dawn
> in order to crumble to pieces)

To this second period, a period of "controlled boldness," of experiments without loss of control over the materials, belong also the *Odes*. In them images are also very important. Up to the New York period Lorca was to emphasize them. As John A. Crow, his fellow student at Columbia University, has written:

> he thought . . . that new metaphors were the core and mainstay of any new poetry, and since most of the old comparisons were already noticeably frayed on the edges, Lorca's central idea in writing was to employ phrases which had never been used before. The sample he gave that day was: "My love is like a pair of old shoes!" He laughed at our reaction, then went

on to explain that it was merely an attempt to place together two things which had always been considered as belonging to two different worlds, and in that fusion and shock to give them both a new vitality.

3) The third period is basically the period of *Poet in New York*. Free verse replaces traditional rhythms; the images become more personal, obscure, sometimes disappear and are replaced by "inventories," long lists of disparate objects. Chaos and anguish reign inside the poet's heart as they rule the outside world as he sees it. It was essentially the poet's troubled heart that gave rise to this new style. It is good to keep in mind, nevertheless, that other outside influences were at work in Spain at that time, influences tending toward a freer expression of the subconscious.

Gómez de la Serna was not the only innovator whose work Lorca had assimilated: in Madrid there lived or had lived Vicente Huidobro, Juan Larrea, Gerardo Diego, and especially Salvador Dalí, all of them influenced by Imagism, Dadaism, and Surrealism. Dalí tells us that he showed his colleagues and professors at the School of Fine Arts the first study on Braque and Cubism they had ever seen. Having subscribed to all the magazines, Dalí had been able to follow every change in artistic and literary fashion, and though he was still a Cubist in 1926 and 1927, many of his ideas were already Surrealistic *avant la lettre* or partially inspired by the movement. The friendship between Dalí and Lorca was an intense and troubled one, with ups and downs and periods of enmity. Lorca has told us little of this aspect of his life, but it is obvious that each influenced the other and that this friendship was a traumatic experience for both of them. With his usual truculence, Dalí writes in his *Secret Life*:

> The shadow of Maldoror [Lautréamont's Byronic and perverse hero, a forerunner of Surrealist ideas and attitudes] hovered over my life, and it was just at this period that for the duration of an eclipse precisely another shadow, that of Federico García Lorca, darkened the virginal originality of my spirit and of my flesh. . . . This was the culminating moment of his irresistible personal influence—and the only moment in my life when I thought I glimpsed the torture that jealousy can be. Sometimes we would be walking, the whole group of us, along El Paseo de la Castellana on our way to the café where we held our usual literary meetings and where I knew Lorca would shine like a mad and fiery diamond. Suddenly I would set off at a run, and no one would see me for three days. . . . No one has ever been able to tear from me the secret of these flights, and I don't intend to unveil it now—at least not yet . . .

Lorca left for the Waste Land of the big city and wrote *Poet in New York* in a style derived in part from the French Surrealists, which he used to express solitude, anguish, chaos in the modern world. This is a theme which, as has been said many times, awakened a profound echo in the poet, responding to his loneliness, melancholy, and homesickness. Yet it would be an error to believe that his reactions to New York City were totally negative. Had Lorca been completely unhappy in New York, had he believed that his experience in New York was to be fruitless and inassimilable, he would not have remained there more than a few weeks. The scion of a wealthy family, little drawn to formal study and academic degrees (he frequently cut classes at Columbia), he could go where he liked, and if he stayed in New York it was because he found there an almost inexhaustible source of experiences for the two opposing but complementary sides of his personality, the tragic and the gay, even frivolous. In its tragic aspect, New York allowed him to effect his "descent into Hell." Our modern poets, beginning with Baudelaire, can no longer carry out this descent vertically, as did Dante and Virgil, but must satisfy themselves with a horizontal trip through the world that surrounds them, and preferably through a world that is most alien and antagonistic to their personalities. If Hell, as Sartre has said, is "the others," the more "otherness" there is in a landscape or in a culture the better the possibilities will be of reaching Hell. At the same time, we must not forget that Lorca found many frivolous, gay, and exotic experiences in New York. Crow reminds us of the positive reactions of the poet to life in the United States: his passionate interest in American films, which, because of his ignorance of English, he interpreted through his own imagination; his admiration for the beauty of the women in New York; his intense fascination with jazz; his deep respect for the tenacity of the American character. Indeed it is very possible that Lorca owes to his experiences in America much more than is generally suspected. It is certain, for example, that they contributed to the aura of prestige that surrounded the poet. His trips through Latin America strongly reinforced his fame at home. Almost everyone in Spain could make a trip to Paris; but to travel through America was something altogether different. And to triumph in Latin America was the dream of every Spanish actor and every Spanish writer.

Besides this, it is altogether possible that his stay in New York proved the decisive factor in his metamorphosis from poet to playwright. After his return to Spain his plays concerned themselves almost exclusively with a single theme: the suffering and the frustration of the Spanish woman. Is it not possible, and indeed probable, that Lorca learned to understand the situation of the Spanish woman by thinking about her in New York and comparing her position with the situation and the possibilities, so completely different, of the North American girl? Between Bernarda Alba's daughters and the career girls of New York City there was a world of difference. Lorca's American friends at Columbia University quickly realized that the poet only half understood the independence and apparent coldness of the young women in New York.

But after living in the United States the position of the Spanish woman living within the confines of the traditional family must have seemed to him somewhat absurd and at times difficult and tragic. Like Cervantes and Molière, he became, without preachiness or moralizing, a defender of womankind. He certainly did not wish to build his dramatic works exclusively upon local color; he wished to create universal feminine types. But types that were rooted in the Spanish background. And this background stood out more clearly, more rigidly, more poignantly from the vantage point of his American experience. The difference between the happy and carefree eroticism of Belisa in *The Love of Don Perlimplin* (a work which apparently was written or completed in 1929) and the tragic feminine characters in Lorca's plays written after his return from New York is a fact of enormous importance.

4) The fourth period in Lorca's career includes the *Lament for the Death of a Bullfighter* and the poems he wrote after his return to Spain in 1930. In these he goes back to traditional metric forms and Spanish subjects. But his melancholy has not been dissipated. The *Lament*, probably his best sustained effort as a poet, is a brilliantly orchestrated piece, rich in bold images, where death and destruction are condemned and accepted at the same time. The poet comes face to face with chaos and nothingness, but this time he carries better weapons, and once more is in full control of his style and his emotions.

In 1930 Lorca returned to Spain and embarked upon a new life: that of the stage. He was not altogether unprepared for it; as a child his first toy had been a puppet theater, and if his first work, *El maleficio de la mariposa* (The Butterfly's Spell),[5] had failed in 1920, *Mariana Pineda* had achieved a *succès d'estime* in 1927, partly because liberal theatergoers found in the play political allusions it did not really contain.

Lorca may have brought back from America one or two plays still in the preliminary stage of composition. According to Jean-Louis Schonberg, the Rivas-Cherif theater group had announced the premiere of *Don Perlimplín* as early as 1928. Lorca may have been dissatisfied with his first version and have withheld the play until it could be retouched. *The Shoemaker's Prodigious Wife*, dated 1930 in the Aguilar edition of Lorca's complete works, may also have been started or reworked during the New York period. Be this as it may, Lorca's capacity for work during his first months back in Spain was astonishing, and it is not impossible that the texts we now possess were entirely rewritten by him at that time. His blue mood had disappeared, he was rapidly reaching maturity, filling with incessant activity a life devoid of deep personal attachments. He became a successful lecturer, rewrote some old poems,

---

[5] Not translated into English to our knowledge.

published the *Poem of the Cante Jondo* and worked at several of his new plays. The political situation in Spain was changing rapidly. The dictator Primo de Rivera had been dismissed by the King and replaced with a much more benevolent despot, General Berenguer. Lorca's friend and mentor, Fernando de los Rios, had been given back his professorship and was soon to become Minister of Education under the Republic. In April 1931 after a municipal election that gave the Republicans strong majorities in the cities, the King fled the country and the Republic was proclaimed. For the first time Lorca was to have friends in power.

The Shoemaker's Prodigious Wife, staged in 1930, was a complete success. Lorca had finally gained confidence in himself as a playwright and invested most of his energy and talent in the stage during the rest of his career. This did not entail a radical change in his technique as a writer, since for him the boundary between lyrical poetry and drama was hazy and often nonexistent. In 1935 he declared to a journalist who interviewed him: "I have started working as a playwright because I feel the need to express myself through drama. But this is no reason why I should neglect pure poetry; on the other hand one can find pure lyrical poetry in a play as well as in a poem." He announced at the same time his plans for a play dealing with problems closer to the present situation of Spain, "tackling problems everybody is afraid to speak about."

Lorca, born a poet, became a playwright through incessant toil and personal involvement: he had to "learn by doing"; he had to become a stagehand, a set decorator, a director, an actor, before he could master all the aspects of stage technique and write his most ambitious theatrical works. The obstacles were almost insurmountable. First of all, a psychological block: he had failed at the very beginning of his career with The Butterfly's Spell, and the memory of that first failure was to haunt him all his life. Having known success in every other field, he was reluctant to face the theater-going public again. Moreover, the public for the sort of poetic plays he had in mind was very limited: the Spanish audiences were conditioned by Benavente's drawing room comedies and by the pleasant but somewhat superficial "local color" plays of Arniches and the Quintero brothers. This applied especially to enlightened theatergoers. For most others the dramatic ideal was still old-fashioned melodrama as reinterpreted by Echegaray (who had managed to win a Nobel Prize on the strength of his almost inexplicable success with the Spanish public) or harmless but nonsensical one-act plays of low comedy enlivened by puns and turned out mechanically by dozens of specialists. Spanish actors were even worse: they prided themselves on overacting, which was fatal to Lorca's plays since they demanded great sensitivity and shading in the expression of emotions. Margarita Xirgu was one of the few Spanish actresses who understood and liked Lorca's plays at all. Moreover, Lorca's forte was the creation of poetic mood—of no advantage to an actor who wishes to upstage the rest of the players—and his emphasis upon women's roles displeased male leads. Ultimately as far as professional interpreters were concerned, he could rely only upon Margarita Xirgu and the Rivas Cherif group.[6] It therefore seemed a sound idea to create his own company.

In 1931-1932 he did just that. He called it *La Barraca* (The Hut). It was an unpretentious group of amateurs, mostly students playing during vacation time. The Republican government had granted a subsidy, enough to buy or rent a truck and a few costumes and props. Lorca and his student friends did all the rest. Their project was as generous as it was difficult: to bring the classics to the people. *La Barraca* played mostly to rural audiences, in the middle of the square of Castilian villages. Lorca adapted and directed Calderón, Cervantes, Lope de Vega, adding occasionally as a modern touch *L'Histoire du soldat* by Ramuz in its Spanish version and with Stravinsky's score. Lorca directed, acted, took care of lighting effects, pleaded with old peasant families so that he could borrow their authentic eighteenth century costumes for one night. The settings were extremely simple and very effective. The techniques of modern theater had finally reached Spain and were applauded first not in its big cities but in the improbable setting of Spain's remotest villages. Lorca's aim, first of all, was to reach an unsophisticated but sensitive and emotionally responsive audience and, secondarily, to achieve for himself and his friends grass roots experience in the difficult trade of stage directing. Juan Chabás quoted him: "I am happy to create, to be doing something. This does not distract me from my personal work. I go on writing and taking care of my projects. Moreover this activity with *La Barraca* is an excellent lesson for me. I have learned so much from it. Now I am a real stage director." This was in 1933, perhaps the most glorious year in a career that had allowed the poet to taste success almost from the very beginning. It was the year of his great stage successes: *Blood Wedding, Don Perlimplín, Love the Sorcerer,* an opera in which he collaborated with the great De Falla, and finally his trip to South America. Buenos Aires applauded Lola Membrives in her roles as heroine in several of Lorca's plays: *Mariana Pineda, The Shoemaker's Prodigious Wife, Blood Wedding.* Margarita Xirgu played Lope's *La dama boba,* adapted by Lorca, to vast enthusiastic crowds. Lorca himself made several lecture tours in which he drew large crowds and abundant applause. He had become an Ambassador of Spanish culture, the symbol of Spanish intellectual and artistic awakening. His departure from Argentina was highlighted by a public ceremony with toasts and speeches. The most famous Argentine writers were there to see him off. Far away, on the

---

[6] Another experimental group was formed later around the playwright Alejandro Casona and shared some of Lorca's ideals. Casona, too, tried successfully to bring the classics to the Spanish villages. The military uprising put an end to the group.

Spanish shores, the political thunder and lightning was only beginning. The witches were yet to enter the scene.

It is fashionable for American intellectuals of liberal inclination (and also for official Soviet commentaries) to see in Lorca a symbol of the Spanish Republican regime, of the golden hope of the Thirties which the forces of reaction in the United States and Western Europe condemned to death, either by intention or default. But his reputation inside and outside of Spain hardly requires such uncritical and in fact unliterary approval to survive. He does not depend on social movements for his place in history as does, for example, Mayakovsky in his complete identification with the Russian revolution, or Steinbeck in his associations with the problems of the United States in the Thirties. What if Lorca had never been killed by the Fascists? Had never written his attack on the Spanish Civil Guards? What if he had lived out his life, probably in exile like Jorge Guillén, and quietly died a very unpolitical death?

The chances are that fewer people outside of Spain would have heard of him so soon. For the majority of the world's population he would have remained another Spanish poet, who, unless he received a Nobel Prize, would not be known even by reputation. But in the long run his reputation would have been certain to make its way. He can be read by Spanish Fascists or Republicans, by European Communists or democrats, with equal pleasure. And this, from Lorca's viewpoint, is just as it should be. Lorca, as we have mentioned, tried to hold himself aloof from history, or to encompass all of history, which amounts to the same thing. He becomes an impartial observer of all happenings on his planet, with omnipotence to dissolve past and future in one everlasting moment. He refuses to identify with his own age, with his own country. Yet he does not seek to shrug off responsibility thereby. On the contrary, he wishes to assume a wider responsibility, to suffer not only as a Spaniard of the twentieth century, but as an American, as a gypsy, as a primitive man for whom myths are still alive, as any one of the million amorphous souls caught in the dilemmas of an impersonal industrial society, as any of the millions of souls throughout all history whose distinctive loves, hopes, and beings have been sacrificed to one impersonal goal or another—from Antoñito el Camborio cruelly bound and carried away by the rural guards to the slum dwellers in Brooklyn. It is this breadth of sympathy and imagination that makes Lorca a "democratic" poet, a universal poet, rather than any determined historical commitment on his part. To be sure, he was an anti-Fascist; his religious poems are anything but orthodox; he would have opposed Franco and helped the cause of the Spanish Republic. As Pablo Neruda, the famous Chilean poet, put it, "those who in shooting him wanted to hit the heart of his people made the right choice." Nevertheless, Lorca was not an *engagé* poet or propagandist like Mayakovsky or Neruda or even like Camus. This is something the heated political atmosphere of the Thirties, the period when he became really famous outside of Spain, has made us forget. Lorca at that time became a political symbol, not much more.

On the other hand, we would err if we thought of him as an ivory tower dweller. He did not retreat from the social or political problems of his time. He simply saw them, as in *The House of Bernarda Alba*, in terms of a conflict between tradition and individual desires. Unlike Brecht, he would not expect people to rush from the theater to right the wrongs portrayed there. His most "socially conscious" play, *Bernarda Alba*, has, for any Spaniard born and bred in one of Spain's main cities, a rather unreal and strained atmosphere. I would not go so far as to say that the play is not believable, but both Barcelona and Madrid in his time had their share of "emancipated" young girls, girls with jobs and a certain amount of freedom, who were light-years away from the intensely desperate characters selected for the play. Lorca never claimed to hold any social, political, or moral truth that could change the world. If he was not a party man—and kept his Falangist friends until the very end—he was a believer in solidarity, he had great faith in the artistic responses of his people; he thought it was the poor, the humble, who were the best public for his plays. And, as he stated a few days before the civil war, he refused to "go and live in a star": he was firmly rooted in the present, even when refusing to portray it *as such* in his works.

When we compare Lorca to his literary contemporaries in Europe and America in the Twenties and Thirties, we realize what this ahistorical or antihistorical attitude meant (or rather would have meant had Lorca lived). Not identifying himself with any specific social situation (as for example Steinbeck with the problems of the unemployed in the Thirties), Lorca could suffer no drying up of the creative instinct when the urgency of the problem disappeared. Having no illusions about any paradise, earthly or otherwise, he could never have been driven to the extreme step taken by Mayakovsky of committing suicide, motivated largely by disenchantment with the political situation and the difficulty of reaching the "promised land." His love for life was too profound, too broad to be based on the success or failure of any social or political institution. Yet even Lorca, in spite of his desire to avoid any entangling alliances with history, could not avoid being caught. Time and history took their revenge, just at the moment Lorca was reaching a perfect maturity. "Now I see clearly in which direction my theater is going to develop," said Lorca to Guillén in the summer of 1936. Guillén comments:

> His maturity unfolded like an opening, like the entrance to his Kingdom. The *Lament*, the *Divan of Tamarit*, *Bernarda Alba*, and then . . . God only knows! A plenitude of future. He worked toward it with decision and

joy. Every obstacle surrendered to his personality and his angelic *daimon*. He only had to fight the normal difficulties of expression. What could stand in his path? That is why I prophesied to Don Federico, the poet's father (he reminded me of it later, on American soil), in a moment of exaggeration that can be explained by the fact that Lorca seemed to have only friends: "In case there is a rebellion, if there is one single Spaniard who gets out of it alive, Federico will be that Spaniard."

His memory and his influence *are* still alive. The reason why the fame of some writers endures and the name of other writers progressively fades away seems to be always the same: the writer who endures is the one who can tell us something about man. Not about an abstract intellectual idea of man: about concrete man, in his time and his place. But in a way that permits us to draw conclusions for our own time, our own place. To catch a glimpse of something permanent and solid while talking about what is evanescent and frail is a difficult accomplishment. It is achieved by only a few artists.

In Lorca we learn about eternal Spain while he is trying to express the relationship of what has changed little or not at all in Spain with the ever changing twentieth century in which he lived and we live. Lorca's roots are firmly planted in the Spanish past; his sensitivity allowed him to bring that past alive for us, to show us in what ways that past can still bloom today. For the Spaniards of his generation, he was the best introduction to the twentieth century; for us, he may be the best introduction to eternal Spain. "The original genius," Gilbert Murray once observed, "is at once the child of tradition and a rebel against it." Lorca was precisely this: at home with Spanish tradition, still wishing to go beyond it, to connect it with our anguished present. Whether he succeeded or not it is for his readers to say.

The writing on Lorca is extensive. Yet most of the articles and books are not available to the average reader because of the language barrier or because the articles are buried in back issues of magazines. I have tried to provide the reader with as comprehensive a view of Lorca as possible, one in which many facets would complement each other and provide volume, depth, detail. Several of the contributors, notably William Carlos Williams, Dámaso Alonso, and Pedro Salinas, are not only excellent critics but also creative poets, which may add something to their insights into the personality and the work of a fellow poet. Others, like Angel del Río, knew the poet intimately: their reminiscences are also valuable. Sometimes the categories (critic—poet—friend) overlap: this happens with Dámaso Alonso among others.

William Carlos Williams needs no introduction to an American audience. His essay, written shortly after the poet's death, is an especially valuable introduction to Lorca since it places the poet's work within the context of Spanish lyrical poetry from the earliest period, beginning with the epic poem of *Mio Cid*. As usual, his essay combines a sense of proportion with a love for the telling detail. By placing Lorca at the end of a long evolution he explains both the meaning of this evolution and Lorca's role in Spanish lyrical poetry.

The essay, "Lorca," by J. B. Trend, manages to achieve the same result with respect to Lorca's environment, the Granada of 1919, where the author met Lorca for the first time. He also discusses the generation of poets and prose writers that preceded Lorca and prepared the artistic climate in which he developed. Trend deftly weaves anecdotes, analyses of poems and fragments of poems into his essay, as well as background material dealing with modern Spain and the classical tradition in Spain.

Dámaso Alonso's "Lorca and the Expression of the Spanish Essence" underlines Lorca's *Spanishness*, the love affair between the poet and his country. A description of the poet's impact on his contemporaries helps us come closer to Lorca the man. Lorca's success is thus explained and justified not only in artistic terms but also as the triumph of a strong and appealing personality.

"A Poet Crazy about Color," by Louis Parrot, stresses the visual appeal of Lorca's images and descriptions, particularly his use of color, now lavishly, now sparingly. Whether he uses strong primary colors or subtle shades Lorca is always interested in color: color as description of external reality or as symbol of hidden meanings.

"The Early Poems," by Roy Campbell, is an analysis of the early Lorca, in whom the "power of enthusiastic perception" was already developed and who was attracted by his immediate surroundings. Campbell underlines the difference between a Latin "nature poet," like Lorca, and an Anglo-Saxon one, like Wordsworth; he discusses the faintly diabolical and Byronian attitude of the adolescent Lorca, and his conception of poetry as a static inward illumination.

"Triumph of Sensual Reality—Mature Verse," by Edwin Honig, treats chiefly the period of the *Gypsy Ballads*, during which Lorca acquires a mastery over his technique and materials, enlarges his subjects, and develops a personal style. Sensuality and the theme of death are presented as a re-creation of folklore subjects within the framework of bold images and dramatic situations. The essay contains accurate and feeling translations of numerous poems, as well as an analysis of the artistic quality of Lorca's mature style.

"Lorca and the Poetry of Death," by Pedro Salinas, states the importance of the theme of death within what one might call the "Existential tradition" of Spain and its culture—and is also marginally an indictment of the modern world in which this attitude, which makes poetry possible, has been neglected or crushed.

"The Ritual Sacrifice in Lorca's *Poet in New York*," by Richard Saez, is a subtle and convincing contribution to the field of comparative literature. Lorca's book is analyzed side by side with references to T. S. Eliot's *Waste Land*, whose attitude toward the modern city was in many ways similar to Lorca's, and an effort is made to unravel the difficult symbols with which Lorca expresses his rejection and his hope.

"Lorca's Theater," by Angel del Río, is a clear and detailed account of Lorca's unfolding dramatic talent, from his early unsuccessful efforts to his last plays, where his talent for dramatic expression is finally realized. His scope, his technique, and his limitations as a dramatist are described in terms of the evolution of his ideas and style.

"Lyrical Primitivism: García Lorca's *Romancero gitano*," by J. López-Morillas, was written in order to find an answer to this question: "Is there, indeed, anything original and common to all men? Is it possible to discover in human life an irreducible core which acts as a center for man's disparate activities?" Lorca's poetry answers the question in the affirmative, and his answer tallies with the result of recent speculations on the nature of myth.

Lorca's poetry has often been qualified as gloomy, morbid, obsessed with death. Susan Smith Blackburn's essay, "Humor in the Plays of Federico García Lorca," is a rebuttal of this generalization Lorca the dramatist is shown to possess a robust sense of humor, a *joie de vivre* that appeals both to the senses and to the mind; his "love of death" was balanced by his "joking with death."

Finally, "*Don Perlimplín*: Lorca's Theater-Poetry," by Francis Fergusson, points out the subtle method by which Lorca manages to write a "romantic farce" in which a lusty, even lewd subject is raised to the level of poetry.

Federico García Lorca

by William Carlos Williams

In 1936 Lorca was dragged through the streets of Granada to face the Fascist firing squad. The reasons were not obvious. He was not active in leftist circles; but he was a power—he was a man of the people. His books were burned.

There are two great traditional schools of Spanish poetry, one leaning heavily upon world literature and another stemming exclusively from Iberian sources.

Lorca was child of the latter, so much so that he is often, as if slightly to disparage him, spoken of as a popular poet. Popular he was as no poet in Spain has been since the time of Lope de Vega. He belonged to the people and when they were attacked he was attacked by the same forces. But he was also champion of a school.

The sources whence Lorca drew his strength are at the beginnings of Spanish literature. In the epic conflict which the Spanish maintained in over four thousand battles for the reconquest of the peninsula from the Moors, there stands out an invincible leader who was, and continues to be in the memory of the people, the great national hero: Rodrigo Díaz de Vivar, called *El Cid Campeador*. His popularity is justified not only by reason of his qualities as a man of audacity and power but also for his having been the champion of popular liberties in face of the kings, one who disdained and despised their sovereignty under the dictates of reason and protected the people. The periods of the greatest deeds of this hero make up the *Cantar de Mio Cid* or *Poema del Cid,* the oldest work that survives in the Castilian tongue. The types are intensely human, the descriptions rapid and concrete:

> *Martín Antolínez mano metió al espada:*
> *Relumbra tod' el campo. . . .*

The flash of a sword lights the whole field.

This *Song of My Cid* was written, tradition says, by one of his loyal followers, not more than forty years after the death of the hero it celebrates: and there Spanish literature gives a first and striking proof of its ability to make poetry out of the here and the now. This quality it has never lost. Lorca knew it in his *Lament for the Death of a Bullfighter.*

Not only is *Poema del Cid* the first preserved to the Castilian language but it sets at once the standard in point of form for all Spanish poetry to follow. Sometimes out of favor but always in the background, its meters have become imbedded inextricably in the songs of the people— and there is no Western poetry in which the popular has a greater bulk and significance than the Spanish. Its line is famous. It is of sixteen syllables assonanced sometimes for long periods on the same vowel. This line, divided in half as usually written, becomes the basis for the *romance* or ballad, many of the *romances viejos* being, in all probability, as old as *Poema del Cid* itself or even older. It was a form much used by Lorca whose reassertion of its structural line, unchanged, forms the basis for his work.

Writing in the old meter eight hundred or a thousand years perhaps after its invention, García Lorca was pleased, as he stood in the street one night before a wineshop in Seville, to hear the words of a *copla* which he himself had written sung word for word by an illiterate guitarist, syllable for syllable in the mode of the twelfth century epic.

And I remember one night in 1910 in Toledo listening in the same way before a cubicle opening onto one of the plazas where a few men were sitting drinking. One of them was singing to the beat of a guitar. I went in, a young man not very familiar with the language and an obvious stranger, but they became self-conscious so that I took my drink and left soon after. They looked like the shepherds I had seen coming in that afternoon across the narrow bridge with their big wolfish dogs.

Toward the middle of the thirteenth century Alfonso X, called the Wise, first gave due honor to the language of the country by ordering all public documents to be written in the common tongue rather than in Latin as formerly. It is typical of Spain that many blamed precisely this change for the disorder and disasters which followed. It was Alfonso who, in 1253, gathered a whole book of *cantigas* or *letras* to sing in the *dialecto gallego*. He was dethroned by his own son and driven an exile to die neglected in Seville, after which for close to a hundred years, "in that miserable epoch," so it is said, "the men of Castile seemed to possess hearts only to hate and arms only with which to kill."

Yet it was appositely enough during this distressed period that there appeared the second of Spain's great early poems, *Libro de buen amor, The Book of Good Love,* the work of that most arresting personality in Spanish medieval literature: Juan Ruiz, archpriest of Hita. This is the portrait he gives of himself among the many contained in his famous work: corpulent, a big head, small eyes under heavy eyebrows black as coal, a big nose, the mouth big also, thick lips, a short, thick neck, an easy gait—a good musician and a gay lover.

If Lorca has rested his poetic inspirations firmly in the structural forms established by *Poema del Cid,* much of his mood and spirit can be discovered in the nature of the old reprobate archpriest of Hita.

Juan Ruiz was a priest of that disorderly type which his time tolerated, his favorite company the people, always the people, and particularly that part of the Spanish population, says Madariaga, "which it is so difficult to imagine today, in which Jews and Moors and Christians mixed in an amiable fraternity of mirth and pleasure." Such a population is perhaps less difficult to imagine today in the South, where Lorca was at home, than those not fully initiated might have supposed. For it is the home of the Andalusian folksong which Lorca so ably celebrated, that curious compound of the "philosophical desperation of the Arab, the religious desperation of the Jew, and the social desperation of the gypsy." With these elements he was thoroughly familiar.

The major work of the fourteenth century in Spain, Ruiz' *Libro de buen amor* is in reality a picaresque novel in verse and prose, much of it in dialogue full of laughter, full of movement, and full of color, a vast satirical panorama of medieval society. The poet, for all the faults and indignities of the priest, is a great one. He knows the secrets of that direct plunge into action which is typical alike of *Poema del Cid,* of Spanish *romances* no less than of Spanish comedies, and, nowadays, of popular song, to all of which Lorca owes much of his inspiration.

To understand fully all that is implied in Lorca's poetic style, what he rejected and what he clung to, the development of Spanish poetry subsequent to the work of the early masters must be noted. There was a sharp revulsion from the "old taste" which they exemplified up to the time of Juan de Mena. As always in matters of this character geography must be recognized as playing a leading part.

Spain is a peninsula dependent from the extreme lower corner of Europe, cut off from Europe by the Pyrenees which make of it virtually an island. It is, besides, far to the west of all direct European influences. From the South the Moorish invasion, with its softening influences, failed, being driven back after four centuries of temporary supremacy into Africa whence it had come, though its mark remains still in a certain quarter of Spanish and all European thought. Lorca, whose home was Granada, knew this inheritance. The Moorish invasion stopped short and receded while Latin thought, following the tracks of Caesar, had in the main gone east of Iberia up the Rhone valley through France to the north. Thus the flexibility and necessitous subtlety of the French, their logic and lucidity of ideas, remained unknown to Spain. Enclosed within themselves, Spaniards have remained basically limited to a reality of the world at their feet from which there was no escape (save across the sea, which failed them) and that second steep reality of the soul in whose service they have proved themselves such extravagant heroes.

Little affected by the Renaissance and not at all by the Reformation, early Spanish literature reached a stop, just prior to the discovery of America, in the work of Juan de Mena (1411-1456). For two hundred years thereafter, during the fifteenth and sixteenth centuries or until the time of Góngora, the "old taste," characteristic in its resources, limited in its means, succumbed, and the influence of Italy held an ascendancy. As Quintana says in the introduction to his *Poesías selectas castellanas* (1817),

> The old assonanced versification of octosyllabics, more suited to the madrigal and the epigram than to more ambitious poems, could not be sustained without awkwardness and crudeness—as Juan de Mena had found. It was unfit for high and animated conceptions. Force of thought, warmth of feeling, harmony and variety, without which none can be considered a poet, all were lacking.

But Cristóbal de Castillejo in a violent satire "compared these novelties of the Petrarquistas, as he called them, to those Luther had introduced into the Christian faith."

Great names abounded in Spanish poetry following this breakdown of the old modes, some of the greatest in Spanish literary history, all under the newer influence, all working as they believed to enlarge and enrich the prosody and general resources of the language. Fernando de Herrera celebrated the majesty of Imperial Spain. There was the mystic Fray Luis de León and among the rest Saint Teresa, that greatest of Spanish mystics, whose few poems, not more than thirty in all, ignoring grammar, logic, ignoring everything but the stark cry of the spirit, wrung direct from the heart, make them seem its own agonized voice crying in our ears. It is the same recurrent, unreasoning note found in the strident, bright colors and tortured lines of El Greco. Escape! As ideas come into Spain they will stop and turn upward: "I proceed," Unamuno says still in the twentieth century, "by what they call arbitrary affirmations, without documentation, without proof, outside of Modern European logic, disdainful of its methods."

But toward the end of the sixteenth century the typically Spanish reaction occurred. It is curious and interesting to note how the otherwise mildly acquiescent Quintana responds to it, how for the first time he really warms to his subject and his style glows when he records:

> At this time (1570-80) corresponding with the youth of Góngora and Lope de Vega it happened that a new interest began to appear in the old *romances*. . . .

Stripped of the artifice and violence which the imitation of other modes
had necessitated; its authors caring little for what the odes of Horace or
the *canciones* of Petrarch were like; and being composed more by instinct
than by art, the *romances* could not possess the complexity and the elevation
of the odes of León, Herrera, and Rioja. But they were our own lyric
poetry; in them music found its own accents; these were the songs one
heard at night from windows and in the streets to the sound of the harp
or the guitar. . . .

"There are in them more beautiful expressions and more energetic, ingenious, and delicate sallies than in all our poetry besides. But curiously
enough in a few years this revival of a taste which popularized poetry, and
rescued it from the limits of imitation to which the earlier poets had reduced it, served also to make it incorrect and to break it down, inviting to
this abandon the same facility as in its rehabilitation.

Góngora was the man!

It was Luis de Góngora who as a lyric poet brought the new adventure
to its fullest fruition and then attempted to go away, up and beyond it
—to amazing effect.

Góngora is the only Spanish poet whose inventions, at the beginning
of the seventeenth century, retain a lively interest for us today, one of
the few poets of Spain of world reputation and lasting quality of greatness. Look at his picture: chin deep in his cravat, his forehead a
Gibraltar, the look on his face slightly amused but formidable, not to
say invincible, his person retracted into an island of strength resembling
nothing so much as the map of Spain itself. There you have the spirit
that sustained Lorca in our day.

A master in his *romances,* one of the greatest masters of the burlesque
and the satire, Góngora had already established a redoubtable reputation
when toward the latter part of his life he set out to elevate the tone of
Spanish poetry, illustrating it with erudition and new conceptions,
enriching the language with those tones and turns which distinguish
it from prose. It was the same ambition which had inspired Juan de
Mena and Fernando de Herrera; but Góngora lacked, as they said, the
culture and moderation possessed by those predecessors.

Be that as it may Góngora, who to the end of his days continued at
times to write his lovely *romances,* "developed a style—turgid and difficult, infuriating his age, which became known as *Culteranismo.* And
inasmuch as Góngora was the great representative of *Culteranismo* it
became known as *Gongorismo.*"

What else but the same escape upward! As in the poems of Saint
Teresa! When Góngora found himself confined by the old, unwilling to
go back to the borrowed Italianate mode, he sought release in an illogical,
climbing manner, precursor of today. He could not go back to Latin,
to Greek or the Italian. Never to the French—so he went up! steeply,
to the illogical, to El Greco's tortured line. So that when Luzán and

those other humanists (who after a century were restoring good taste) applied themselves to destroy the sect and its consequences—denouncing its founder—they took Góngora and detestable poet to be one and the same thing.

It was for Federico García Lorca, in our day, to find a solution. Like the young Góngora, Lorca adopted the old Spanish modes. I have taken his book *Llanto por Ignacio Sánchez Mejías (Lament for the Death of a Bullfighter)* to be touched upon for the conclusion of these notes.

There has always seemed to be a doubt in the minds of Spaniards that their native meters were subtle enough, flexible enough to bear modern stresses. But Lorca, aided by the light of twentieth century thought, discovered in the old forms the very essence of today. Reality, immediacy; by the vividness of the image invoking the mind to start awake. This peculiarly modern mechanic Lorca found ready to his hand. He took up the old tradition, and in a more congenial age worked with it, as the others had not been able to do, until he forced it—without borrowing —to carry on as it had come to him, intact through the ages, warm, unencumbered by draperies of imitative derivation—the world again under our eyes.

The peculiar pleasure of his assonances in many of the poems in this book retains the singing quality of Spanish poetry and at the same time the touch of that monotony which is in all primitive song—so well modernized here: In the first of the *romances* which make up the book's latter half, "La casada infiel," the play is on the letter o; in "Preciosa y el aire" upon e; in "Romance de la Guardia Civil Española" upon a; etc., etc. This is straight from *El Cid*; but not the scintillating juxtapositions of words and images in the three "Romances históricos" (at the very end), where the same blurring of the illogical, as of refracted light, suggests that other reality—the upward sweep into the sun and the air which characterized the aspiration of St. Teresa, of El Greco, and the Góngora whom none understood or wished to understand in his day, the "obscurities" which Unamuno embraces with his eye toward

Augustine, the great African, soul of fire that split itself in leaping waves of rhetoric, twistings of the phrase, antitheses, paradoxes and ingenuities . . . a Gongorine and a conceptualist at the same time. Which makes me think that Gongorism and conceptualism are the most natural forms of passion and vehemence.

The first stanza of Lorca's greatest poem, the lament, has for every second line the refrain: *A las cinco de la tarde*—"at five in the afternoon."

That refrain, *A las cinco de la tarde*, fascinated Lorca. It gives the essence of his verse. It is precise, it is today, it is fatal. It gives the hour, still in broad daylight though toward the close of the day. But besides that it is song. Without reading Lorca aloud the real essence of the old and the new Spanish poetry cannot be understood. But the stress on the first syllable of the "CINco" is the pure sound of a barbaric music, the heartbeat of a man's song, *A las* CINco *de la tarde.* What is that? It is any time at all, no time, and at the same time eternity. Every minute is eternity—and too late. *A las* CINco *de la tarde.* There is the beat of a fist on the guitar that cannot escape from its sorrow, the recurring sense of finality translated to music. The fatality of Spain, the immediacy of its life and of its song. *A las* CINco *de la tarde,* Mejías was killed! was killed on a bull's horns. *A las* CINco *de la tarde,* he met his end.

This is the brutal fact, the mystical fact. Why precisely *a las* CINco *de la tarde?* The mystery of any moment is emphasized. The spirit of Góngora, the obscure sound of the words is there.

Much in the examples of Lorca must have been in the mind of the elder poet when he strained at the cords of the old meter, the old thoughts, refusing to adopt the Italianate modes of his immediate predecessors until the words broke like a bridge under him and he fell through among fragments—wisely.

Two years after the event the Spaniard takes a man killed in action—a bullfighter killed in Mexico—for his theme.[1] No matter what the action, he was a man and he was killed: the same ethical detachment and the same freedom from ethical prejudice which characterized *El Cid* and *The Book of Good Love.* The same power also to make poetry of the here and the now. The same realism, the same mounting of the real, nothing more real than a bullfighter, mounting as he is, not as one might wish him to be, directly up, up into the light which poetry accepts and recasts. That is Lorca.

In the "Romance of the Faithless Wife" is reflected the same aloofness, the same reality, the same reserve—not the superficial passion that is surface only: The gypsy takes the woman, the ecstasy he wins from her and of which she speaks to him are real, but she made him believe she was a virgin and he found that she was married. So he enjoyed her realistically and paid for it, like a gypsy, but he would not love her thereafter—just as in a song from the high valleys of the Asturian Pyrenees, a man sings:

> Una niña bonita
> Se asomó a su balcón.
> Ella me pidió el alma,
> Yo la di el corazón,
> Ella me pidió el alma,
> Y yo la dije adiós.

[1] Actually the bull-fighter Sánchez Mejías died in Madrid in August of 1934; Lorca's poem, written soon afterwards, was published in 1935. [M.D.]

> (A pretty girl
> Came out to her balcony.
> She asked me for my soul,
> I gave her my heart.
> She asked me for my soul,
> Then I said good-bye.)

He gave her his heart but when she asked for his soul he said good-bye.

In reading Lorca the whole of Spanish history must be borne in mind, Saint Teresa with her bodiless thrust of soul, the steadfastness, the chastity—*but* also the reality of the Spaniard. Spanish poetry, says Madariaga, is both above and below the plane of thought. It is superficial to talk of Lorca as a sensualist. He is a realist of the senses and of his body but he is far from the common picture of a sensualist. The cold and elevated plateau which has bred the chastity of the *copla*, such as that quoted above, enters into all of Lorca's work. Read carefully, the icy chastity of Spanish thought comes through the reality of the event from which the man does not flinch—nor does he flinch before the consequence. He will give the body, yes, but the soul never! The two realities, the earth and the soul, between these two the Spaniard swings, firm in his own.

These are the influences that made Lorca. The old forms were bred of and made for song. The man spent his life singing. That is the forgotten greatness of poetry, that it was made to be sung—but it has been divorced from the spoken language by the pedants.

Lorca honored Spain, as one honors a check, the instinctive rightness of the Spanish people, the people themselves who have preserved their basic attitude toward life in the traditional poetic forms. He has shown that these modes, this old taste, are susceptible of all the delicate shadings—without losing the touch of reality—which at times in their history have been denied them. In such "obscurities" of the words as in the final *romances* in his book, the historical pieces addressed to the saints, he has shown how the modern completes the old modes of *The Cid* and *The Book of Good Love*. He has carried to success the battles which Juan de Mena began and Góngora continued.

Federico García Lorca, born in 1899 in the vicinity of Granada, produced a number of outstanding works in lyric poetry, drama, and prose between his eighteenth year and the time of his death in 1936 at the age of thirty-seven. He was a pianist, the organizer of a dramatic troupe, and a distinguished folklorist of Spanish popular songs of great distinction.

Many stories are told of him. He was loved by the people. His murder by the Fascist firing squad in Granada is perhaps as he would have wished it to be: to die on the horns of the bull—if a man does not put his sword first through its heart. Like most men of genius he went about little recognized during his life but he has left us a weapon by which to defend our thought and our beliefs, a modern faith which though it may still be little more than vaguely sensed in the rest of the world is awake today in old Spain, in proud defiance of destruction there. By that Lorca lives.

Lorca

by J. B. Trend

I

Some writers on Lorca can recommend themselves to their readers by the claim that they never met the poet or knew him personally. They mean, I think, that they have not been dazzled by his personality or by a tourist's vision of Granada, and so can see Lorca steadily and see him whole. I have neither of those advantages. I knew Lorca personally when he was beginning, and have been about Spain enough to know that it can never be seen wholly or steadily; while the truth about Granada was apprehended by Lorca himself when he said that it was a "Paradise closed to many, with gardens open to few": *Paraiso cerrado para muchos, jardines abiertos para pocos.*[1] By accident, or sheer good luck, I happened to be one of those few.

I have described that first meeting with Federico García Lorca before. It sounds, now, too romantic to be true; but it was true in 1919. Granada at that time was living its own life, without tourists; and conditions which seemed to be normal proved afterwards to have been highly exceptional. There was no radio, the gramophone was still a primitive affair with a tin trumpet, and poetry was read aloud or recited among friends. Gardens were open for the performance of poetry and music.

That evening there had been a concert at the Arts Club, the Círculo de Bellas Artes. The performers were a trio of what Shakespeare called "twangling instruments"; two Spanish lutes and a guitar. Falla, the composer, was there in the audience. Actually it was he who had brought me; and afterwards it seemed that "of course" we were to go to someone's garden in the oldest and most picturesque part of Granada, the Albaicín. It was already midnight, but we dawdled in the main street, eating prickly pears which someone had bought off a barrow; and then

"Lorca." From *Lorca and the Spanish Poetic Tradition* by J. B. Trend (New York and Oxford, 1956), pp. 1-23. Reprinted by permission of The Macmillan Company, New York, and Basil Blackwell & Mott, Ltd., Oxford.

[1] The title of a poem by Soto de Rojas (1652). The Granada of this chapter should be compared with the Granada of today, described by Mr. Gerald Brenan in *The Face of Spain* (New York: Farrar, Straus, and Cudahy, Inc., 1951).

were led up the steep, cobbled streets to a plain door in a high wall. It opened into a large dark garden full of the sound of running water. The three musicians were there and played some of their program over again, particularly the pieces by Falla. Then a poet was called upon. He declaimed something by Villaespesa; the verse was an unending succession of amphibrachs. Once or twice the reciter hesitated, but he recovered, until the awful moment when he dried up altogether; and a hoarse voice—that type of southern Spanish voice which has grown voiceless from uncounted *cañas* of dry sherry—was heard imitating the rhythm:

| ¡Se pierde . . . | se pierde . . . | se pierde . . . | perdió! |
| ¡*You'll lose it* . . . | *you'll lose it* . . . | *you'll lose it* . . . | *it's lost*! |

The audience dissolved in laughter and the poor poet vanished, though he was to be seen afterwards by a trestle table where there were several demijohns—*damajuanas* the Spanish call them—of dry sherry; and a pleasant individual, I remember, embraced me and asked (in German) if I could tell him the publisher of the *Gesammelte Werke* of Walter Pater.

Then we were hushed and a rather shy youth recited. He did not declaim, but spoke in a soft, warm, eager voice: *la obscura, cálida, turbia, inolvidable voz de Federico García Lorca,* Gerardo Diego said long afterwards. It was a simple ballad with striking but easily intelligible imagery. "Who is it?" "Federico García Lorca. You must meet him." The evening ended after 4 A.M., with the poet and myself, arm in arm, helping one another down the steep streets of the Albaicín, to the main street and the bottom of the Alhambra Hill. ¡*Noche, que noche nochera*!

That was my introduction to modern Spanish poetry. It was followed a year later by a book called *Libro de poemas,* with an autograph inscription—a precious book which is kept out of sight at the back of a bookshelf. Soon after that I reviewed the book, in an article which an American bibliographer has claimed to be the first ever published outside Spain on Federico García Lorca. Later the review was rewritten for a book, and I should like to quote from it now.

A stray traveler [it said] should be the last to claim that he has discovered a new poet. I must confess, indeed, that I opened Sr. García Lorca's book with certain misgivings. I had made the acquaintance of his poetry . . . in circumstances which were so exceptional . . . that they seemed never likely to be repeated. I was afraid of meeting it again in cold print. In that corner of Europe to which the poet belongs, poetry, like music, is a thing to be performed. It is read aloud in gardens on summer nights. . . . in surroundings which are like Mr. Walter de la Mare's "Arabia" come true. To understand García Lorca, an English reader must begin by saying that exquisite English poem over to himself. He must "decry her gliding streams," he must

> Hear her strange lutes on the green banks
> Ring loud with the grief and delight
> Of the dim-silked, dark-haired Musicians
> In the brooding silence of night.

That was the background against which García Lorca's poetry was performed. The experience of it, therefore, was a composite experience; the printed page of today is only a part.

This, of course, is begging the question. A poet has no right to expect you to know his own particular corner of the world. But he has the right to expect you to look at things from his point of view—if you can; and to assume that you know something of what his contemporaries are doing: especially his older contemporaries. You must try to realize his poetic environment, and discover what sort of poetry he was likely to have heard and read.

The poetic environment of a Spanish poet at that time might be said to consist of two gliding streams. There were the nursery rhymes, the singing games, and the short, epigrammatic *cantares*: and those, in García Lorca's home in "Arabia," people sang to a guitar—not the guitar of national legend, but a guitar played seriously as a serious instrument. On the other side were Rubén Darío and Villaespesa, with contemporary poets like Antonio Machado and his brother Manuel, Enrique de Mesa, Valle-Inclán and Juan Ramón Jiménez. The field was wide— wide as Spain and Spanish-speaking America; and there was plenty of room for poets to cultivate their own corners of it independently. García Lorca's corner was a place of trees and falling water, of dreams, and children playing.

Poetry was a social, friendly accomplishment, natural to the society into which García Lorca was born; and later, in Montevideo, he told another poet that he wrote poetry because he wanted people to like him; and that, too, was part of the explanation of his poetry.[2]

It is difficult for a foreigner to judge [the review went on] but these verses seem less reminiscent than many first books of verse. There are reminiscences, of course; but they are reminiscences of sound rather than of sense. . . . It is seldom that this poet writes the poetry of other people's

---

[2] "Lo hago para que la gente me quiera; nada más que para me quieran las gentes he hecho mi teatro y mis versos, y seguiré haciéndolos porque es preciso el amor de todos." ["I do it so people will love me; only for this love have I written my plays and my poems, and I will go on writing them because I need everybody's love."] *Poema del cante jondo* (2 ed.: Madrid: C.I.A.P., 1937), p. 146; said to Alfredo Mario Ferreiro in Montevideo.

poetry, or the erotic mysticism of other people's passions; and he never uses forms that have to be filled out with padding. There is a curious distinction about his writing; yet it is combined, as a rule, with an engaging simplicity.

That review was a youthful indiscretion: a shot in the dark, perhaps —or in a dark garden at Granada—but I do not wish to withdraw it. I did not know at the time—indeed, it has hardly yet been realized outside the Spanish-speaking countries—that García Lorca was not alone. He was, in fact, or became later, a member of a brilliant circle of contemporary Spanish poets, the most brilliant for three hundred years; though now, in consequence of the civil war and the persecution which followed it, nearly all those poets are either dead or in exile, while one of the best books about them is called *Tríptico del sacrificio* (A Triptych of the Sacrifice) by Guillermo de Torre who afterwards edited the complete works of García Lorca in Buenos Aires.

This revival of Spanish poetry followed the revival of the novel which began in 1868; the best pages and most typical characters of Pérez Galdós, though still (with two recent exceptions) largely untranslated, are to my mind almost on a level with the great Russians. After the novel came the essay. The condition of staleness and frustration which led to defeat in the Spanish-American war of 1898 stimulated Unamuno and contemporary essayists to some of their best writing; while the new sympathy of the Spanish-speaking American countries for the people of Spain disposed Spaniards to read the Central American poet Rubén Darío. Darío had revolutionized Spanish prosody, something in the way that Swinburne had revolutionized prosody in English; and though poets in Spain did not follow him in his Parisian Greek subjects or his expansive Spanish-American manner, they learned from him how to write alexandrines and hexameters and other forms of verse which had been little used in Spanish. On the formal side, they nearly all began to write like Rubén Darío, though on the other side they were more like their own poet, essayist and philosophical writer, Unamuno; and Unamuno, though he wrote sonnets as if he were heaving bricks at a wall, yet had his roots firmly planted in the soil of Spain and in his own everyday Spanish thoughts.

The first result of the new poetry in Spain was Juan Ramón Jiménez. Though some of his early alexandrines sound like Rubén Darío, he soon became something very different; more finished, more subtle and more penetrating, with a poetical world of his own; and he is still the central figure among contemporary Spanish poets, though frowned on in Madrid for preferring exile to the régime of General Franco. Then there was Antonio Machado, who developed in directions where he met no one else. He followed the winding galleries of his own mind, the wide and windy uplands of Castile, the social satire on certain types in

Andalusia, and the premature existentialist philosophy of a great teacher who was entirely imaginary, and invented by the poet himself.

Lorca belonged to a younger generation. He was born near Granada at the end of the nineteenth century—he liked to keep the date unspecified—and there is little or nothing of Rubén Darío about him, even on the rare occasions (such as the "Ode to Salvador Dalí") when he wrote alexandrines. Like his contemporaries, his favorite verse was the characteristic eight-syllable line with varying accentuation—"hovering stresses," Mr. MacNeice calls them—and assonance: rhyming on the vowels but not on the consonants. That use of assonance instead of full rhyme has been one of the great advantages which poetry in Spanish has had over the poetry of almost all modern languages. In English, we are only just beginning to use it, and still finding that imperfect rhymes or "pararhymes" in the style of Wilfred Owen may suit us better; but in Spain, assonance has been used by poets for eight hundred years. Assonance does not exclude rhyme, which is valued for certain effects; but it saves poetry from the abuse of rhyme in a language where rhyming is too easy and almost always feminine and two-syllabled, while it helps to keep verse natural and within speaking distance of people in general.

What distinguished Lorca from his contemporaries was that he followed every suggestion and evocation which word or verse could give him. That led him to popular verse and also to plays in verse, but above all it led him to ballads; and his book of ballads about gypsy ways and the "gypsified" customs of southern Spain, the *Romancero gitano,* will probably be his most enduring achievement.

II

Most readers and critics of García Lorca have tried to place him in the Spain of the "black legend": the Spain of blood, lust, death, and all the "isms." I confess that, from my first long visit to Spain in 1919 down to the civil war of 1936, I took things in Spain as I found them. I regarded Spanish things and Spanish ways as natural, and did not go about looking for "isms." In 1919, after four and a half years in uniform, Spanish ways seemed not only natural but friendly and delightful; for even the 1914-18 war was a crescendo of horrors, and the fearful casualties among one's friends made Spain seem not a country of war and lechery, but of a new Age of Reason.

The new Age of Reason has not yet arrived. At this moment it seems further off than ever; and what we have now is an age of mysticism, showing itself incidentally in unscientific psychoanalysis and unconvincing popular theology. There is room for both of these if they are real and genuine; but neither of them can help us to tell a good poem from a bad one, and attempts to make deductions from Lorca's poems by amateur psychoanalysis or popular theology are apt to mislead, if not checked by evidence from other sources. The word *verde* (green), for instance, has been taken for a psychoanalytical symbol. Actually, when Lorca said that a thing was green, we knew that it *was* green, and that was that; it did not occur to us that he was consciously or deliberately symbolizing anything. The ballads on Tamar and Santa Olalla, again have been brought forward in evidence of Lorca's preoccupation with sex; and above all there is the ballad of the faithless wife: "La casada infiel." [3] In fact, the point of that poem is the high gypsy standard of manners. The gypsy, looking back on the affair in a cool hour, considers that he acted correctly, *como gitano legítimo* (as a true gypsy). He made his companion a present afterwards. "But I didn't know she was married." The Lorca I knew was certainly not oversexed. On the contrary.

The story of Tamar—"Atamares" of the gypsies—came originally from the Old Testament; she was the sister of Absalom, but was forced by her half-brother Amnon. An earlier Tamar was married to Onan, and afterwards solicited her father-in-law, Judah. The first of these edifying stories was sung to children of the well-to-do by their nurses who came from remote villages. The poet tells us so himself. There is a ballad about it, which was sung to put children to sleep. The grim and bloodthirsty words of Spanish cradlesongs have been remarked; but are they any more bloodthirsty than our own?—that well-loved rhyme for instance, for playing "Oranges and Lemons":

> Here comes a candle to light you to bed,
> And here comes a chopper to chop off your head.

Lorca's gypsy ballads did not come first. The *Libro de poemas* of 1921 prepares the scene. The *Canciones* (1921-24, published in 1927) gradually introduce human figures; and human figures are there, in all their full-blooded life, in the *Romancero gitano* (begun in 1924, but not published until 1928) and in the *Poema del cante jondo* of 1931. These poems fill the scene, already prepared in the earlier volumes, with real people; gypsies, horse copers, smugglers, civil guards; and the civil guards are only too real, even though their souls—like their three-cornered hats— are (Lorca said) made of patent leather: *almas de charol*. Yet the ballads are all—and one is actually called that—*romances sonámbulos*[4]: sleep-walking ballads. Life is still a dream. The gypsies are formed from bronze and sleep, *bronce y sueño*.

Lorca came from a family of large and successful farmers. His mother had been a school-teacher; but among his aunts and uncles were people extremely well-acquainted with popular poetry. He spent eleven years—

[3] *Oxford Book of Spanish Verse,* ed. James Fitzmaurice-Kelly (2d ed.; New York: Oxford University Press, 1940), No. 251.

[4] *Ibid.,* No. 250.

nearly a third of his life—in university colleges. The first was the
Residencia de Estudiantes at Madrid (1918-28) where he met the most
prominent poets of his generation; for the President of that College, Don
Alberto Jiménez, besides being an ideal head of a house, had the genius
to attract to it many of the best poets of the time. It was the poet Juan
Ramón Jiménez who had designed the gardens between the College
buildings; and Unamuno was often to be seen and heard there, during
his visits to Madrid, particularly after his return from exile in 1931.
Antonio Machado and Alfonso Reyes were frequent visitors; so were
Enrique de Mesa and Pérez de Ayala; while Moreno Villa, Pedro Salinas,
Jorge Guillén, Emilio Prados were all at one time or another actually in
residence at the College, together with Buñuel and a painter who had
considerable influence on Lorca: Salvador Dalí.

Then, after ten years' desultory study of what were known in Spain
as "Philosophy and Letters," Lorca moved to America. It is said that he
went there because he had made a mess of his love affairs. That may
be or may not; the same has been said of Rupert Brooke. Lorca spent a
year at Columbia University, New York. To him, the American scene and
the American way of life were shattering—far more than they had been
to Rupert Brooke, or to Juan Ramón Jiménez in 1915. It was all so
"un-Latin." The only kindred spirit among the poets was the ghost of
Walt Whitman, with his beard full of butterflies, Lorca said:

> tu barba, llena de mariposas.

The only part of New York he really liked was the negro part, Harlem.
His book, *Poeta en Nueva York,* profoundly influenced by Whitman in
form and deeply tinged by Surrealism in approach, is taken by many
foreign critics for his most important poetic achievement. It may be; but
I am inclined to agree with Guillermo de Torre that *Poeta en Nueva
York* is really a work of transition. He was certainly doing what other
poets of the time were doing, in Europe and America; but these poems
are the saddest and most tragic he ever wrote. The poet in New York
was a lost soul. Confirmation for this view can be found in another
Spanish critic, José Bergamín, who edited the first edition of *Poeta en
Nueva York,* in Mexico in 1940. He regards it as "a borderland book,"
un libro fronterizo:

> The words [he says] have not the same clear and exact value that they
> have in the best poems. . . . While he sings, he stammers words of terror,
> which suddenly seem to become cradlesongs; but the thing he rocks in his
> arms is some inhuman creature: a dead dog or a dead chicken. . . . The
> poet in New York, once the poet in Granada, remembering his lost Paradise
> of streams and skies . . . but now alone in a strange city, becomes a child
> once more; he would scream, if he could, in his immense, lethal nightmare.

Lorca fled from New York, and reached Havana, waltzing, he said, toward civilization. In Cuba he found himself at home once more; not only because Cuba speaks Spanish, but because the colored people there are so much happier and more natural than they are in the north. "We Latins," the Mulatto Cuban poet, Nicolás Guillén, said to him. He breathed again.

It is usual, in speaking of García Lorca, to point out how he turned away from "culture" and sought the society of singers and dancers. He certainly had a passion for *cante jondo* or *cante andaluz*—the "deep song" of southern Spain—and wrote a book of poems inspired by it. But a passion for *cante jondo* is not turning away from culture. Many "cultured" people have frequented the performance, and—if they were able—the society, of Andalusian singers and dancers, not because they were tired of "culture," but because they wished to acquire something of the oldest culture in the Peninsula. There is no room for conjecture about this; Lorca has told us quite clearly what went to the formation of his poetry and his mind, and popular poetry had a large share in it. It did not begin with *cante jondo*, however, but with the kind of poetry known in Victorian England as "nursery rhymes." *Nanas,* he called them, *nanas infantiles*: songs sung by a mother to put her baby to sleep. In the late Twenties, Lorca went about Spain collecting *nanas,* and formed the impression that, in Spain, they "use melodies of the most melancholy and bloodthirsty description." That, we have seen, applies to other countries, too. The chief singers of these songs, he found, were the women who went out for nurses.

> These nurses and domestic servants have long been performing the important task of bringing ballads, songs, and stories to the houses of the well-to-do. The old ballads of Gerineldo, Don Bernardo del Carpio, Tamar, the Lovers of Teruel—children hear all these from those admirable nurses and maids who come down from the mountains or up from the rivers to give us our first lessons in Spanish history.[5]

García Lorca described this to an audience at Havana with such simplicity and conviction that it must have been what happened in his own home at Fuente Vaqueros, in the country near Granada.

> The mother or nurse often turns the song into an abstract landscape, almost always at night, and there she puts—like the oldest and simplest interludes and mystery plays—one or two characters who perform some sim-

[5] *Obras completas,* Ed. Guillermo de Torre (Buenos Aires: Losada, 1938-48), VII, 122: "Las nanas infantiles." An "omnibus" edition, preface by Jorge Guillén, appeared in 1954. "El hombre" Alfonso Reyes had said, "sólo quiere oír lo que sus abuelos contaban; y los narradores de historias buscan el Arte Poética en los labios de la nodriza" ["Man wants to hear only what his grandparents used to talk about; and the storytellers look for their Poetic Art in the lips of their nurse"], *El descastado* (1916).

ple dramatic action, generally with the finest but most melancholy effect
that can possibly be imagined.[6]

On this diminutive stage come the types which will stay in the child's
head for the rest of its life: the man who led his horse down to the
water, but left him with nothing to drink

> de aquél
> que llevó el caballo al agua
> y le dejó sin beber.

Or the man who tried to feed his horse "on the leaves of a green lemon,
and he wouldn't eat them at all."

> A mi caballo le eché
> hojitas de limón verde,
> y no las quiso comer.

The mother [Lorca said] evokes a landscape by the most simple means,
and makes a personage pass across it whom she hardly ever names; . . .
and the child has a poetic game of pure beauty before going to sleep.
"That man" and his horse go off into the distance along the road under the
dark branches down to the river, and he comes back to ride again when-
ever the song begins once more. The child never sees him face to face. It
always imagines him in the shadow: the man's dark clothes and the bright-
colored saddle blanket.

No one in these songs ever shows his face. They must go off into the
distance and take the road to places where the water is deeper, and the
birds will never fly any more.

In other songs the child recognizes the man, knows him by sight; for
the outline of his figure is familiar—even his features and the flat curl
on the forehead, like Antonio Torres Heredia in one of the gypsy
ballads. But it is a world of poetry inaccessible to us: one without a
grain of reason to destroy it

. . . where [Lorca says, in a way very characteristic of him] the white horse,
half nickel and half smoke, suddenly falls wounded with a swarm of bees
buzzing furiously over his eyes.

Sometimes mother and child themselves go off on an adventure.

Danger threatens. We have to grow smaller and smaller; the walls of the hut
touch us all the way round. Outside they're watching us. We have to live
in a very small space. If we could, we should live in an orange, you and I.
Or better in a grape. . . . And at that point sleep comes.

[6] *Ibid.,* VII, 126.

It is fascinating to find Federico García Lorca describing the formation
of his own poetry from the ways he has heard mothers and nurses put
their babies to sleep. It applies to his earlier poems; it applies to his
ballads, and seems like a description of what the mother is saying to
her baby in the first act of his play, *Bodas de sangre*. One of the ballads
is called "Romance sonámbulo," "a sleep-walking ballad." But all of
them are that: all have dream vision and dream logic, and the dream
is induced by the poet telling the story to put us into a condition in
which dream vision and dream logic are only natural. That applies to
nearly all Lorca's poems, not only the ballads, but the ballads are the
best examples.

Romance de la luna, luna

The moon came down to the smithy, crinoline of tuberoses. The child
was looking and looking, the child kept on looking. The air grew more and
more excited; the moon kept moving her arms, and showed, lascivious yet
pure, her hard and tinny bosom.

"Moon, moon, run away! If the gypsies found you here, they would steal
your heart to make their metal rings and collars."

"Child, let me dance awhile! If the gypsies really come, they would find
you on the anvil with both of your eyes shut tight."

"Moon, moon, run away! Now I hear their horses coming."

"Go away, don't put your feet on my stiff and starchy whiteness."

Nearer, nearer, came the horsemen, drumming the drum of the plain.
In the smithy, the small boy was waiting with eyes shut tight. Through the
olive-grove they came, bronze and dream: they were gypsies. Their heads
were thrown back proudly, but their eyes were all turned inwards. How
the little owl was hooting there, as it sat on a bough! Through the sky the
moon was marching, while a small boy held her hand.

But there were tears in the smithy, tears and shouting: they were gypsies.
And the air was watching, watching; the air kept watching her go.

Romancero gitano

The "Romance sonámbulo" plays on the Spanish overtones of the word
for "green," like an early poem of Juan Ramón Jiménez. Yet the feeling
is essentially Lorca, with a suggestion of Falla's ballet *El amor brujo*.

Romance sonámbulo

Green, green, how I love you! Green wind, green branches. The ship
far out on the sea, and the horse upon the mountains.

With the shadow in her girdle, dreaming at her window-bar, green cheeks
and green hair, and eyes of the cold silver.

Green, green, how I love you!

Under the gypsy moon, things utrn to look in her eyes, yet she cannot see them too.

Green, green, how I love you!

See the great stars of hoar-frost, coming with pitch-dark shadows, opening the road to dawn. Now the fig-tree strokes the wind with the smoothness of its branches; the mountain's a thieving wild-cat, fur on end with cactus prickles.

But who's that? How could he get there?

Still she's at her window-bar, green cheeks and green hair, dreaming in seas of bitterness.

"Neighbor, I would change with you: change a good horse for your house, change my saddle for your mirror, my long knife for your blanket. Neighbor, bleeding all the way, I come from the passes of Cabra."

"If only I could, young man; here's a deal that's quickly done. But I am no longer I, and my house is not my house."

"Neighbor, neighbor, let me die, decently and in bed. An iron bed-stead let it be, and the sheets be linen sheets. See the gaping wound I have from my navel to my neck."

"Ay, three hundred roses red, frill the front of your shirt; and I smell the smell of blood, oozing round about your sash. But I am no longer I, and my house is not my house."

"Let me go up, at least, to the high barred window: Let me go up, let me pass to the high green window; to the window-bars of the moon and the roaring waterfalls."

Then the two neighbors went up to the high barred window, leaving a trail of blood, leaving a trail of tears; while the little tin lanterns trembled there on the roof, and a thousand drums of crystal beat on the early morning.

Green, green, how I love you! Green wind, green branches.

So the two neighbors went up, and the wide wind left with them a rare taste in the mouth, of gall and mint and sweet basil.

"Neighbor, neighbor, tell me now, where is your daughter, bitter-sweet? How long shall I wait for you! How long, how long have I waited! That pale face, that coal-black hair, at the green window bar!"

Out on the edge of the cistern the gypsy girl was swinging. Green cheeks and green hair, and eyes of the cold silver. An icicle from the moon held her above the water.

The night had become friendly like the turn of a back street. The Civil Guards were drunk when they came and knocked at the door.

Green, green, how I love you! Green wind, green branches! The ship far out on the sea, and the horse upon the mountains.

Romancero gitano[7]

Yet this is a ballad. The gypsies are not only bronze and dream; they have knives. There has been a fight, a *reyerta*; and the girl's lover is

[7] *Oxford Book*, Nos. 249, 250.

bleeding to death. "Señores," the Civil Guards are told in another ballad, "here it has been the old, old story. The dead were four of them Romans, with five that were Carthaginians."

> Señores guardias civiles:
> aquí pasó lo de siempre.
> Han muerto cuatro romanos
> y cinco cartagineses.

The ballad of the martyrdom of Santa Olalla (Eulalia) begins with a reference to a roughly illustrated religious leaflet—a "tract," almost—showing Flora, stark naked, ascending "a little old stairway of water":

> Flora desnuda se sube
> por escalerillas de agua

The diminutive -*illas* does not mean that the stairs are particularly narrow, but that the poet had an affectionate feeling for them: a memory, perhaps, of those in the garden of Generalife, where the water runs down the banisters. The same love of diminutives can be heard in the everyday speech of Argentina, Chile, and Mexico: *adiosito,* "goodbye, my dear"; *ahorita,* "I'll do it for you in a moment"; *despacito,* "gently, gently." The Romans knew this way of speaking, too, and called it CAPTATIO BENEVOLENTIAE; to Lorca it came naturally. We never find him "talking bronco."

III

Lorca, from the first, was fascinated by what children sing in the streets. Granada is—or used to be—full of the sounds of falling water and children playing; and it was a blend of those two sounds that reached you if you leant over the walls of the Alhambra. "Clear runs the river, oh!—fountains are falling."

> Arroyo claro,
> Fuente serena[8]

You feel that Lorca would have given everything to have been the only begetter of a real Spanish "nursery" rhyme like that, or a piece of pure verbal magic like "Moon, moon—bells in the moon"

> Luna, lunera
> cascabelera.

[8] *Obras completas,* II, 95. "Balada de la placeta," his first published poem.

Even the grim Unamuno fell to this, though on his rough tongue it turned to bitterness: "Moon, moon—lunatic moon"

> luna, lunera, lunática.

The poetry of children's games was frequently an inspiration to Lorca like the poetry of cradlesongs. The "Ballad of a Day in July" is unintelligible, unless one knows that game of *Viudita*, the Widow. In that game, a ring of children dance round the "widow," who sings:

Yo soy la viudita	Oh, I am a widow,
del conde Laurel,	The Countess Laurelle,
que quiero casarme:	I want to be married;
no encuentro con quién.	To whom, I can't tell.

The ring of children answers; and the widowed countess, looking round the circle of intense Spanish faces says: "I choose . . . you!" making a dive for the chosen one who becomes the countess in her turn.

García Lorca brought this into his early ballad of a July day—it was in 1919—when, to the tinkle of silver cowbells, a voice asks:

> "Where are you going to, my pretty maid,
>   All sun and snow?"
>
> "I'm going to pick daisies, sir," she said,
>   "In the green meadow."
>
> "The meadow is very fearful
>   And far from here."
>
> "For the rough wind and deep shade
>   My love has no fear."
>
> "He'll fear the sun, my pretty maid,
>   All sun and snow."
>
> "But he has gone from my sight
>   Now long ago."
>
> "Who are you, then, fair maid,
>   And where is your home?"
>
> "From deep loves and fountains
>   Do I come."

> (*A tinkle of silver cow-bells*)

"What have you got on your lips
    That burn so red?"

"The star of my true-love,
    Who's alive, yet dead."

"What do you bear in your bosom,
    So light and fine?"

"The sword of my true-love,
    Who's dead, yet alive."

"What have you got in your eyes,
    As black as jet?"

"The sorrow of my thoughts
    That wound me yet."

"Why do you wear that mantle,
    As black as death?"

"Oh, I'm a widow, gentle sir,
    In want and sorrow.
My true-love, he was Count Laurelle
    Lord of the Laurel."

"But who are you looking for, my pretty maid,
    If you've no lover?"

"I seek the body of Count Laurelle,
    Lord of the Laurel."

"So then, you look for a lover,
    My pretty widow?
You look for a lover too far,
    For I am with you."

"The stars of heaven are my delight,
    Oh, sir," she said.
"But where can I find my own true-love,
    Alive or dead?"

"Your true-love, he lies in the stream, pretty maid,
    All sun and snow;
With maiden pinks about his head,
    And his great sorrow."

"Alas, my wandering knight-at-arms
    Of the cypress tree,
One night beneath the moon, your soul
    You offered me."

> "Oh, Isis of my long dream,
> Maid without honey;
> You, in the speech of children,
> Your dream have told me.
> My heart I offer you,
> A heart that's human;
> One wounded by the eyes
> Of every woman."

> "Oh, knight of gallantry,
> Good-bye to you.
> I go to look for Count Laurelle,
> My love so true."

> "Good-bye, good-bye, my pretty maid,
> Rose ever sleeping,
> You go to look for your true-love,
> And I for dying.

> *(A tinkle of silver cow-bells)*

> My heart will bleed to death
> Like the stream below."

Libro de poemas[9]

That sort of poetry is not Federico Lorca's great poetry—not his final achievement—but it was the everyday stuff out of which much of his mature poetry grew. Yet it is misleading. The version given above is not translation, but transplantation; it is Lorca transplanted from Granada to England: a Spanish tune harmonized like an English folk-song, and translators ought *not* to do that sort of thing. They should resist the temptation of turning these poems into an English which gives all the wrong associations. Lorca's poems, if ever they are to be translated adequately, must be put into an English which (the phrase comes from R. C. Trevelyan) is "disinfected" from all English suggestions; only then can it convey the exotic suggestion of the original Spanish. One must firmly avoid both English rhyme and Scottish ballad meter.[10] To my mind the most successful translations, so far, are those of Stephen Spender and J. L. Gili; yet this literal version, with some attempt at

[9] *Ibid.*, II, 65: "Balada de un día de julio."

[10] The disinfection, however, must be done with care. "All words," a correspondent wrote—words as used in poetry—"are boats laden almost down to the water-line with suggestions—and if they are English words they must necessarily carry a cargo of English suggestions; and if you throw them overboard you have a barren, unevocative, prose kind of a word."

conveying the vowel harmony of the original, and beautifully printed
with the Spanish on the opposite page, seems—to Spanish readers—
"colorless." They miss the rhythm. Actually, the rhythm is the one thing
which an English translator can follow, and more or less reproduce.
Translation of Lorca's poems should, above all, be rhythmical, following
as far as possible the movement of the original. The ideal English version
would be one which would fit a setting of the original Spanish to music.

Lorca's poems were recited—first to friends, and then in public—long
before they were printed. His poetry is for the ear, not for the eye; and
that should be taken into consideration by those who translate him.
But one thing in his poetry is frankly untranslatable: the verbal magic.
In this respect the recent Spanish poets have all been conscious of their
forerunners; particularly the Renaissance poets Garcilaso and Góngora,
and the primitive poets of the Middle Ages. Some of the early Spanish
poems—some of the refrains of the early Spanish poems—are little
more than jingles: delightful jingles signifying nothing. That is true
of a great deal of primitive and popular poetry; but there is a magic,
too, in the mere sound of Spanish words, however charged with
meaning and association they may be now. Mallarmé wrote to Degas
that sonnets were not made with ideas, but with words; and in medieval
Spain (and in later times too) words themselves have an effect, a power,
a magic, which no amount of "meaning" can explain away. The sound
may mean more than the sense. The poetry is not in the meaning, but
in the evocation.

There remains the imagery; and that, a translation should be able to
convey. Lorca's imagery came originally from popular poetry and
children's games; and also from the semipopular poetry of an earlier age,
which, in his time, was being recovered from the sixteenth century music
books. It often has the *curiosa felicitas* of country speech. Then Lorca
found that Góngora had done the same thing. He saw that language is
formed on a basis of imagery, and that the people in his part of the
world—Granada and the south of Spain generally—had a magnificent
wealth of imagery. "Green voices," for instance. We should say now
that they were an invention of García Lorca; but they are already in
Góngora. So are the hours all "dressed-up in numbers," *las horas ya de
números vestidas*; and eyes like Federico's own "with much night in
them": *los ojos con mucha noche.* Yet those are in Góngora, too; while
the phrase "an ox of a river," *un buey de agua,* an Andalusian image
admired by Lorca and extolled by all his critics for its startling originality, had already been used by Horace and before him by Sophocles.[11]
It is old, and Mediterranean; for rivers flowing down from the mountains

---

[11] *Odes,* IV, xiv, 25: "Trachiniae," 10-14.

in Mediterranean countries rush like a bull, in spring, though in summer they run bone-dry or a little trickle in the sand.

Lorca was a man whose strongest impressions were visual. In this, he was like other Spanish poets of his time, like Rafael Alberti, whose first thought was to be a cubist painter; like Juan Ramón Jiménez, who worked in a studio at Seville, and like Moreno Villa of whom it would be hard to say whether he was primarily a painter or a poet. García Lorca's metaphors are almost always conditioned by sight. So are the metaphors of cradlesongs. It is a view which limits the field of vision and gives it a sharper outline, though it foreshortens the perspective and concentrates the light, like a view through prismatic glasses. One thinks of Keats, doing much the same thing. Lorca knew that, too. His knowledge of English was limited, yet he divined that Keats had concentrated his vision in the same way. He wrote—rather oddly—that

> . . . even the most evanescent [*sic*] English poets, like Keats, must draw an outline and limit their metaphors and figurations; and Keats is saved, by his admirable plastic sense, from the dangerous poetical world of his visions.

"Imagery," he said later, in a talk on Góngora at the Residencia de Estudiantes, "is a change of dress or occupation, between things and ideas."

> They have their own planes and their own orbits; but metaphor joins them through the imagination taking a high fence on horseback (*un salto ecuestre de la imaginación*) . . . The poet harmonizes two different worlds, and gives them plastic form, in a way that may often seem violent; but in his hands there is no disorder nor disproportion. He holds, like toys, seas, and geographical kingdoms and hurricane winds.[12]

Francis Thompson said much the same of Shelley in his famous essay in the passage beginning: "The universe is his box of toys." Lorca's religious imagery, also, is that of a child. Rather than from the statues in country churches, it came from the domestic plaster saints on the family altar or chest of drawers, and the little clay figures which children put into their toy "Bethlehems" (*nacimientos*) at Christmas. There were also the rough woodcuts on those broadsheets which used to appear at certain seasons of the year, and were known as *aleluyas*.

---

[12] It has been observed that this passage in Lorca's "Imagen poética de Góngora" is not far from Valéry in "Eupalinos ou l'architecte." That Lorca had Valéry in mind is probable, because he mentions him by name; and he was at the Residencia in 1924 when Valéry came there to lecture.

IV

To the end, Lorca kept something of the wide-eyed wonder of a child, in a world where many of the others were mad.

I said: "Why, it's afternoon!"
But it wasn't.
The afternoon was something else
which had already gone.
        (And the daylight
shrugged its shoulders like a girl.)

It's afternoon! But no, it's no use!
This is a sham one; this has
a half moon like lead.
The other won't come back ever.
        (And the daylight—we all saw it—
played at being a statue with the mad boy.)

That one was little,
and munched a pomegranate.
This one is biggish and green, and I can't
take her in my arms or dress her.
Won't she come back? Why won't she?
        (And the daylight, as it went—for a joke—
separated the mad boy from his shadow.)

                                        Canciones[13]

Campana

In the tower,
        the yellow tower,
a bell is tolling.
In the wind,
        the yellow wind,
bell-notes everywhere falling.

Stroke of resounding dagger,
opening a wound in the distance.
And yet they tremble, like
the breasts of girls playing.

[13] *Oxford Book*, No. 247. The translations were made for a friend twenty-five or thirty years ago, when the poems were new and no one had thought of putting them into English; but the sense is a poor substitute for the sound.

In the tower,
the yellow tower,
now the bell stops ringing.

The air out of the dust,
is making ships of silver.

Poema del cante jondo[14]

Canción de jinete

Córdoba.
Far-off and lonely.

Coal-black mare and big full moon;
Olives in my saddle-bag,
Even though I know the roads,
I'll never come to Córdoba.

Along the plain, along the wind,
Coal-black mare and blood-red moon.
Death's always watching me now
From the towers of Córdoba.

Alas for the long long road!
Alas for the valiant mare!
Alas for the death that awaits me
Before I come to Córdoba.

Córdoba.
Far-off and lonely.

Poema del cante jondo[15]

No child was ever more affectionate than Lorca, or could inspire more affection in others. I repeat the remark: "I write poetry because I want people to like me," that he made to a friend in Montevideo. Yet the writing of poetry was a serious business, the most serious thing in life.

"The poet who is going to write a poem," Lorca said—and added that he knew it from his own experience—"has the vague sensation of going to a nocturnal hunting party in a wood a long way away. An unaccountable fear whispers in his heart. To calm himself, it is always useful for him to drink a glass of cold water, and make black pen strokes with no meaning."

[14] *Obras completas*, IV, 102.
[15] *Oxford Book*, No. 246.

Lorca kept his head, and held on tight, even in the most overpowering moments; and he was always careful of his technique.

"I am not unconscious of what I am doing," he told Gerardo Diego, the editor of an admirable anthology. "On the contrary, if it's true that I'm a poet by the grace of God—or the devil—it is also true that I'm one by the grace of technique and effort, and of knowing exactly what a poem is." [16]

Poetry (he said) felt like fire in his hands; yet he understood it and could work with it perfectly. *Mira. Yo tengo el fuego en mis manos. Yo lo entiendo y trabajo con él perfectamente.*

His most complete account of poetic inspiration came in a lecture at Havana: Theory and practice of the *duende,* or familiar spirit. [17] In many parts of Spain there was a saying "He has a *duende*" or "has much *duende.*" "You have a voice," a young Andalusian singer was told—a singer of *cante jondo.* "You know the styles; but you will never have a success, because you have no *duende.*" In Andalusia people talked perpetually of the *duende,* for they found it in whatever came out with the irresistible effectiveness of instinct. An elderly gypsy dancer exclaimed one day, on hearing a record of the pianist, Brailowsky, playing Bach: "*Olé!* That has a *duende*"; but she was unmoved by Gluck, Brahms, or Darius Milhaud. And Miguel Torres, the gypsy, "the man with the greatest culture in the blood I have ever known," Lorca said, declared when he heard Falla playing one of his *Nights in the Gardens of Spain*: "Everything that has black sounds has the *duende.*" These black sounds, needless to say, have nothing to do with the black notes on the piano. They are the mystery, "the roots (Lorca said) held fast in the primitive slime we all know (but which none of us really knows) from which comes everything that is substantial in art." The *duende* is not quite *das Dämonische* which Goethe told Eckermann he found in the playing of Paganini. Nor should anyone confuse it with the demon of theological doubt at which Luther threw a bottle of ink; or with the conventional devil of popular theology, which Lorca thought so absurd and unintelligent because he disguised himself as a little dog to get into convents.

> The duende (he said) is a power, not a method; a struggle, not a thought. . . . It is not in the gypsy's singer's throat, but rises from within him, from the soles of his feet. . . . For every artist, every step he climbs in the tower

[16] Gerardo Diego, *Poesía española . . . contemporáneos* (1931), p. 298; (1934), p. 423.
[17] The Spanish *duende* has generally been identified with the Latin DOMITUS, house-spirit; but see the article by Yakov Malkiel in *Estudios hispánicos: homenaje a Archer M. Huntingdon* (Wellesley, Mass., 1952), pp. 361-92. Alfonso Reyes speaks somewhere of "la hora del duende" and we may remember Calderón's play, *La dama duende.*

of perfection costs him a struggle—not with the angel, or with the muse, but with the *duende*.[18]

Falla had the *duende* and Juan Ramón Jiménez has it; but in few has it risen so often from the soles of the feet to produce the "black sounds" that we get in Federico García Lorca.

The *duende* rises unmistakably in many of the plays. If he had lived, Lorca would have been the poet who returned Spanish poetic drama to the heights where it was left by Lope de Vega; for after his lyrics and ballads, Lorca's highest flights were in tragedy; and *Bodas de sangre, Yerma*, and *La casa de Bernarda Alba* have restored tragedy to the Spanish stage. Many of his plays suggest the Irish plays of Synge, both in the language that people talk and the kind of people who talk it. (An English writer in the Argentine, Mr. Patrick Dudgeon, first pointed this out.) Lorca is unlikely to have known Synge in the original; but there is an excellent Spanish translation of *Riders to the Sea (Jinetes hacia el mar)* by Juan Ramón Jiménez. It came out about 1920, and Lorca is bound to have read it; there is, in fact, an extraordinary likeness between the mother in *Bodas de sangre* and the mother in *Riders to the Sea*. Their thoughts run on the same lines and they say much the same things. One thing is clear, at any rate: the proper language for translating Lorca's plays is Anglo-Irish. Yet one looks in vain for that beautiful choice of simple words, and those appealing Anglo-Irish cadences, in the translations of Lorca's plays that are printed and performed.

Yerma and *Bodas de sangre* were great experiences when one saw them on the stage; and so was the interpretation of Margarita Xirgu, who showed from the first that she believed in the poet, and did not, like some others, insist upon alterations. *Yerma*, another of his interpreters said, was the tragedy of Federico himself.[19] Again, the early play, *Mariana Pineda*, is also a beautiful and moving experience. It already shows the poet's power over the ballad; and incidentally gives the lie to those who would like us to believe that he had no political convictions. The play was, in fact, produced at a time when it could only have been taken for a protest against the dictatorship of Primo de Rivera.

---

[18] *Obras completas*, VII, 142-43.

[19] One of the critics who was present at the first performance of *Yerma* has written to me as follows: "La Argentinita, la noche del estreno de *Yerma*, nos decía esto: 'La obra es la propia tragedia de Federico. A él lo que más le gustaría en este mundo es quedar embarazado y parir . . . Es ello lo que verdaderamente echa de menos: estar preñado, dar a luz un niño o una niña . . . Yo creo que lo que más le gustaría sería un niño . . . Yerma es Federico, la tragedia de Federico.' " ["Argentinita told us the night of the *Yerma* premiere: 'This play is about Federico's own personal drama. What he would like best in the world is to become pregnant and give birth . . . That's what he misses in life: to be pregnant, to give birth to a boy or a girl . . . I suppose he would like to have a boy . . . Yerma is Federico, Federico's tragedy.' "]

In a way the whole of Lorca's theater is a political conviction, or at any rate a social service; and his *Barraca*—a traveling or fit-up theater—was "a theater for everybody," like the Old Vic; a protest and a contrast to the commercial Spanish theater, where it used to be impossible—and once more seems to be impossible—to perform Lope or Calderón or any of the great plays of the past without copious additions or *refundiciones.* Lorca proved, with his amateur or semiprofessional *Barraca,* that Lope de Vega has only to be put straight on the stage, by intelligent people of good will, to have an overwhelming effect on a modern audience. *Fuente Ovejuna* and *Peribáñez,* produced by García Lorca, had a message for a Spanish audience of the Thirties, which neither their original creator, nor any subsequent producer, is likely to feel again. "He sat on the grass in a circle of blue dungarees," one of them told me, "the student members of *La Barraca* theater workshop, who did *Fuente Ovejuna* in the open air."

Lorca achieved the height of his poetic expression in his lament for the bullfighter Sánchez Mejías. This is not merely a piece of local color or traditional *popularismo.* Sánchez Mejías was no ordinary bullfighter, though he had reached the top of his profession. He had written an original and successful play; he was a fine and noble character and enjoyed the friendship not only of García Lorca and Rafael Alberti, but of other poets and writers of their generation. So, too, had the cattle breeder Francisco Villalón who, after writing some shorter poems which derive (though not too closely) from one of the earlier manners of García Lorca, suddenly revealed himself as a most original poet, with *La Toriada (The Toriad),* an epic, in the language of Góngora, on the life of wild bulls in the long grass of their native pastures. Villalón was a poet, even in his professional relations. He declared that he had always had an ambition to breed a bull with green eyes, and he lost a fortune over it.

The death of Sánchez Mejías in the ring brought consternation to his friends; but it led to two of the finest poems in modern Spanish literature: the *Llanto (Lament)* of Garcia Lorca and the *Elegia* of Rafael Alberti. Both poems are in several movements like a symphony; Lorca's four movements in different meters are a summing up of his whole poetic achievement. The first has one short line repeated like a bell; though it is so plain a statement of fact—the time of day—that he may have read it first in a newspaper. The second is in the traditional Spanish ballad form; the third, in the long lines of Spanish alexandrines; the fourth mainly in blank verse.

This poem should finally confute those foreign critics who try to fit Lorca into the traditional black legend of Spain: that it is all blood, lust, mysticism, and death. The second movement is called "The blood spilt"; but the whole burden of it is "No! I won't *look* at it!" The last movement is not an apotheosis, for the dead man's soul is absent. It is a poem difficult to judge on its own merits, for it is inevitably confused in one's mind with the poet's own death a year later: dragged out and shot by some blundering adherents of General Franco.[20] Lorca's poetry remains, in his own words, "a conscious rocket of dark light, let off among the dull and torpid": *un cohete inteligente de luz oscura en la tonta modorra de las gentes.*

[20] Brenan, t.c., 127-48. See also, Marie Laffrangue, *Textes en prose tirés de l'oubli.* Bordeaux: Bull. Hisp. LVI, No. 3 (1954).

Lorca and the Expression
of the Spanish Essence

by Dámaso Alonso

In Lorca's works Spain turned out more bitter, more impregnated with its own character, more closed, more tragic, more obsessive
than any other nation. This does not mean that he was prejudiced in
favor of Spain, because as much bad is depicted as good. And it is not
Spanish boasting on my part, because so many dazzled foreigners, so
many readers attracted from elsewhere, have already said the same thing.
From Spain's highly intense and even dangerous concentration of vital
forces there sprang a dramatic necessity for a differentiated kind of expression, a national expression, in all forms of life, in all forms of art.
Every race needs to express itself: life is no more than expression. But
in general in the other European countries which have an important and
ancient national culture, the expression of their essential qualities is
carried out without interruption. In these countries the expression of
subject matter takes shape more through nuances and chiaroscuro than
through radical contrast. When, on the other hand, we wish to characterize Hispanic self-expression, we must resort to torrential and erup-
tive images: the overflowing of a stream which sweeps away fields and
towns; or seething lava which cracks rocks and burns everything. So
much for the mood and the form of expression; with respect to the subject itself, we must point out that the color of the national essence
impregnates even Lorca's smallest details in such a way that these become visible and acquire significance through this coloration.

There is a terrible intensity in his concrete details, an almost brutal
violence in his expression. We see in it the presence of Spain. His is the
torrential genius of Spain which bursts out from time to time, producing
strange contorted beings, visionaries whose power of expression in national as well as universal terms reaches the highest conceivable peak.

"Lorca and the Expression of the Spanish Essence." Translated by Gloria Bradley.
From *Poetas españoles contemporáneos* by Dámaso Alonso (Madrid: Editorial Gredos,
1952; 2d ed., 1958), pp. 271-80. Reprinted by permission of the author and Editorial
Gredos.

What can European art offer, within this violent framework, which equals an El Greco possessed by the Spanish spirit, or a Goya?

And nowhere can this general principle be seen more clearly than in literature, in this art which is made of words, that is to say the shadow of our thoughts, the breath of our emotions, a sort of fragment or emanation of our very souls.

Throughout Spanish literature, regardless of whether we follow the line of "popular" writers or that of so-called "cultivated" ones, in the epic poems as well as in the ballads or in the modern songs, in the *Lazarillo* as in the novel of the nineteenth century, in Berceo or in Fray Luis de León, in Quevedo and Góngora as in Bécquer, there is, near the surface or deep in the entrails, this strict sense of closed distinctive autochtonous expression. But things happen as if the hidden, guiding purpose were not satisfied with these forms of continuous and normal manifestation of the tightly closed Spanish peculiarity. From time to time in sudden convulsions deep abysses are opened; an earthquake shakes loose an implacable inner vitality in a real outburst of the Hispanic core.

An explosion of this kind of genius took place in the fourteenth century with the Archpriest of Hita who, at the height of a period in which the individual was still scarcely differentiated, projected his gigantic figure in which personal expression and the Spanish essence are equally triumphant.

Down through the centuries other nuggets of incontestably Hispanic substance have become heavier within the main lode of our literature: such were the Archpriest of Talavera, the *Celestina*, the *Lazarillo*, and finally, above all others, the illustrious Cervantes, whose *Don Quixote* produced the major miracle of world literature: the greatest intensity in the local sense united with the most penetrating search into the universal soul of man.

But, for various reasons, Lope de Vega is the best example of such writers. In Lope's genius are united all the elements of the Hispanic character which had appeared before him in Spanish literature. He fathomed the hidden recesses of the common soul and mastered the language of the average honest man with as much malice and thoroughness as the Archpriests and the *Celestina*. And thus he held the great treasure of our folklore. He infused artistic animation into all our social classes with their struggles, their pleasures, their jealousies, and their wavering. He saw and rendered with a marvelous instinct for local color—something which we believed to be a modern invention—the regional variety of Spain with the particular light and odor of its fields and seas, from the mountains of Leon and Vizcaya to Cadiz, from Salamanca to Valencia. In short, in Lope a work of art was a rendering of the Spanish spirit. This is so not only in that part of his work dedicated to the masses, or inspired by them, but also in his cultivated poetry. Here there is a human warmth, a passion. To a certain extent his work gives us a fore-taste of Romanticism and is full of the sun and the salt of Spain. Seen in this way, Lope de Vega is the most genuine representative of that which is most Spanish in literature and the first of our great poets.

After Lope de Vega many years were to pass. They were years little adapted to literary creation; the eighteenth and nineteenth centuries favored only the novel and produced but a few isolated poets. The law of Spanish literature, its irrepressible necessity, Hispanic expression be-fore universal expression, did not stop during these two centuries. But the great personalities in whom are concentrated the essences of the country were lacking.

Many years were to pass. It was necessary to reach the beginning of the twentieth century to witness a great poetic movement, a movement as genuine and widespread as anything Spain had seen since the be-ginning of the Golden Age, a great tide of poetry begun by Antonio Machado and Juan Ramón Jiménez which has not yet ebbed. There, in the dawn of the third decade of the century, it happened that two young men who were to become great poets, Rafael Alberti and Federico García Lorca, did not merely turn their eyes to folk and traditional inspiration, but rather penetrated to the very depths of the national spirit. They intuited it and created it with assurance and depth, speaking with the authentic voice that had been lost since the period of Lope de Vega. But the art of Alberti successively offered a series of points of view which at times departed from the popular vein. There was no one who thirsted more for change or strove more for perfection than this poet. Almost every one of his books was a new departure. Yet his fidelity to himself was complete, as complete as his fidelity to the spirit of Spanish expres-sion. Of Lorca this is also true.

Lorca's art is an essentially Spanish activity with respect to its pro-fundity as well as its range. It would be convenient but inaccurate to call this art a miracle. Lorca is, within the framework of Spanish litera-ture, a writer who was necessary, who could have been foreseen. Spanish literature from time to time needs to express itself in a more intense and pure form. And so it produces an Archpriest of Hita in the fourteenth century, a Lope de Vega in the seventeenth century, a Lorca in the twentieth. In our time, therefore, the essences of Hispanic thought drew together again; our diluted tradition condensed; the salt of our wit, the wisdom and irony of our peasants, the inflexion and rhythm of our songs concentrated in one man; and out of them came forth Lorca's art. It came forth because it had to. It had to fulfill the law of our destiny. Spain had expressed herself once more.

This strange concentration of the essences of the nation can be seen above all in Lorca's personality. His social success is more than anything else a Spanish success. In Spain he becomes the center of attraction of any group of friends, of any meeting he attends. A treasure-house of charm, he laughs with loud contagious peals of laughter which affect even the most melancholy. Now he imitates Valle-Inclán's white beard with a napkin; now he flutters his eyelashes and speaks, swallowing his pauses, like Gerardo Diego; now he rolls guttural *r*'s like Max Aub; now he scribbles Surrealistic drawings. These talents are not the disjointed and insignificant talents of an entertainer but the formidable powers of a man who could capture every means of expression. Hear him speak of the "madness of water" in the Generalife Gardens or of the "swept light" of dusk in Granada. His imagination places on the threshold of our fantasy landscapes, men, and atmosphere. But we are now in New York City, at a wild party given at the caprice of an American millionaire. Through the spacious rooms people wander in little gesticulating groups, and the beverages begin to take effect. Suddenly this maddened and disparate mass converges toward a piano. What has happened? Lorca has begun to play and to sing Spanish songs. These people do not know Spanish nor do they have the least idea about Spanish culture. But his force of expression is such that light penetrates those minds that had never seen light, and the smooth bitterness of the Spain they had never known reaches their hearts.

In Spain, at the piano, with a few friends, for two, three, four hours, without tiring, songs and songs pour out from Lorca. There was never a better way of realizing how deeply he felt about the whole of Spain: he sang Andalusian songs, gypsy songs, Castilian songs, songs of Leon, of Portugal, of Galicia, of Asturias, with the *sardanas* and the *zortzicos*. All the antiquity of the *Cancioneros,* all the modernity of today's songs, all the wealth of Spain, were there, felt and interpreted with his bad voice, his voice so immersed in the depths of Spanish emotion that whoever has heard him will never forget him and will find false and insipid anything that he hears afterwards.

He drinks from all of Spain, and he gives back of himself to all of Spain. He exhibits his sensitive sketches in Barcelona and impresses the artistic circles of Catalonia. He spends some time in Galicia and writes, without knowing the Galician language, the best poems in that tongue which have appeared in our time. His arrival at Madrid is greeted by enthusiastic applause. There is no city he visits that he does not charm. And what about his lectures with musical illustrations or the purely literary ones? What he does not know, he invents. I remember now his lecture on Góngora. He does not let anything stop him, and he produces for a few fragments of the *Soledades* an interpretation completely divorced from the obvious meaning. But that does not matter. The lecture is beautiful and his general interpretation of the art of the great seventeenth century Spanish poet is perfect and indisputable. Success goes with him everywhere.

And so far this was still the very limited success of a poet. The dramatist arises in him. His name passes to the lips of the great masses, not

only in the Spanish peninsula but also in every country that has had a
historic tie with Spain. He had already been sympathetically and en-
thusiastically received in Cuban poetic circles. Now it is Buenos Aires
which acclaims his theatrical productions during hundreds of performances. A patriotic effort of cultural propaganda: this is what he accomplishes—unintentionally, and thereby of course most effectively, and
better than anyone else could have done, through the sheer miracle of
his charm and his great Spanish art.

He knows all of Spain. In large part this is through direct contact,
through the instantaneous grasping of the intimate sense of the people's
forms of expression. And the rest he invented. What he invented becomes
in his work as authentic as everything else. Lope de Vega had done the
same many times. Today it is often hard to know what was invented
by Lope and what was taken by him from folklore and tradition. In
The House of Bernarda Alba, Lorca's last dramatic play, completed
shortly before the start of the Spanish civil war, there is at one point a
salmodia or traditional song. When he read it to us someone asked him
where he had got it. He said he had made it up: nobody could distinguish it from an authentic one. And in the same fashion he often
made up the melodies for the lyrics in the plays he directed: some I
have heard sung by people who were themselves ignorant of the author-
ship and are now on the way to becoming truly popular among many
different groups. This power of creating or inventing the folk traditions,
the power of the great artist immersed in the creative roots of his people,
was always lacking among the pseudocreators of folklore in the nineteenth
century, in whom you can see the pastiche at ten miles' distance, and it
is this power that distinguishes the true masters, the great interpreters
of a nation's spirit: Lope de Vega, Lorca.

The same power can be seen in his dramatic dialogue, above all in
the works in which he begins to ripen as a dramatist: *Blood Wedding*,
Yerma, *The House of Bernarda Alba*. The dramatist in Lorca restrains
the poet from an excess of lyricism which still at times interrupts the
action in *Blood Wedding* but which has almost completely disappeared
in his last work, in which the dialogue has a laconic, mathematic, schematic perfection. As usual, Lorca follows here a long tradition of com-
petence in the rendering of the popular idiom. Perhaps no one has
succeeded in doing so with more restraint, with less artificiality. In the
works of even a great artist like Valle-Inclán we detect the effort to
reproduce the common vernacular and perceive the labors of a cultivated
poet. Not so in Lorca. He has grasped the deepest secret of the inner
form of language: the placing of a verb, the introduction of a particle
are at times the way in which his sentences acquire all their meaning and
flavor. There is no verbosity in Lorca, none of the archaic aftertaste that
follows pseudodialogue inspired by an exaggerated super-Hispanicism; on

the contrary, we find in his works an absolute fidelity to the national and individual psychology of his characters.

This genial trace of the Spanish character in his dialogue is supplemented by his insuperable intuition for what one might call general dramatic language. By this I mean anything that can be expressed on the stage. For Lorca was a great stage director. Sometimes he had to struggle against the inexperience of the young actors in his company (an inexperience compensated for by their dedication and affection) and at other times against the paralysis and the detestable mannerisms of so many professional actors. He triumphed over every obstacle, sometimes by dint of sympathy, sometimes through his contagious enthusiasm. Even acting groups already entrenched in old habits worked miracles when taken over by Lorca. And the young actors of his theater group, constantly on tour, brought the gospel of true art to the heart of Spain. I can still see it now: in the town square, a few seconds before the start of a performance given out of doors, a fine rain begins to fall. The actors become drenched on the stage, the townswomen cover their heads with their loose clothing, the men contract and huddle together: the raindrops keep falling, the show goes on, nobody leaves. Lorca concerns himself with everything: the tone of voice, the position of each actor on the stage, the total effect. Nowhere is his talent more clearly seen than in those hollow passages of written drama, in the dead letter that only a great director knows how to bring to life. Remember that gradual crescendo "wake up the bride" which the guests cry out in *Blood Wedding*; remember the gathering in *Fuente Ovejuna* and Lorca's way of animating passages which if read in a book would hardly leave a mark in our imagination. Who can forget a certain scene of *En las almenas de Toro* in which through the same technique he could underline both the national tradition and the poetic and plastic beauty of the work? What would have become of such dramatic highlights if left to the vulgarity of our professional hams? Lorca destroyed the cardboard monsters and threw a dazzling white Spanish light on the fairyland of the stage.

The goal of Lorca's artistic personality, to be the voice of Spain, is reached above all in his lyrical poetry. To what degree and in which way is he a lyrical poet? He is almost never a poet who feels compelled to write in order to bare directly the inner recesses of his own soul. His poetry is lyrical and subjective, only inasmuch as we can always find in it the unique stamp of his personality: a slenderness, a nervous subtlety which make him the finest, the most sensitive of our contemporary writers. But the soul which sings in his poems, both hiding itself and revealing itself in the mysteries of poetic creation, is not the soul of the poet: it is the soul of his Andalusia, it is the soul of his Spain. His intense and penetrating images, when clear, carve the image of Spain; when

obscure and elusive, still manage to suggest Spain from their mysterious
subterranean sources. The half-sleeping music and the blurred rhythm
make Spain shimmer amidst the beat of the *cante jondo* or the ancient
monotonous rhythm of the ballad. The atmosphere, as in

> Cordoba,
> distant and lonely . . .
>
> Only sighs row
> through the waters of Granada . . .

is evoked by soft restrained chords, framing Spain in a bittersweet vague-
ness full of distance and memories. Lust, darkness and death assault her;
destiny and magic mystery wait, lurking in a night full of perfume. The
soul of Spain—Andalusian, Gypsy, Roman—clear and dense, scent and
light turned to music, is what Lorca's poetry offers us. In it the soul of
Spain fulfilled once more the law of its destiny, its irrepressible need for
expression.

A Poet Crazy about Color

by Louis Parrot

Lorca's colors! It is too bad that Valery Larbaud, who did not have the chance to finish his *Domaine espagnol*, his study and anthology of new Spanish poetry, discovered Lorca's colors too late. How many philological or pictorial insights might he not have drawn from the comparison of Lorca's poems and the paintings that he had seen during his travels on the Iberian Peninsula. Larbaud stopped at Ramón Gómez de la Serna, and surely his curiosity could not drag him away from the Café Pombo where I brought Paul Eluard one day and where Gómez de la Serna, one of the most brilliant prose writers of his generation, gave a performance each evening. The theme of Lorca's colors still remains to be dealt with. Perhaps one day a student will attempt to draw a comparison of the blue of the moon along the route taken by Don Quixote and the reddish and golden light of Madrid's Main Square discussed by Ramón de la Cruz in his *sainetes* and the shimmering radiance of fruits Lorca describes for us in the myriad arabesques of a Matisse.

Still lifes, sleeping guitars, a silhouette simplified to the extreme, landscapes with graceful lines dominated by the gamut of reds and yellows, Lorca's first paintings, the pastels that he sent to his friends from Granada when he had just arrived in Madrid, these are the sketches for his poems. When he was a very young man he used to decorate his letters with designs, with little watercolors. Perhaps he wished to show by this that for him painting was inseparable from poetry. Salvador Dalí, who knew Lorca when he was twenty, describes for us Lorca's intensive efforts to imprint his paintings on his poems. There was no poetic image which did not appear to him without a vibrant color, surrounded by a musical rainbow. More than any other Hispanic poet, Lorca succeeded in making us feel this rainbow around the most familiar words.

Without a doubt this rare gift for giving back to colors their purest brilliance was constantly strengthened by his memory of the brilliant scenes of his childhood. He was always to preserve faithfully the picture of that old city of Granada near which he was born and upon which

"A Poet Crazy about Color." Translated by Gloria Bradley. From the preface of *"Lorca"—Les Poètes d'aujourd'hui* by Louis Parrot (Paris: Editions Seghers, 1947), pp. 43-61. Reprinted by permission of Editions Seghers.

all the colors of the prism multiply as upon a jewel with a thousand facets. During his travels, his long stays in Madrid and abroad, these colors of the South continued to live in him. He remembered the Alameda at sunset, the Albaicín, the Alhambra and the Generalife Gardens, gardens where all the Andalusian flora weaves an incomparable Persian rug upon which the Darro River is placed cautiously as if it were an ancient sword.

One discovers again all this flora in his *Gypsy Ballads*, in his *Book of Songs*, as in an herb garden where it loses none of its fragrance. In the only page that he dedicates to Granada, Théophile Gautier had been forced to resort to the simple enumeration of colors: he could not, it seems, suggest them. As Lorca was to do later on, he employed at first an original color scheme of basic colors to paint the neighboring mountains: pale sea green, light brown, red, dark brown, striped pink, from which, little by little, the new "veiled tones" come, submerged by a vast liquid purplish wash. He uses a second gamut for evoking the city with variegated façade: vermilion, apple green, rosy white, jonquil; these are, he claims, the colors of the satin slippers of the Andalusian women, of the flowers and the shrubs of the Alhambra, the jasmines, the myrtles, the pistachio trees, the laurels, the rose bushes. Finally he resorts to a third gamut, more subtle and finer still, since when the evening comes it clothes, he says, the country and "the mountain with a silk gown fringed with silver," with all the iridescence of mother-of-pearl: frosty pink, opal, ancient pearl, sapphire, agate, the infinite nuances which Lorca was to rediscover in his memory and with which he was later to paint his *Gypsy Ballads*. But just as these colors do not appear simultaneously to the traveler, they do not appear all at the same time before the poet. It is only after a long struggle that he uncovers them. As his work progressed, the new colors appeared in it, just as a day from morning to sunset will witness successively all the possibilities of light.

For this reason it may be useful to draw a chart of the colors used by the Andalusian poet, to show how they are born, how they grow, how they vanish in his poetry. The progressive changes in coloration, and throughout his work the appearance of new shades, might shed light on the nature of his intent. In the first poems, as in certain of his gypsy ballads, where the landscape of olive trees and cypresses forms the backdrop of the action, colors are deliberately made poor and take the form of objects—dull silver, lead blue, moon gray dominate. The landscapes are lighted by a moon "with breasts of hard tin"; only the important features are indicated by reddish shadows; the faces are white or yellow. The popular elements in these poems, which belong to a childish world of images, demand primary and clean colors without running into each other. The words seem to be encircled by the musical background of the poem, but they are scrupulously separated and none of their shades mix. It is only later that the nuances appear, when the poetry becomes richer, the horizon expands, and the landscape becomes complex. The wind and the water, the Andalusian rivers, intervene then, and the primary colors of his adolescence poems are not enough to bring to light the allegorical figures who enter the scene. The sunlit words are now adorned with new tints; they light up with a thousand variegations. In the *Cante Jondo*, the "River Guadalquivir with his garnet beard," appears; the "Virgin of Solitude opens like an immense tulip"; the "dark Christ with his prominent cheekbones and his white pupils is changed from a lily of Judea into a Spanish carnation." We are sometimes reminded of Rouault.

Thus each book of the poet will be presented with different colors and with a gamut that grows constantly richer. In the *Gypsy Ballads* these colors reach a variety and a violence that are dazzling. Lorca, like Van Gogh, is a painter crazy about colors. Any subject suits him, provided it gives him a pretext for using the luminous tints which vibrate in us long after we have closed the book. All these shades which he juxtaposes with an unconscious art could seem to us excessive if we did not know that they are often truer than those we see; our eyes have been tired for a long time—our vision has become blunt and no longer allows us to distinguish the shimmering shades with which the solar spectrum surrounds the surfaces of even the most lusterless objects. Like Van Gogh, Lorca knows how to see them, and he gives them to our eyes. All are polished to their highest brilliance. The wind is not only green-hued, but so strongly so that it becomes an emerald old man who chases Preciosa. The fruits are a yellow velvet. If the houses are white, they are like chalk. No shadow can rest on the "indigo walls of the side streets of his secret neighborhood," Juan Ramón Jiménez later will be able to say. And among all these colored masses there is an interplay of multiple shades which take on fleeting forms: mother-of-pearl fish, a tie that is not red but crimson, a straw-colored gilliflower that is to be found again and again in his poems and in his plays. As for the famous green which appears so often in Lorca's landscapes, Jean Camp suggests an ingenious explanation for its frequency. "Might it not be," he says, "the memory of the green Prophet's turban which floated in time gone by over all the minarets of Granada and on the lances of all the Moorish warriors? Is not green still today the sacred color of Islam, and did not Lorca wish by this device to underline the imprint of Islamic fatalism upon this land of the *Santísima,* one-third Christian, doubtless, but according to the ancient couplet two-thirds Mohammedan?"

Later, in the "Ode to Walt Whitman," which makes one think of a painting by André Masson, with its corduroy draperies and its birds pierced by arrows, and in his less well-known poems about New York, strange colors are superimposed on the primary colors that he had brought from Andalusia, and give them the vital depth, the warmth, and richness of enamel. As the work of the poet matures, his colors become more subdued. They do not disappear, nor fade, but rather become fused with the words; they return to the shade. They mass there as a thousand luminous spots in the moving crowd at a bullfight when the sun begins to set.

Moreover, the crowd is for Lorca a spotted fruit, spattered with gold dots, speckled with black, with scars that are slow to close—a fruit which turns slowly beneath the sun. In the magnificent poem about the death of the bullfighter Ignacio Sánchez Mejías colors take on a muted vibration. The great bullfighter died in August of 1935 in the arena of Madrid. I remember with what grief Bergamín learned the news at the Escorial and how he returned hurriedly to the deathbed of his friend. Sánchez Mejías was a very cultivated man, a friend of all the young poets of his time, and his death sent all of Spain into mourning. In the poem dedicated to him the colors do not vibrate; they are mute; they no longer speak to our eyes. They are grouped silently around the luminous circle in which the tragedy of death takes place, in which the sunset, suggested by a bloody cape and a sword still vibrating on the woolly neck of the beast, seems to be scribbling with charcoal on the sand these funereal lines from which all color has been withdrawn:

> Oh white wall of Spain!
> Oh black bull of sorrow!
> Oh hard blood of Ignacio!
> Oh nightingale of his veins!
> No. I do not want to see it!

Only two spots of color remain on the whiteness of the design. One is the head of pale sulphur of the "dark Minotaur" resembling those which Pablo Picasso was then drawing. The other was the spot of blood which the poet did not wish to see. This poem, one of the last which Lorca wrote, no longer makes use of the simple and dark colors that he employed in his first verses.

Between these first poems and the *Lament for the Death of a Bull-fighter*, in which today we can discover so many allusions to his own death, there stretches a whole shimmering world, a brilliant profusion of colors. Birth, then profusion, then abandonment of colors. Having proved himself a master of dazzling color, Lorca renounces little by little the overabundant use of his favorite shades. And it is only when our enchantment is over that we can distinguish, intertwined among all the themes which provide the lifeblood of this poetry, the theme of death of which he has given us so many tragic and painful variations.

The theme of death, constantly nourished by a fundamental melancholy constituting one of the most typical traits of the Spanish character, is present in all his work. It is blended with the happiest images, those that express the most candid joy. Nevertheless Lorca is not a tormented man. But in the Southern lands "Andalusian hearts/ always seek old thorns."

It is this constant preoccupation which is expressed in his *coplas*, where one finds the voice of a whole people who can no longer speak for themselves, and the words that have been forgotten, but whose echo remains in us. The death Lorca evokes in his poems is shown to us in the most carefree colors, hidden under familiar words which are used to express in one way or another our daily share of sorrow and happiness. For him death is the shadow dragging to the ground the sun-bathed objects, and it is even more visible when the light is brightest. It is over this shadow that the fragile landscapes which he describes with such restless love are painted. Painted in the fear that he will not have enough time to tell us about them, tell us how they were and how they will be forever: the olive tree growing above the yellow wall, the grotto where the gypsy forge burns, a group of adolescents in a field of stones. In each of these poems the tools of death find their work. A dagger burns in the hand of every true gypsy and it plays a great role in the ballads and the theater of Lorca. Like a sunbeam, the "dagger lights up the terrible depths." It is again a dagger which trembles "at the heart of the crossroads where the streets vibrate as a rope." The cathedral of Granada is made of golden knives; the most humble fishermen see clearly at night thanks to the brilliance of their blades. Seville is "a tower full of fine archers," where yellow cannons are juxtaposed with Andalusian arrows. In the air the "roses of black powder" burst. The heart of the Virgin is pierced by arrows and carnations. Saint Eulalia, whose martyrdom he depicts with the colors of a stained glass window, with the shades of an old tapestry, is only a bit of tortured flesh. She hangs from her tree before a vast landscape of snow and "her burned nudity fans the icy air." Everywhere, utilized with an innocence that is never cruel, we find these allegories, these images of a bloody death, of a voluptuous sense of tragedy with which the theme of love is always connected. Death and love face each other and penetrate each other so intimately in Lorca's poems that it is impossible to separate them from each other: they are expressed, fused, in images which often convey a double sense, that which is understood immediately when one reads these poems, and that which we discover later in ourselves when we have absorbed them.

But is it not the medley of these two themes that more than anything else characterizes his poetry? In a letter to the Colombian poet, Jorge Zalamea, he wrote:

Now I am going to create poetry that will flow like blood when you cut your wrists, poetry that has taken leave of reality, written with a feeling that reflects all my love for things and my amusement at things. The love of death and the joking with death. Love. My heart. It's like that. All day long I work in a factory of poetry. At times I throw myself into the subject of Man, of the pure Andalusian, of the bacchanale of flesh and laughter. Andalusia is unbelievable: the Orient without poison, the Occident without action. Every day I have new surprises. The beautiful flesh of the South forgives you and thanks you after you have abused it.

A large part of his work was written under the signs of *ardor* and *brio*. All the themes which occurred to him and which he treats in his poems have a passion full of tenderness. He dreamed of expressing all of these themes in all their forms. The poet Lorca was a musician and a painter. From the moment of his arrival in Madrid and during his travels abroad he never stopped painting and he never forgot the long visits that he had with Manuel de Falla, when he was only a college boy.

Lorca had all the qualities of his race and also all of its defects. It is not impossible that there ran in his veins some drops of that Moorish blood which once created the grandeur of Granada. And he was certainly never displeased when people believed him to be of gypsy origin.

Now legend has turned him into a gypsy, and for a gypsy, music and poetry are one single medium of expressing the cruel tenderness, the maternal sweetness, the poverty and the beauty of these Southern lands whose unity is made of contrasts. As there are many Spains there are many Andalusias—the classic Andalusia of Seneca, the baroque one of Góngora, the maritime Andalusia of Juan Ramón Jiménez; then there is the Andalusia of the Sierra Morena Range, that of the orange groves, that of the great rivers and of the legends. There is also the grieving Andalusia which Lorca describes in his poems and whose sadness can sometimes be contained in a song, an Andalusia in which all the others are united, vibrant and golden as a guitar full of prayers and sighs. And it is to this Andalusia that Lorca always remained faithful. He left to others the care of singing in loud, gaudy verse of the easy exotic nature of the province of his birth, or of describing its picturesque quality and its poverty in novels widely read outside Spain. He never ceased thinking of that gypsy land when he painted in Madrid or wrote the first stanzas of the *Poem of the Cante Jondo*. In a few lines he sketched a lost village in the mountains, the calvary on the Bald Mountain, the men who pass wrapped up in their capes, and on top of the towers the weather vanes that never stop turning in the cold wind. For him objects, the spots which trees make on the sky, houses, animals, are so many luminous hollows surrounded by a delicate halo of golden light. "All the light of the world can fit in an eye"—"the cock crows, and his crow lasts longer than his wings." But also: "the emptiness that an ant leaves can fill the air." On the horizon there appears "the very white hollow of a horse—surrounded by spectators whose voices are full of ants." Only he can see

> A thousand concrete forms seeking their emptiness,
> stray dogs, bitten apples.
> I see the anguish of a sad fossil world
> which no longer can find the sound of its first sob.
>
> *(Poet in New York)*

He painted Andalusian landscapes. He sang old Seville airs. He added some touches of color or some musical accompaniment to the drawings that Salvador Dalí brought him to Granada one day. The painter Dalí was for him "a marvelous friend" who wrote him: "You were a Christian spasm and you needed my paganism. I will go and get you to take a sea cure. It will be winter and we will light a big fire. The poor beasts will be numb. You will remember that you are the inventor of marvelous things and we will live together with a camera."

At Cadaqués, on the level Catalan square carefully painted egg-yellow as in the poems that he had written in Madrid, Lorca took these strange color photographs that the painter Dali was to reproduce in his canvases. Shortly after exhibiting his own paintings in Barcelona in 1927, Lorca wrote an ode in praise of his friend lauding the landscape that inspired him.

This was the period when Salvador Dalí painted his rocks with human faces on the livid beaches, where one day finally the ghost of Vermeer of Delft appeared to him. He measured his "invisible, fine, and average harp" with his yellow yardstick and found on that very beach the first metamorphosis of his Narcissus, his soft watches, the edible furniture, all the elements of his "lugubrious game" which should, he said, lead him to the "conquest of the irrational." The least objects, the pebbles of the Cadaqués beach, these he painted with affectionate care, and Lorca described for us his "palette with its wing—pierced by a shot." Dali hated simplicity in all its forms. He said so himself, but Lorca was no dupe.

In his Ode, Lorca conjured up the first paintings of his friend, and one can still see, arising from under his pen, the allegorical personages of Dali's canvases, the apparitions on the deserted beach, the strange objects, the torn forms, the hollow rocks, like hollow sponges holding crutches which are thrust in the sand. "I sing," he said, "of your marvelous effort to capture Catalan lights and of your love for everything that is unexplainable."

Throughout the poem, which was published in Madrid by José Ortega y Gasset in his *Revista de Occidente* (a magazine which was during all those years the most active spiritual center of the Peninsula), Lorca exalted this friendship that he shared with Dalí and which was more important, he added, than "the painting which you are designing so

patiently." Lorca at that time had as yet published only the *coplas* of
the *Cante Jondo*. Dalí did not yet dream of going to live in Paris. Long
afterwards, the poet was to remember with nostalgia those "obscure and
golden hours" that he had lived with such fervor and which had united
the two men with a common thought, a common intention: to express
"everything that is unexplainable." Shortly after the Ode appeared, the
painter went off to Paris, to the conquest of the irrational, and Lorca
published his *Gypsy Ballads* which brought him back to his birthplace
and made known to every attentive Spaniard all the "marvelous things"
that he had invented.

The Early Poems

by Roy Campbell

In the collected edition of Lorca's works, printed as a prefatory introduction to his *First Poems*, we find a quotation from Lorca's spoken conversation with his friend and contemporary, the very excellent poet Gerardo Diego. It is revealing, not of any preconceived and conscious system by which Lorca worked, but of his total freedom from any such system:

> But what am I going to say about poetry? What can I say about these clouds, about this sky? To gaze, to gaze, to gaze at them, to gaze at it, and nothing more. Understand that a poet cannot say anything about poetry—that must be left to critics and professors. But neither you nor I, nor any poet, knows what poetry is.
>
> Here you are: listen. I have fire in my hands. I understand it and work perfectly with it, but I can't speak about it without literature. I understand all poetics; I could speak about them if I did not change my mind about them every five minutes. I don't know. One day bad poetry may please me very much, just as today bad music pleases me (and us) almost to madness. I would burn the Parthenon tonight just to begin to rebuild it again tomorrow, and never finish it. In my lectures I've sometimes spoken of poetry, but the only poetry I can't speak about is my own. And not because I'm unconscious of what I'm doing. On the contrary, if it's true that I'm a poet by the grace of God—or of the devil—it's because I'm also a poet by the grace of technique and effort.

In this reported speech, which rings very true, we are reminded of the instinctive opportunism of Apollinaire, who also wrote like Lorca, straightforwardly, with grammatical structure, in the vernacular, and to whom all things whether beautiful, ugly, comic, or repugnant were potential subjects for poetry. Both wrote in simple language bordering on plain everyday speech—the antithesis to "Hopkinese" or to Dylan Thomas' highly stylized personal language. They saw whatever was commonplace or quotidian with the fresh eyes of children. Sophistication and

"The Early Poems." From *Lorca* by Roy Campbell (New Haven and London, 1952), pp. 29-50. Copyright 1952 by Yale University Press. Reprinted by permission of Yale University Press and Bowes & Bowes Publishers Ltd.

experience never exhausted that gift of wonder and genuine interest that transformed for the townsman and soldier, Apollinaire, the cavalry defenses outside his trenches, or the lights on the tramlines in the suburbs, into the magical substance of poetry; or for the countryman in Lorca the commonplace objects of his landscape, such as sisal into "petrified octopus," or prickly pears into "multiple batsmen" and "savage Laocoöns."

This power of enthusiastic perception is merely a matter of vitality—it is not an adopted attitude. In calling Lorca a "nature poet" I mean something very different from what is meant in England. The influence of the natural landscape on a romantic northern poet generally, not always, results in a "brown study," a blending of the intellectual attributes of the poet with the rocks, trees, and mountains around him, until they seem to become more articulate, reasonable, intelligent, and sentient than the poet himself. There is a sort of "merging" and self-annihilation in which the un-intelligent part of the landscape gets the better of the intelligent part of it, the poet, and finally swallows him. The poet disappears completely, into an inhuman mist which gets thicker and thicker, undisturbed by his dissolution, and apparently impenetrable to any supernatural rays from above. This operation is commonly practised by German, Scandinavian, and Anglo-Saxon poets; and it is judged to be highly laudable to be able to extinguish oneself in this way, as I know from far better poets than myself, though I have never been able to see the point of this self-immolation to an insensate universe. As a Celt and a Latin, nature leaves me cold, except as something to be dominated, confined, made to fructify, and loved, if at all, for the sake of the benefits it confers when it is properly treated, kept in its place, and rationed with water and manure. I like to see the sierra terraced from top to bottom by the skill and strength of men's hands, not lying uncultivated and wasting. I like to see a horse brought to the fullness of its strength and expression by having a skilled rider on its back, not running about as a brumbie trying to fend for itself on the backveld.

That is where Latin "nature poets" differ entirely from the German and English Romantics. When I read Wordsworth, I feel that all his rocks, trees, and mountains are more intelligent than human beings, whereas his human characters, wherever they can be unearthed, are almost without exception imbeciles and nitwits. I feel that there is something deeply perverse, intellectually suicidal, and misanthropic about this transposition of values. In fact I think the whole Romantic principle (in its bad sense) can be defined as something perverse, a sort of centrifugal panic in which the poet escapes from himself: a principle that subordinates the immediate to the remote, the evident to the occult, the normal to the abnormal, the lucid to the obscure, the moral to the immoral, and the present to some Utopianized future or romanticized past. It necessitates many, or most, of these falsifications to credit a mountain, or a cloud, with having a quarter of the intelligence of an ant, let alone of a man. Aldous Huxley says that Wordsworth would never have written his poems on the benevolent intelligence of nature, if he had lived in the tropics among cobras, tarantulas, and scorpions. But Huxley commits as sentimental a perversion in seeming to ascribe a malignant intelligence to tropical "nature." I had two years as a jungle coast-watcher, almost entirely on my own, in the tropical fever forests, and another eighteen months in a shepherd's cot in the Welsh mountains, well within sight of Wordsworth's hills. Nature was equally severe and clement in both places. What would have disturbed me in either case, and maybe sent me off my head, would have been to imagine that nature outside was evilly or kindly disposed to me, and consciously stalking me with misfortunes or trying to bestow benefits on me; for those are the very superstitions that make savages so miserably unhappy; and they return in the form of fetishistic credulity, where Europeans have lost their faith, as in Huxley's case. The difference in the Latin-Mediterranean type of "nature poetry," seen at its best in the *Georgics* of Virgil, is that there is no brown study, no Buddhistified blurring and blending with "the Whole," to the detriment of all outlines and sane values. Where a Latin poet creates a darkness, as in Saint John of the Cross's *Dark Night of the Soul*, it is not for the sake of merging with that darkness alone, nor the losing of all contours in a brown study; it is simply to rid the mind of a less intense form of reality, so as to give it all the more power to seize the more intense reality of God. The proof is in the fact that this kind of mystical poetry makes you wide awake, and the other soothes you almost to sleep; and this is the difference between the mystic and the mystagogue. The nature poets of the Latin races tend to differentiate, to particularize, and even to anthropomorphize the objects about which they write, as Virgil did with his bees, bringing them out clearly from their background. The tendency of the northern poets is to let nature envelop them around with moss, clouds, weeds, and flowers, until we and they disappear in a dream of mental vegetation and vapor.

Lorca, who had known intense suffering in childhood and throughout the rest of his life, since he was never to know the normal command of his muscles and limbs, grew up among those countrymen who, different from the poetical excursionists, know the particular in nature, and not a single entity with a capital N. The things that attract his attention most as a poet are always in his immediate surroundings, with their peasants and their animal population of bees, butterflies, nightingales, cicadas, frogs, and lizards. The poems in his first collection were written between the ages of eighteen and twenty-two. In dealing with the smaller creatures of the earth, he affects a sort of Lilliputian minuteness, almost Franciscan in its intimacy, which in its detail reminds one of the exquisite treatment of bees by Virgil and Góngora, or the even more perfect treatment of the fable of the Town and Country Mouse by Horace in his satires. We are reminded of the pre-Romantic poets in our own literature, the exquisite Drayton of the *Nymphidia*, the speech of Mercutio about Queen Mab, and certain passages of *A Midsummer Night's Dream*. The very important difference is that we are torn by Lorca between a comic grotesqueness and a heartrending pathos with which he invests these slightly humanized, tiny creatures of the fields. He notices on the lizards their "little white aprons," calls them "drops of crocodile," and "dragons of the frogs," seeing their "green frock-coat of a devil's abbot." But Lorca's small animal and insect world, though conceived with a childish directness of vision, is no dream world of Titanias and fairies, but the real old world we inhabit ourselves, seen in miniature, with startling clearness, as through the wrong end of a telescope. Its fierceness remains undiminished by microscopic proportions, and becomes all the more startling because of them and because of a sort of Goyaesque and Bosch-like mixture of the human with the Lilliputian.

The description of the voices of the frogs "freckling the silence with little green dots" is another uncanny but perfect image to those who have heard the frogs of the southern marshes, at sundown, start up their chorus with the twinkling of the stars. When I say Lorca partly humanizes his creatures, I do not mean that he detracts from their peculiar frogginess, lizardliness, or whatever it may be. The touch of humanity seems to enhance and emphasize their innate quality as frogs, snails, or ants, by the sheer force of contrast. I have mentioned how Lorca used to love harrowing and terrifying the peasants by imitating the priest's "hell-fire sermons." Some of his poems, of a seemingly trivial nature, are so poignant that one sometimes indignantly and resentfully accuses the poet of going out of his way to make one suffer.

In one of his earliest poems describing the Odyssey of a snail, we are made to enter the nightmare world of suffering. The snail, "the peaceful bourgeois of the meadow," feels a sudden curiosity about the world and decides on seeing, if he can, "What is at the end of the path." He meets two frogs, one of which is blind and both of which are beggars; after a depressing argument with them which brings on a mood of pessimistic doubt, he meets some ants. I quote this passage in a literal prose translation, since it is too hard to translate into verse:

> Now over the path
> An undulating silence
> Flows from the olive grove.
> With a group of red ants
> He next encounters.
> They are going along angrily,
> And dragging behind them
> Another ant with his
> Antennae clipped off.

The snail exclaims:
"Little ants, have patience.
Why do you thus illtreat
Your companion?
Tell me what he has done,
And I will judge in good faith;
Relate it, little ant."
The ant, by now half-dead,
Says very sadly,
"I have seen the stars."
"What are stars?" say
The other ants uneasily.
And the snail asks
Pensively, "The stars?"
The ant repeats,
"I have seen the stars.
I went up to the highest tree
In the whole poplar grove,
And saw thousands of eyes
In my own darkness."
The snail asks again,
"But what are stars?"
"They are lights which we carry
On the top of our heads."
"We do not see them,"
The other ants remark.
And the snail says "My eyesight
Only reaches to the grass."
The ants exclaim,
Waving their antennae,
"We shall kill you
You are lazy and perverse;
To labor is your law."
"I have seen the stars,"
Says the wounded ant.
And the snail passes judgment:
"Let him go free,
Continue your work.
It's likely that soon,
Worn out, he will perish."

Across the mild wind
A bee has passed.
The agonizing ant

Inhales the vast evening
And says, "It is she who comes
To take me to a star."

The other ants run off
On seeing he has died.
The snail sighs
And goes off amazed
And full of confusion
At the eternal. "The path
Has no end," he exclaims . . .

This disconsolate mood recurs with insistence and power in Lorca's early
work: and it returns even more powerfully in his later plays in which he
invariably deals with what we call "unpleasant subjects." But in these
later plays, the cruelty which he flings in one's face almost aggressively,
as if to relieve his own sufferings, is tempered and balanced by the
Euripidean stature of the protagonists, their innate strength, their willingness to accept suffering (since there is always a way out by cowardice or
compromise) and their capacity for resignation. We accept his plays as
we would accept them from scarcely anyone else dealing with the same
subjects. It is his sheer artistic mastery which makes us accept them, and
the realization that his compassion is, after all, one of the main motives
for burning both himself and us with such anguish.

In his *Romancero gitano* we get the same cruelty and suffering. Ben-
jamín Janés calls these poems "Little pictures drawn in ice by a refined
savage." But in these perfect little pictures we are removed from the
direct anguish of the emotional stab, since Lorca is not telling us the
tale himself, but, as it were, through the mouth of a gypsy, whom he is
parodying and burlesquing at the same time. This removes the impact
so that we receive it at second hand, as we do the very real tragedy of
"Tam O' Shanter" in Burns, which if it had been written straight out
in the vernacular by Chekhov, Maupassant, or Liam O'Flaherty would
be an extremely sordid and harrowing tale. But Burns, whose native
language was English, not Lallands (as we see from his letters to his
intimates), puts the whole story into *patois,* and tells it through the mouth
of a slightly naïve, comical personage, so that we receive the gruesome-
ness on a shield or cushion of laughter. In the same way the personality
of the gypsy whom Lorca impersonates in all his native mannerisms and
naïveté protects the reader from the full impact of the terrifying apparitions, the crimes, the brutal murders, the martyrdoms described in the
Romancero. In the end it is clear that Lorca is not deliberately inflicting
pain on the reader, in order to shock or annoy him; but that he feels so
poignantly that he has to share this feeling with others. This is the
motive underlying his insistence on themes of cruelty. We know that in
his life he was cheerful, full of fun, a radiant and kindly personality, and

that considering the extent and nature of what he had to suffer, there was not much perversity in his make-up, as modern poets go.

Together with this sense of pain one feels almost everywhere in Lorca's poetry, even at its gayest (and it can be very gay) there goes also the sense of a lurking, imminent, and violent death. Even in his most vernal poetry, the shape and presence of death is always there, as in this "Spring Song":

> On the lonely mountain
> A village cemetery
> Appears like a field
> Sown with seeds of skulls
> And cypresses have flowered
> Like gigantic heads,
> Which, with empty eye holes
> And green hair,
> Pensively and sadly
> Contemplate the skyline.
>
> Divine April, who comest
> Charged with sunlight and perfumes,
> O fill with golden nests
> These flowering skulls.

Like Webster in Eliot's poem, Lorca is "much obsessed by Death," and not only "sees" but actually "feels" and "tastes" "the bones beneath the skin." In the "Ballad of the Little Square" ("Balada de la placeta") the children ask him:

> What do you taste in your mouth
> So ruddy and thirsty?

and he replies:

> The taste of the bones
> Of my enormous skull.

Again, in the most voluptuous of all Lorca's early poems, the "Canción oriental," which owes perhaps a debt to Paul Valéry's *Douces grenades entrouvertes* in which the jeweled seeds of a pomegranate are compared to thoughts ripening in the brow of a poet, we get a triumphant image of the pomegranate as half a heart and half a skull. This is one of Lorca's richest poems, glittering with the plunder of other poets such as Góngora, Valéry, and Darío, yet at the same time burning with Lorca's own personality, for he has already fully digested these outside influences; and the plunder already belongs to him by *right of conquest:*

> The fragrant pomegranate! in it
> A heaven seems to crystallize
> (In every seed a star is lit
> In each red film a sunset dies).
> It seems a tiny hive that drips
> With live blood soaking through its mesh
> Because the bees have formed its pips
> Of women's mouths and kisses fresh:
> And when it bursts, a thousand lips
> Are laughing in its crimson flesh . . .
> The pomegranate is like the hoard
> Of the old goblin of the glade
> That in the pathless woods abroad
> Met with the solitary maid.
> It is the treasure whose red rays
> The green leaves guard within their hold,
> It is the ark of gems that blaze
> Within the dim-seen casque of gold.
> The corn ear is the bread. The Christ
> In death or life lies there concealed.
>
> The olive stands for hardness, spliced
> With strength and labor in the field.
>
> The apple is a carnal thing,
> The sphinx's fruit, the food of sin,
> The drop of juice that aeons wring
> With Satan's touch upon the skin.
>
> The orange burns with grief untold,
> Grief that white blossoms were profaned,
> Since now it's flushed with fire and gold
> That was so spotless and unstained . . .
>
> Chestnuts for peace by the fireside
> And bygone things of yesterday:
> The crackle of old logs, the sigh
> Of pilgrims who have lost their way.
> The acorn is the poetry
> Of what is ancient and mature.
> In the pale yellow quince we see
> The cleanliness of health that's pure.

> But in the pomegranate the fierce
> Blood of the sacred heaven gleams,
> Blood of the earth which waters pierce
> With the sharp needles of their streams,
> Blood of the boisterous winds that sweep
> From the rough mountains that they rake,
> Blood of the ocean's windless sleep,
> Blood of the hushed and drowsy lake.
> The pomegranate is the prehistory
> Of our own blood. So gashed apart,
> Its bitter globe reveals the mystery
> Both of a skull and of a heart . . .

The obsessional presentiment of death is pre-eminent even in Lorca's most lush and pastoral descriptions. It is to be remembered that death was very much in the air in the twenty years that preceded the civil war. *Viva la muerte,* the cry of the anarchists, was frequently heard, and their skull and crossbones chalked up everywhere. The sense of death is deeper in Lorca than in most other Spanish contemporary artists. Someone has said jestingly that Death is the patron saint of Spain; and Barrès says that the Spanish consciousness is founded in voluptuousness, blood, and death. To accept this would be to discount such seraphic personalities as Saint John of the Cross, Saint Teresa of Avila, Saint Francis Javier, and Saint Ignatius of Loyola, who are among the most ethereal and purely spiritual creatures in history. The great Castilian mystics had transcended death. Their attitude to death is the very opposite of Lorca's: it is one of longing for death not out of tiredness but because of an intenser life promised after death.

> I die because I do not die

says Saint Teresa, expressing the very opposite of the terrified thrill of anguish which Lorca expresses at the thought of death, and which Goya depicts with such violent force and horror.

In Lorca's first book of verse, *Libro de poemas,* is a most interesting experiment in the shape of an "Elegy to Lady Joan the Mad." Joan the Mad was the daughter of the great queen Isabella; she was driven mad partly by lover's jealousy for her warrior-husband; and in this elegy, while suppressing any historical allusions which would tend to anachronize or "date" the theme, Lorca tackles the subject in a grandiose manner, with full orchestration, almost as if he were toying with the idea of the epic treatment of some such subject. It is powerfully moving and reminds one for a moment of Camoes's passage referring to the unfortunate historical figure of Inez de Castro in the *Lusiads*; or of the

broad full stream of Espronceda's rhetoric in his *Canto a Teresa*. The
following lines are selected from the closing verses of the elegy:

> You had that passion which the sky of Spain confers.
> The passion of the dagger, the listening ear, and the dirge.
> O divine princess of the crimson twilight
> Whose spinning wheel was iron, whose thread was steel.
>
> You never knew the bower or the sad madrigal,
> Nor the troubadour's praises sobbing in the distance.
> Your troubadour was a lad with silver scales
> And the echo of a trumpet was his wooing.
> Yet without doubt you had been formed for love,
> Made for the sigh, for spoiling, and for fainting,
> To weep your grief on a beloved breast
> While you tore a scented rose between your lips . . .
>
> Granada keeps you like a holy relic,
> O dusky princess sleeping in the marble.
> Heloise and Juliet were but as two daisies,
> But you a red carnation full of blood
> Who came from the golden earth of Castile
> To sleep between the snows and the chaste cypresses.
>
> Granada was your deathbed, Lady Joan,
> She of the ancient towers and the still-hushed garden,
> She of the ivy dead on the red walls,
> She of the blue mist and the romantic myrtles.
>
> Princess that loved without the due reward.
> Red carnation in a deep and desolate valley.
> The tomb that keeps you oozes forth your sorrow
> Through eyes which it has opened in the marble.

These powerful alexandrines remind one of the vitality and verve of
Rubén Darío. In spite of some immaturities such as the use of "poetical"
words, like "romantic myrtles," there is a surge of movement and color
in this poem which makes one wonder why Lorca never returned to this
type of elegy orchestrated with epic undertones, like Shelley's "West
Wind." But it seems that already in his first book of verse Lorca had
defined for himself the limits within which he was to write from then
onward; and the only time he ever approaches the same broad and
solemn treatment of such a theme is much later in the *Three Odes*, two
to the Blessed Sacrament, and one to Salvador Dalí, though these are

sustained by a succession of unconnected images which do not fuse into one another dynamically, as here in this elegy with its cumulative and one-way stream of images, increasing in momentum.

Everywhere in the *First Poems* one is conscious of Lorca's growing powers of imagery. Sometimes the imagery is there for its own sake; and sometimes there is a slightly obsessional repetition as when the *chopo* or black poplar tree, with its swaying gestures, is more than once compared to an old man, a music master, or a schoolmaster, and once we see it aiming a box at the ear of the moon for disturbing a music party of frogs, crickets, and trees. One wonders of what teacher or master it is the affectionate souvenir. Poplar trees are so much a part of the landscape in Andalusia, with their perpetual nervous fidgeting, that instead of getting annoyed by the repetition (for Lorca seldom makes a repetition inadvertently) we begin to feel an amused affection for the presiding schoolmaster of so many of his evening classes, group parties, and concerts of trees. Here is a brief passage in which a mere visual fancy or image sustains and performs the function of a poem, like one of those short Chinese or Japanese poems which are satisfied with producing a single vivid picture:

> Trees.
> Have you been arrows
> Let fall from the azure?
> What terrible warriors shot you forth?
> Were they the stars?

He addresses the passionflower as the "anvil of the butterflies" and mosquitoes as the "Pegasi of the dew." A straight road is a "lance wounding the horizon." Donkeys, the most fatalistic and resigned of creatures, are called "Buddhas of the fauna," and the high road with its countless tracks, and spoors, and cart ruts, an "enormous chiromancer" and the "Flammarion of footmarks." Throughout the later poems in the *Libro de poemas* we feel Lorca perfecting his command of these terse and vivid epithets, of which he showed such mastery in his later work that they become his very style itself.

In poems such as "Prólogo" Lorca affects a faintly diabolical and Byronic attitude, probably through the influence of Baudelaire, Lautréamont, and perhaps Salvador Dalí in his early youth; but in this swashbuckling pose, as in most of his erotic poetry, until we come to that one brilliant exception, the "Casada infiel," and to love scenes in his plays which treat love objectively, Lorca is self-conscious and ill-at-ease. He gave up this occasional Byronic pose after his first book; why it did not suit him is probably explained in his self-analysis in one of his very earliest poems where we see him oversensitive and gentle, and something like "El desdichado" in Gérard de Nerval's famous sonnet:

> The waif, the shade, whose grief is absolute,
> The prince of Aquitaine whose tower fell down.

Now follows Lorca's portrait of himself. It is instinct with a deep sorrow which his outwardly radiant and pucklike cheerfulness concealed from his friends:

> I go weeping down the street
> Grotesque and bewildered
> With the sorrow of Cyrano
> And of Quixote,
> The redeemer
> Of impossible infinities.
> With the rhythm of a clock
> I watch the lilies wither
> At the contact of my voice,
> And in my lyrical song
> I wear the trappings
> Of dusty clown. Love,
> So beautiful and handsome,
> Has hidden under a spider. The sun
> Like another spider hides me
> In tentacles of gold. No!
> I'll never prosper in my venture
> Because I am like Love himself
> Whose shafts are lamentations
> And his quiver the heart.

There is no dramatized self-pity in this portrait. Both Lorca's suffering and his capacity for suffering were very great. He did not suffer morbidly, but as a true poet should, by trying to turn his suffering into poetry, and he did this better than most other contemporary poets. His eternal wrestling with the theme of death had its justification, just as Keats's preoccupation with the same theme. It came out of strength rather than weakness. The event proved that it was no illusion. His own violent death, and that of nearly three million Spanish men, women, and children, could already be sensed in the air, like a coming thunderstorm, for many years before the Terror was unleashed. It was publicly threatened on all the walls. One could not escape from being confronted with skulls and crossbones with bloodthirsty inscriptions chalked up everywhere. In his "Song for the Moon" ("Canción para la luna") and in many other poems, he senses and prophetically describes the event, play-fully apostrophizing the moon, and yet clearly foreseeing the desolation of his country. Even in this playful piece of moonshine, we feel the imminence of disaster:

> Living lesson
> For anarchists!
> Jehova has the habit
> Of scattering his farmyard
> With dead eyes
> And the little heads
> Of contrary
> Militias . . .
> Live in the hope,
> Dead eyeball,
> That the great Lenin
> Will be the Big Bear
> Of your landscape,
> The bleak ridge
> Of the sky
> Which will tranquilly drift
> To give the last embrace
> To the Old Man
> Of the Seven Days.
>
> And then, O moon,
> So white, will come
> The unsullied reign
> Of dust and ashes.

In this and other passages is a definite fore-sense of the useless chaos about to be precipitated over Spain. In the repeated wrestling with the idea of death, Lorca generally increases the stature of life, and intensifies it. All those people who repeatedly seek out death to risk their lives do so chiefly because they are overflowing with a surplus of life. They get a stimulus from the presence of death as a healthy body does from a cold bath.

In Lorca's time, the men who risked their lives most consistently were the priests and the great matadors; several of the latter were killed in the exercise of their profession; as were the majority of the monks and priests also, who did not even receive the pay of the lowest artisans for the most dangerous vocation of all. In Lorca's greatest sustained lyrical poem, the *Lament for the Death of a Bullfighter* (*Llanto por Ignacio Sánchez Mejías*), we see a duel between Life and Death, enacted almost as a ritual dance between the superb, overflowing vitality of the matador and the cold shadow of Absence, while each augments and enhances the stature and the mystery of the other. In all his early poems in which he treats the subject of death we feel that the dual process is at work, which he carries to such a supreme triumph in the *Llanto*. Many of the earlier poems are rehearsals of this towering spiral in which the two forces contend in a sort of ecstasy; but there are also heights of serene lyrical contemplation which are exceptional in such a young poet, above all in these lines from the poem "Mañana" ("Morning"):

> But the song of water
> Is an eternal thing.
>
> It is light become the sound
> Of romantic illusions.
> It is firm, yet soft,
> Meek, and full of heaven.
> It is the mist and the rose
> Of the eternal morrow.
> Honey of the moon which flows
> From buried stars.
> For some good reason Jesus
> Realized himself in water.
> For some good reason Venus
> In its breast was engendered.
>
> Christ must have said to us:
> "To whom better, my brothers,
> Can we confide our sorrows
> Than to her who rises up to heaven,
> Arrayed in a spiral of whiteness?"

Ideas are continually suggested to Lorca by the sound of water, to whose endless dropping he compares the sound of a far-off guitar in one of his finest poems, the *Cante Jondo*. The sound of rain in the poem "Lluvia" evokes the following significant passage concerning the fall of rain:

> It is the dawn of fruit. It is that which brings us flowers
> And anoints us with the holy spirit of the seas,
> That which sheds life over the down lands
> And in the soul a sorrow which is not known.
>
> The terrible nostalgia for a lost life
> And the fatal sentiment of having been born too late,
> Restless illusion of an impossible tomorrow
> With the close inquietude of fleshly pain.

Love is awakened in the greyness of its rhythm.
Our interior sky contains a triumph of blood.
But all our optimism turns to sorrow
To contemplate the dead drops on the glass.

And those drops are eyes of the infinite; gazing
Back into the white infinity which is their parent.

Each drop of water trembles on the dim glass
Leaving divine wounds of diamond.

They are the poets of water who have seen and meditate
Things which the vast crowds of rivers ignore.

That image of the inactive drop of water filled with conscious light as contrasted with the blind strength of the brawling rivers gives us an idea of Lorca's conception of the poet's function in the scheme of things —that of static inward illumination, lit up even by one's own sorrow.

Triumph of Sensual Reality—Mature Verse

by Edwin Honig

Romancero gitano (*Book of Gypsy Ballads*) (1928) is the realization of poetic sensibility which has achieved technical mastery over its materials. Here the poet's restless imagination has at last found a form in which to cast his personal cosmology. Less slavish to the letter of folkloric devices, Lorca has begun to create a respectable folklore of his own. The characteristic concentration upon a theme in single monotone, which occurs in the conventional Andalusian song, is replaced in *Romancero gitano* by a solid variety of thematic materials. These are elaborated in subtle musical patterns with a personal emphasis which marks the matured poetic spirit. Written in the traditional octosyllabic meter, these ballads become a series of reinvented *cantares de gesta*. They partake of the anonymous folk character upholding a tradition distinctive for its magical re-creation of language and its exaltation of natural phenomena and pagan feeling. Spanish poets beginning with Jiménez sought to eschew the anecdotal qualities of the old *romance* and to reshape the form according to new inventive techniques. And this is Lorca's first accomplishment in *Romancero gitano*. He has re-created the classical style of the old ballad and given it a new tonal quality which is distinctly modern.

Romancero gitano reflects the sorrows of a persecuted people living on the margins of society, who maintain their old tribal primitivism intact. Hounded by the police, their conflict is symbolized by the silver steel of their knives and the Mausers of the law. The civil guard which hunts them through the night pervades like a plague:

> Black are their horses
> and black their horses' hooves.
> Upon their capes stains
> of ink and wax glisten.
> Because their skulls are made
> of lead they do not weep.

> With patent-leather souls
> they come down the road.
> Hunched and nocturnal,
> wherever they stir they compel
> silences of dark India rubber
> and fears of fine sand.
> They pass, if they wish to,
> and hide in their heads
> a vague astronomy
> of indefinite pistols.

The constant struggle of the gypsies is against a universal repression whose edict is death. They themselves, however, own the moon's proud body which they hammer on a forge in the intimacy of the surrounding night. A people whose innocence is as endless as their misery, they know no argument more final than the fatal message of the dark-winged angels:

> A sharp light of cards
> cuts into the bitter green
> profiles of riders
> and furious horses.
> In the bower of an olive tree
> two old women weep.
> The bull of argument
> climbs over the walls.
> Black angels were bearing
> scarves and water of snow.
> Angels with huge wings
> sheer as knives from Albacete.
> Juan Antonio Montilla, dead,
> is rolling down the slope,
> his body full of lilies,
> between his temples, a grenade
> Now a cross of fire mounts
> the highway of death.

> *   *   *

> The afternoon, mad with fig trees
> and warm murmuring,
> faints in the horsemen's
> wounded thighs.
> And black angels were flying
> through the west wind.
> Angels with long tresses
> and hearts of oil.

Nothing sleeps where the gypsies ride; every image, every stone conceals some threat of danger. Thus, the wind itself suddenly grows lustful and chases Preciosa, the gypsy girl, clear down the mountains into the house of the English Consul. And the iconography of some obscure Byzantine retable depicting the martyrdom of Saint Eulalie is immediately transformed in the erotic symbolism of Lorca's balladry:

> A nude flower climbs
> the water rack.
> The Consul asks a tray
> for the breasts of Eulalie.
> A spurt of green veins
> bursts from her throat.
> Her sex trembles like a bird
> caught in the brambles.
> On the ground, now undisciplined,
> leap her cut-off hands,
> which can still cross themselves
> in soft decapitated prayer.
> Through red pin-holes
> where were her breasts,
> miniature skies
> and milk white streams are seen.

The austere agony of a Catholic martyr's death is turned into a daylight-flushed scene of a bright little Roman orgy, such as might appear commemorated on a Goya tapestry. The same splendor of a reanimated Romanesque landscape permeates the ballads on the three Andalusian saints, Michael, Raphael, and Gabriel:

> In his tower room, full of lace,
> San Miguel displays
> his handsome thighs
> ringed by lantern light.
>
> .   .   .   .
>
> Fashionable wenches come eating
> sunflower seeds,
> their big hidden behinds
> like copper planets.
> Distinguished lords go by
> and ladies sad in aspect,
> dark-pale with longing
> for a past of nightingales.

Into each of these three ballads are woven the alternate patterns of background and the action of figures, while here and there a popular vignette is interspersed. Meanwhile, an entirely new geography has been created for the purpose, so that history itself stares out with sudden interest. It is as if a legend had been garnered from the past and a particular crystallized world invented through which a select species of plants and animals and peoples of every race in Andalusia might promenade. But the stylization of imagery which contains them is never utterly fixed as in Góngora. The secret of fluidity is revealed in the poet's own relentless pursuit of a nature which never finds its rest. Lorca's vision never betrays him into accepting a half-awakened reality as an ultimate form of permanence. This vision triumphs only when the poem has entered the province of song, and all artifice has been merged into the quick movement of feeling and rhythm. The stratagems he uses are attempts to construct an aesthetic frame that will at once dignify a people whose genius is so little understood and interpret their ancient spirit in modern form. The poet hopes to come upon a permanent facet of emotion, and perhaps thereby to define his own temperament more closely. In "La casada infiel" ("The Faithless Wife"), for example, he reveals the quiet essence of gypsy dignity which an innate eroticism can never completely overcome:

> It was on the night of St. James
> and almost as if so arranged.
> The streetlights were doused
> and the crickets lit up.
> On the outskirts of the town
> I touched her sleeping breasts,
> and they opened to me quickly
> like a branch of hyacinths.
> The starch of her petticoat
> sounded in my ears
> like a piece of silk
> slashed by ten knives.

> .　　.　　.　　.

> Past the bramble bushes,
> the rushes and the thorns,
> under her long, thick hair
> I made a hollow in the mud.
> I took off my tie.
> She took off her dress.
> I my revolver and belt.
> She her four underwaists.
> Not spikenard or snails

have skin so fine,
nor do moonlit crystals shine
with such brilliance.
Her thighs escaped me
like two fishes surprised.

. . . .

As a man of honor, I won't divulge
the things she told me.
The light of understanding
has made me quite prudent.
Stained with kisses and sand,
I carried her from the river.

. . . .

I behaved as I am:
a true gypsy.
I gave her a large sewing box
of straw-colored satin,
but did not intend to be her lover,
for though she had a husband
she told me she was a virgin
when I carried her to the river.

It is an untutored spiritual grace by which the gypsy lives. Like the
tenth century Arabic poet, he is cognizant of the higher human ethic
which keeps the abandoned beast from entering the garden. The symbols
of Arab and Gypsy are both so intricately entwined in Lorca's sensibility
that it is not always possible to draw a comparative inference from the
manner in which he treats either of them. However, one may perhaps
differentiate between the more studied, decadent eroticism of the Arabic
lover and the eroticism which rises as an earth force to purify the gypsy.
In the historical ballad "Thamár y Amnón," for example, Lorca presents
an episode of incestuous love, a legend of Arabic imagination. Filled
with such an intoxicating air of sensual vibrations, the poem suggests
the depravity into which love falls when ethical discipline perverts the
natural instinct:

—Thamár, pluck out my eyes
with your fixed dawn.
Threads of my blood weave
flounces in your dress.
—Brother, let me be.
Your kisses on my shoulder
are wasps and little winds

in a double swarm of flutes.
—In your high breasts, Thamár,
two fishes are calling me,
and in the cushions of your fingers
the murmur of a hidden rose.

. . . . . .

All about Thamár
the gypsy virgins wail,
while others receive the drops
of her martyrized flower.
White sheets turn red in
the closed bedrooms.

. . . . . .

Amnón, the frightened seducer,
flees on his pony.
Negroes shoot darts
from the walls and ramparts.
And when the four hoofs
became four echoes,
David, with a pair of shears,
cut the strings of his harp.

One folkloric quality of the ballads is their deep anonymity which cannot be easily plumbed; this is the very spring from which their emotional complex issues. It is not necessary to seek directly into the incidents of origin in order to build, as Lorca did, upon the old cultural structures. Lorca's use of the traditional ballad gradually merges with his whole aesthetic procedure. This use is not the mere exploitation of a theme for the discursiveness of some folkloric poetaster; it is a marriage between the language of personal perception and the language of popular feeling. Lorca's aesthetic demands continually enhance a subjective element of gypsy atmosphere in Andalusian life which others have overworked as an exotic attraction without particular spiritual significance. In *Romancero gitano*, Lorca arrived at a unique synthesis between popular subject matter and his own artistic personality. He thereby came upon the main current of the Spanish tradition which unites the old with the new, the popular with the sophisticated, the lyrical with the narrative. But *Romancero gitano* was in no sense a consummation of artistic purpose. Lorca's spirit was still hungry, as is the spirit of every poet who feels the burden of "the song I shall never sing." For Lorca was not interested in the popular elements of Andalusian culture alone. In his restless seeking of a bond between the habits of an older cultural perception and the values of the modern world, he felt compelled to experiment ceaselessly with different forms.

And so, some time during the years 1926-1929, Lorca wrote two odes in classical hexameters which are curiously beyond the range of anything he had done before. They augur the strangely moving idiom of *Poeta en Nueva York,* and illuminate the quest for equilibrium between his already established modes of perception and the objective reality of the changing world outside Andalusia. The first poem, "Oda a Salvador Dalí," is an attempt to celebrate not so much the art of his painter friend as Dalí's faith in the same world of the senses which Lorca was treating with quite a different organization of objective phenomena. Lorca sees the justice of isolating objects from their accepted surroundings, having attempted the same concentration in his own poetry; he feels it, in fact, the only way to give them that instinctive life which is their essence, and which otherwise is lost in the confusion and banality of massive, unmeaning landscapes surrounding them:

> Modern painters in their white studios
> cut the aseptic flower from the square root.
>
> .   .   .   .
>
> We are pleased by the instinct for form and discipline.
>
> .   .   .   .
>
> The world puts stifled penumbras and disorder
> in the foreground where humanity crowds.
>
> .   .   .   .
>
> Time's flow is stopped and ordered
> in the numerical forms of century after century.
> And trembling, vanished Death seeks refuge
> in the narrow circle of the present moment.
>
> .   .   .   .
>
> You love matter defined and exact
> where fungus can make no lodging.
>
> .   .   .   .
>
> But also the rose in the garden where you live.
> Always the rose, always, north and south of us!
> Calm and concentrated as a blind statue,
> unconscious of underground forces which push it up.

> Pure rose, clean of artifice and mere approximation,
> opening for us the delicate wings of the smile.
> (Pinned-up butterfly contemplating flight.)
> Rose of equilibrium hunting no sorrows.
> Always the rose!
>
> O, Salvador Dalí, voice steeped in olives!
> I speak of what your person and your art tell me.
> I praise not your imperfect adolescent brush,
> but sing the firm direction of your arrows.
>
> I sing your handsome energy full of Catalan light,
> your love of what has a possible explanation.

Whether one agrees with Lorca that the art of Salvador Dalí indicates such a "firm direction" is probably not fundamental. What is important is that Lorca, who has been called the "unconscious" artist *par excellence,* could identify himself in the cosmic vision of the new art which Dalí represented. In some sense every artist is concerned with rearranging his landscape, both within and without. But rarely can one express effectively, as Lorca does here, the consciousness of so shadowy a purpose.

The second hexameter poem, "Oda al Santísimo Sacramento del Altar: Exposición y Mundo" ("Ode to the Most Holy Eucharist: Exposition and World"), is still another aspect of the same aesthetic principle. Lorca perceives in the form of the Eucharist the living Christ as a concrete expression of man's agony. But it is not an heroic figure he sees; it is a Christ made diminutive as a doll—the figure which Spanish children carry about on Christmas and Easter—or it is a Christ as small and palpitating as a frog's heart which doctors place in a bell jar:

> Thus would I have you, familiar God.
> Little flour wafer for the new-born child.
> Wind and substance joined in exact expression
> by love for the flesh which knows not your name.
>
> In such a way, concise form of ineffable sound,
> God in infant's dress, diminutive, eternal Christ,
> a thousand times pronounced dead, crucified
> by the impure word of sweaty man.
>
> .   .   .   .
>
> Oh, most holy Form, apex of the flowers,
> where all angles take their fixed lights,
> where mouth and number construct a body's offering
> of human light and muscles of flour!

> Oh, Form limited to express a concrete
> multitude of lights and heeded din!
> Oh, snow bounded by timbrels of music!
> Oh, flame crackling over all our veins!

In the outer world, such a form is constantly overcome by cruelty and murder symbolized by the razor lying on the table and avidly waiting to slit the throat. In that world, "three thousand men came armed with shining knives to assassinate the nightingale."—

> White-faced night. Night void and characterless.
> Under the Sun and Moon. Sad night of the World.
> Two halves opposed and a man who does not know
> when his butterfly will leave the clocks.

> Only your balanced Sacrament of light
> pacified the anguish of unloosed love.

> Because your sign is a key to the celestial plain.

> Because your sign expresses the wind and the worm.
> Appointed meeting place of century and moment.

> World, you now have a goal for your helplessness.
> For your perennial horror of the bottomless hole.
> O, captive Lamb of three equal voices!
> Immutable Sacrament of love and discipline!

Just as Lorca discovered in Dalí's art a courageous instinct to deal with phenomena of pure form, so in the body and spirit of Christ he found committed the "love and discipline" by which he also sought to implement his poetry.

For Lorca, the Holy Eucharist was the religious counterpart of his own aesthetic; in the unity of the godhead was the same concretization of form symbolized. Through this unity one might aspire to find "love and discipline" outside the characterless flux of the world. Lorca was not seeking to dehumanize experience—a fatal thing for a poet—but to attempt some imaginative expression which his former treatment of sensual reality did not admit.

It is interesting to note that in a letter written to a fellow poet during this time, Lorca speaks of his Odes as spiritual exercises, as attempts to overcome a sense of artistic irresolution and personal despair. He counsels his friend, by his own example, not to allow "these ugly things" to infiltrate his poetry, "because [they] will play you the trick of revealing what is purest in you to the eyes of those who should *never* see it. For that reason, and as a discipline, I am now composing these precise *exercises* and opening my soul to the symbol of the Eucharist. . . ." And in another letter concerning the Odes Lorca adds, "I am now writing a kind of *opening-the-veins* poetry, a poetry altogether *averted* from reality, with a feeling which reflects all my love for things and all my *mocking* of things. Love of death and poking fun at it." Yet he also remarks with decision, "After finishing my Odes, in which I have placed so much illusion, I shall close this poetic cycle to turn toward something else." When Lorca describes this poetry as "averted" from reality, reflecting his love of death and his poking fun at it, he makes the strangely pertinent admission of a personality suggesting less the conscientious artist than the sharp wisdom of the peasant. It was this certainty of instinct which preserved for Lorca his cultural roots in Spain, though he sought momentarily the deepening of death's mystery in a foreign landscape completely outside his knowledge. This new attempt might easily have come as a reaction to the localized experience of *Poema del cante jondo* and *Romancero gitano*. Whether it was impatience with what seemed a too easy accomplishment in his field or the fear of repeating himself, there was already impetus enough to prepare him for the strange world of New York. Only later was he to realize, however, that discarding the known aspects of localism for the unknown aspects of the universal is but another way of dealing with the same problem.

Lorca's short stay in New York resulted in the volume *Poeta en Nueva York*. It is the work of a new spiritual insight and of a largely incoherent prophetic vision. Tormented and mutilated, but still sensually realistic, the poems included in this volume carry a peculiarly important message to the modern age. It is easy to think of them as the fabrications of a mind which has lost its balance, as the outpourings of a surrealist gruesomely constructing an antihuman nightmare world. Certainly they are Lorca's most difficult poems. Musically discordant, disrupted in meter, poured into an arbitrary autonomous form, cascading with the fragments of exploded metaphor, they seem to contradict the whole of his previous procedure. But their secret is that a new world of imagery has been created to embody the fervid spiritual effort which informs them. The intricate imagistic and metaphoric terminology of *Poeta en Nueva York* proceeds from a vision of the world which, finding no expressive instrument in the traditions of any communicative medium, demands of the poet a new imaginative invention.

Begun on a note of spiritual defeat ("Murdered by heaven/ between the forms that issue toward the serpent/ and the forms that seek the crystal . . ."), which is still the poet's concern with form and his sense of failure in the struggle to attain it, Lorca drives relentlessly through the metropolitan jungle to emerge with a song of biological renewal in the rhythm of a Cuban chant, the *son*. Thus, what begins as the denunciation of a civilization which has repudiated all natural form, gradually grows into a paean glorifying the instincts of the one race in the New World—the Negro—that has never relinquished such a form. Meanwhile, livid as a scar are the impressions conveyed of the poet's reawakened vision of death, his refuge in a primitive Christ, and a profound Catholic sentiment, which is at the same time a bitter condemnation of the Church of Rome. *Poeta en Nueva York* includes Lorca's finest mystic expression in the same spirit of religious heresy which has always made Spain more Catholic than the letter of the Church's dogma could warrant. Thus Lorca's incongruent language becomes the very instrument with which a deep spiritual unity is sought. It takes on the indefinable quality of all Spanish mysticism: the knowledge of roots deep in the soil, flowering into human integration. It is the unifying element in a work which rises above the equivocations of poetic analysis in its triumphant surrender to the chaos of the modern world.

The insomnia which would not allow the poet to shut his eye to any moment in Granada is transmuted in New York into the fear of death, the fear that what is precious in each passing moment will be eternally lost as soon as one has allowed himself the luxury of believing that the flux has stopped. There is no way for man to escape into a haven of exalted reality, a quickening of the spirit such as Calderón, for example, envisioned in heaven. No. Those who sleep are blinding themselves to the death and perversity which is man's own creation:

> Nobody in the world is sleeping. Nobody.
> I've said so.
> Nobody is sleeping.
> But if someone at night has excessive moss at the temples,
> open the trapdoors so he may see under the moon
> the theaters' false goblets, the poison, and the skull.

For Lorca, New York is a symbol of spiritual myopia, where man is unable to cope with the disease of body and soul because he cannot see the nature of his dislocation, because he has lost sight of those elemental natural forces which a people living close to the soil understand instinctively. Here men use the wrong "juices," and flail themselves with their nerves until they stumble into the arms of the devil—or what is still more probable, some psychoanalyst. Behind the surge of marching facts and gigantically misspent energies, the poet sees the agony close to the bone, the cancer creeping through the body; he is aware of no salvation and can discern only the wound from which half of humanity must die. At such moments he speaks more clearly, as clearly as Christ spoke to His disciples at the Last Supper, when there is no terror of confused panoramas to haunt his eyes, when he is cleansed by the meaning of his own life:

> I denounce all those
> who ignore the other half,
> the irredeemable half
> raising mountains of cement
> where beat the hearts
> of little forgotten beasts
> and where we shall all tumble
> on the last holiday of the blast charges.
> I spit in your face.
> The other half hears me
> devouring, urinating, flying, in its purity. . . .

With Lorca, Death is always a silent wanderer. In his earlier poems Death appears as a monolithic force which triumphantly overwhelms life because there is no opposition. In *Poeta en Nueva York*, everything falsely believed is Death: a thing created by a tradition of incomprehension and blindness. Like the proverbial old beggar woman, it endures because it is so implicitly accepted. In the poem "Danza de la muerte" ("Dance of Death"), Death carries a mask; but behind the mask is the face of a Negro, who, for Lorca, has a special significance in America: a race apart, marytred for its ceremonial purity and primal innocence. Thus, by a curious inversion, the very incarnation of life comes behind the mask of death to liberate humanity. What lives and moves with the earth is the rhythm of the Negro's blood. He alone does not need to learn the secret of nature's flux; only he, bound by a civilization of steel nerves, knows the music and dance of passion which is eternal:

> Ay, Harlem, Harlem, Harlem!
> There is no sorrow like your oppressed eyes,
> like your blood shuddering in the dark eclipse,
> your garnet violence, deaf in shadow and dumb,
> like your great king, prisoner in a janitor's uniform.

For the Negro, the Jew, the Gypsy, the poor; for races and classes as old as the earth, who must taste the gall of poverty and agony and must learn how to suffer; for all these Lorca has an affection which, in proof, is greater than for his Granadine gardens. It is "this other half" that teaches the poet the meaning of his own life, the pain of the searching, unconsummated spirit. And Lorca does find one man in America who expresses the purity and realistic love of the senses. His is the primitive voice: a voice of dignity, conscious and dreaming, in whose compass all that is false must die. He walked the streets of this same New York, and while "no one wanted to be a cloud," and while "no one wanted to be a river," or to love "the great leaves" and the "beach's blue tongue," he paused to become everything he saw. He is the "hidden angel," the "perfect voice" that will "tell the truth of the wheat" in a New York of "wires and death." He is Walt Whitman.

> Not for one moment, handsome old Walt Whitman,
> have I forgotten your beard full of butterflies,
> or your corduroy shoulders worn by the moon,
> or your thighs of virginal Apollo,
> or your voice like a column of ashes;
> old man, beautiful as the mist,
> trembling like a bird
> whose sex is pierced by a needle,
> enemy of the satyr,
> enemy of the vine,
> and lover of bodies under the coarse fabric.

Though a stranger to the scene, Lorca identifies himself with the burly American poet. Obsessed with the same sense of the body's purity, he rises to the greatest pitch of condemnation in his "Oda a Walt Whitman"; for having discovered the purest fruit, he has recognized the worm of perversion eating at its core. Freaks, contortionists of the senses, frauds representing every degree of physiological and psychological disease—they obliterate nature and fill the blood with poison. Through them the world becomes a stark dream of frustration and death, and the spirit, a little limping thing which cries under a hot leaf in the jungle:

> Agony, agony, dream, ferment and dream.
> This is the world, my friend, agony, agony.
> The dead are rotting under the city clocks.
> War goes by weeping with a million grey rats;
> rich men give their mistresses
> tiny dying illuminati,
> and life is not noble, or good, or sacred.

Caught up with all these are also those who might be lovers, who burn but cannot escape; those innocents, those "recluses of casinos who bitterly drink the water of prostitution;/ those of green glance who love man and burn their lips in silence." They will go down, guiltless, to the same death of the perverts, for their voices have been robbed. Only when the killers of the innocent have been denied will there be a new primeval dawn, when man will come upon the first glories of himself and the New World.

Lorca's Catholicism as seen through his "Oda a Walt Whitman" is supremely a thing of the body, a touchstone for the mystic singing body. Viewing the city as a Babylon of false tongues, Lorca insisted on upholding a primitive Christianity. Often his language reverts to the symbolism of the Mass, and to the rhythm of the Christian chant; but it is only the more to prove that the traditional dogma is meaningless here where the first demands of the spirit are scarcely understood. The earth, bread, fire, water, and blood, the nutriments of life without which it is impossible to understand love, have all gone under the hill with the ants. The killer perseveres and his victims are legion. This is Lorca's argument; this is the essential Lorca risen from his struggle with the music and air of the Granadine gardens to hunt the hunter in the jungle of New York.

Fortunately, Lorca had not cut off his own retreat. It was still possible for him to rediscover the localism of Andalusia, from which he had momentarily rebelled, a stronger and more conscious artist. After the cosmic vision of *Poeta en Nueva York,* he was ready to appraise his earlier materials, and to intensify his cultural perception. This was done, after the return to Spain, in his drama and in two significant poetic works.

Shortly before his death in 1936, Lorca was revising a collection of poems which he intended for publication under the title *El Diván del Tamarit (The Diván at the Tamarit).* Although some of these appeared in magazines and anthologies (and more recently, reprinted in Angel del Río's study of Lorca), they are still an unedited work. The insight they provide into Lorca's last stage as a poet is of outstanding importance. The poems reflect Lorca's reinstatement in the land of his birth. They are a reaffirmation of the cultural heritage he had gained from the medieval Arabic poets, and they celebrate again the aesthetic of sensual form in fleeting time, characteristic of the best Arabic issue in Andalusia. *El Diván del Tamarit* renews the attempt to capture the sound and meaning of the spirit's warfare with nature in Andalusia: a land where life and death have only the few disguises which every object, animate or inanimate, alternately has put on and taken off each day for over a thousand years.

The *Tamarit* was the chief administrative office of Arabic power in Spain during the period of Moorish domination. The *Diván* was the Arabic name for the assembly of governors who came periodically to hold council with the *Tamarit. Diván* also has another meaning: "reunion." And it is probably in this sense that Lorca intended it.[1] By celebrating the spirit of all southern Spain, he sought to come to a "reunion" with his past.

---

[1] It is probable that Lorca was also thinking of *Diván* in still another of its meanings—that of an "anthology" or "collection of poems."

They are poems of sheer imagistic delicacy, in the style of the *gacela* and *casida*, two standard Arabic verse forms used for love poetry and Anacreontic odes. The poems in *El Diván del Tamarit* comprising the bulk of the *gacelas* sing of a love no longer incarnate, which is beautiful in escape, mystic in remembered passion:

> Nobody understood the perfume
> of your belly's dark magnolia.
> Nobody knew how you tormented
> a humming bird of love between your teeth.
>
> A thousand Persian ponies fell asleep
> in the moonlit plaza of your forehead,
> while four nights long I embraced
> your waist, enemy of snow.
>
> Between plaster and jasmin,
> your glance was a pale seed branch.
> I sought to give you from my heart
> the ivory letters saying *always*.
>
> *Always, always:* garden of my agony,
> your blood fleeing forever,
> blood of your veins in my mouth,
> your mouth now unlit for my death.

Lorca adopts the conventions although he does not maintain the old imagistic standards. He has already perfected his own. He adds to the Arabic theme a heightened sense of sympathy with the mineral, botanical, and animal worlds which create the immortal conflict in a nature too perfect to be stable:

> The rose
> did not seek the dawn:
> almost eternal on its branch,
> it sought another thing.
>
> The rose
> did not seek science or shadow:
> margin of flesh and dream,
> it sought another thing.
>
> The rose
> did not seek the rose.
> Motionless in the sky,
> it sought another thing.

Hidden in the very being of the real rose are the destructive energies of transience by which nature turns it to decay. Reminiscent of "Oda a Salvador Dalí" ("always the rose, always, north and south of us," "aseptic," a pure form), the rose here attains the same plasticity which the Arabic poets used when they petrified it or turned it into a jewel. Lorca proposed for the undying, permutated rose an ideal counterpart in the human emotion, which though susceptible to decay may conserve its images of desire through "love and discipline." But if his poetry thus turns the external landscape into a solidified image of the inner landscape where all emotion has been depersonalized, it is not the typical romantic anthropomorphism. Lorca knew the rich possibilities which the use of certain limited concrete symbols afforded. He knew that once these became the poet's property, all desire could be poured into them as into a bottomless well if no cessation and no fulfillment were ever expected in the flow. Having appropriated these symbols, Lorca can dispose of the implications of cause and result. This is intentional and should not make the poems seem incomplete; rather, it suggests a vision which endures as an intimate companion of natural flux, and which, as a result, can never lie about the beginning and end of things. Desire becomes the one means of perpetuating all emotion; and emotion itself, serving as a universal human continuant, may vie with the unending tide of increase and decline in nature. In such a manner, death never stands out as a negative passion, but as part of a larger interminable experience which endures, because it is human, as long as any rock or tree endures, or as long as there are men to feel. There are abundance and extravagance in these poems because there is such abundance and extravagance in nature. And like the Arabic poets, Lorca created substance as rich as anything in nature.

This unusual harmony in Lorca's vision was reinforced when, on the occasion of the death of the bullfighter Sánchez Mejías, his close friend, Lorca wrote what is perhaps his most sustained single poem: *Llanto por Ignacio Sánchez Mejías* (*Lament for the Death of a Bullfighter*). He combined the lyrical devices of his earlier poems with the narrative devices of the historical ballad, and used the rhythm of the gypsy lament to carry the emotional impact of the tragedy. It is an admirable elegiac construction divided into four parts, whose individual motifs are fused in the manner of a Bach oratorio.

In the first section, "La cogida y la muerte" ("The Fatal Wound and the Death"), he announces the tragedy with an insistent refrain in every other line, recalling the hour in which the death took place: "at five in the afternoon." It is like a doleful bell rung out to the monotonous chant of a priest. It is an impersonal background to the death, where the wind bears away the shroud and the dove struggles with the leopard: the conflict of one form with another for ascendancy, of life with death, of spirit with matter. Then, as if viewed from above, the corpse of the bull-

fighter is seen lying in a coffin on wheels, the sound of bones and flutes
in his ears, and the bull bellowing against his forehead.

In the second section, "La sangre derramada" ("The Spilt Blood"),
the death is described with time and space symbols through which the
bullfighter sought to find a spiritual form:

> Ignacio climbs the stairs
> carrying death on his shoulders.
> He sought the dawn
> and found it gone.
> He seeks his sharp profile
> and the dream cuts him off.
> He sought his handsome body
> and found his blood wide-opened.

The poet calls on all things white to help him avoid seeing the blood
spilled on the sand. "¡Que no quiero verla!" ("For I don't want to see
it!")—

> Tell the moon to come
> for I don't want to see the blood
> of Ignacio on the sand.
>
> .   .   .
>
> Tell the jasmins
> in their small whiteness!
>
> The cow of the old world
> passed her sad tongue
> over a snout of blood
> spilt in the sand,
> and the prehistoric bulls of Guisando,
> made half of death, half of stone,
> bellowed like two centuries
> tired of treading the earth.
> No.
> I don't want to see it!

The rhythm mounts slowly until it is cut by the refrain, in the manner
of a guitar suddenly struck on the strings with the thumb. Then caught
again on the same note and in the same tempo, it continues to rise and
fall like quick, heavy breathing. During the pauses, Ignacio is compared
in majesty and strength to a prince, an expert mountaineer, and to a
"river of lions":

> There was not a prince like him in Seville
> with whom comparison is possible,
> nor any sword like his sword,
> nor any heart so well endowed.
> His miraculous courage
> like a river of lions,
> and like a sculptured torso
> his dignity was hewn.
> An air of Andalusian
> Rome lit his head with gold
> where his smile was a spikenard
> of wit and of skill.

When the obsession with spilt blood returns, the lines again are plucked like strings in the quick agony of the lament:

> I don't want to see it!
> For there is no chalice to contain it,
> no swallows to drink it,
> no frost of light to freeze it,
> there is no song or flood of lilies
> or mirror to cover it with silver.
> No.
> I don't want to see it!

In the third section, "Cuerpo presente" ("The Body in State"), the poet seems to detach himself from the scene and from the agony of the death. It is as though, in the previous section, he had experienced the death himself, the actual dying, as though he had been inside looking out. Now, however, he is outside looking in. The music of the verse becomes slow and speculative: a fifteen-syllable quatrain adapted to a melodic long line. It expresses a mystical time-space feeling sublimating the corpse into a symbol of all who are mortally injured and of all the exhausted continuity of human transience. Only that murderous solid, the self-repeating constant which is the stone, can endure death:

> The stone is a shoulder to carry time
> with trees of tears and ribbons and planets.
>
> I have seen gray rains run toward the waves,
> raising their tender perforated arms
> in order not to be hunted by the outstretched stone
> which unties their limbs without absorbing the blood.

And now death has come to put Ignacio behind the stone, to shrink his humanity into the head of a minotaur. "Ya se acabó." ("It is finished.") The rain and the mad air, love full of frozen tears may stream over him, but he has become the victim of the stone—the body lying still under the white shroud. Yet the poet cannot accept physical death.

The vision of man's perfection, his dominance over the flux of time and space must provide the secret of some exit behind the stone—a spiritual permanence:

> I want to see men with rough voices here.
> Those who tame horses and train rivers:
> men whose bones ring out, who sing
> with mouths full of sun and flint.
>
> I want to see them here. Before the stone.
> Before this body with broken reins.
> I want them to show me the exit
> for this captain bound by death.

For what is death after all but a spiritual freedom from the customary bellowing of the death-instructed bull? Is man any less eternal than the sea, the sea which "also dies"?

> I don't want them to bind his face in shrouds
> accustoming him to the death he carries.
> Forward, Ignacio: never mind the warm bellowing.
> Sleep, fly, rest: the sea also dies!

Man's spirit may and does conquer death, as it conquers time and space, not because an afterlife has been created as a last refuge, but because Man has left the impression of his spiritual grace on earth where anyone with eyes to see may grasp it, may sing and celebrate and repeat it.

This is the argument of the fourth section, "Alma ausente" ("The Soul in Absence"). Those who still need to be fed by the fluxional energies of life, who can believe only what passes and shoots before the eyes—they will not remember. They will forget the spirit of Ignacio as they forget the dead all over the earth, dying like "snuffed-out dogs."—

> Neither the bull nor the fig tree knows you,
> nor horses nor your household ants.
> Neither child nor afternoon knows you
> for you are forever dead.

> Neither the stone's back nor the black satin
> of your mangling knows you.
> Nor does your silent memory know you
> for you are forever dead.

No one will remember but those, like the poet, who can lift the seal of mortality, who can look behind the stone, who can fix in the spirit's memory the crystal gaze of human grace and beauty, courage and appetite for death—the achievement of permanent form:

> Long will it be before time yields, if ever it does,
> an Andalusian as bright, as full of adventure.
> I sing his grace with moaning words
> and remember a sad breeze through the olive trees.

Llanto por Ignacio Sánchez Mejías is the work of a poet in whose consciousness dramatic and poetic forms have interpenetrated. Even the manner of the poem's division into four parts, each carrying a different imaginative perspective on the death, suggests the architectural pattern of a play. The elaboration of a musical design within the poetic conception; the capture of the quality of *cante jondo* and the refinement of its basic rhythms in the verse; the coordination between narrative-episodic and lyric-elegiac forms; the consistency in the use of symbols—blood, bull, stone, body, sea, animals and trees—to contain as well as to depersonalize the huge impact of death; in all this one sees artifice merged into the imaginative projection itself, and the search for equilibrium become the very substance of dramatic incident and resolution. To appreciate the full dramatic consciousness which Lorca reached in *Llanto por Ignacio Sánchez Mejías,* one must turn to the work he had for some time been doing concurrently in the drama.

Lorca and the Poetry of Death

by Pedro Salinas

The reader no sooner begins to pry into the poetic world
fashioned by Lorca in his lyric poetry, ballads and plays, than he feels
himself being immersed in a strange atmosphere. It is an apparently
normal setting of popular scenes and people, all perfectly recognizable.
But the air is, so to speak, inhabited by forebodings and threats. Metaphors cut across it like birds of ill omen. So, for example, summer "sows
rumors of tiger and flame." Day breaks in a most peculiar manner, like
a shadowy fish: "Great stars of white frost—come with the fish of
shadow—that opens the road of dawn." The wind is an enormous man
pursuing the maiden "with a red-hot sword." These metaphors do not
have a decorative function; they are an extension of meaning. They
herald what is unusual and mysterious in this world. They proclaim that
something is being prepared; they proclaim an imminence of fatality.
For the poetic kingdom of Lorca, so brilliantly illuminated and at the
same time so enigmatic, is under the rule of a unique, unchallenged
power: Death.

Death lurks behind the most normal of actions, and in the places
where it is least expected. In one poem Lorca says, referring to a tavern:
"Death comes in and goes out—and death goes out and comes in." The
poet repeats the same simple idea, merely inverting the word order, as if
to point out the fatality of this act, the inevitability of Death's continually coming in and going out—over and over again—not in the
concrete place of the tavern, but in the life of man and the work of the
poet. The destination of nearly all the characters that Lorca creates,
whether in his ballads or in his dramas, is death. Lorca creates them to
set them on a road whose only possible end is dying. In a poem of his
youth entitled "Another Dream" ("Otro sueño") he wrote: "How many
children has death?—They are all in my breast." ("¿Cuántos hijos tiene
la muerte?—Todos están en mi pecho.") Yes, that is where they are, and,
as his work grows, those children of death gradually swarm from his
breast, transformed into poetic offspring.

"Lorca and the Poetry of Death." From *The Hopkins Review*, V, No. 1 (Fall, 1951),
5-12. Copyright © 1951, 1962 by Jaime Salinas and Solita Salinas Marichal. Reprinted
by permission of Solita Salinas Marichal, Jaime Salinas, and *The Hopkins Review*.

In the famous "Sleepwalkers Ballad" ("Romance sonámbulo") two lovers, a horseman and the gypsy girl of the green flesh and green hair who awaits him, look forward with desire to a lover's meeting; she is in her house. But the strange creature and her lover will never meet. For when he finally reaches the house his breast has been torn open by a wound that will kill him; and the gypsy girl, killed by too much waiting, floats upon the water, borne up by the reflection of the moon. They have not come together in love, but they have in death.

The same end that befalls individuals also lies in waiting for large groups of human beings, for cities. Lorca invents in his magnificent "Ballad of the Civil Guard" a wonderful gypsy city. It is the city of joy, with cinnamon turrets, with lamps and flags bedecking the flat roof. The poet calls it "the festive city." But it will not escape the common destiny. The Civil Guards arrive, symbolizing the forces of destruction; they stab women and children, they knock down the cinnamon turrets, and when dawn breaks, everything is razed to the ground. In this way a city invented by the poet in his imagination comes to an end. But in this ceaseless bustle, in this accumulation of different peoples and activities, the poet senses, too, the terrible destiny of death. The great city bears death within itself. Beneath the quantities, beneath the quantitative weakness, there is blood: "Under the multiplications—there is a drop of duck's blood." And this city of steel and cement, solid as it is, will be destroyed by grief, will die just like that other one with its cinnamon turrets.

After his phase as a lyric poet Lorca focused his attention on the theater. In his dramatic works we shall find the same themes of death, repeated time and again. If he chooses an historical character for his first important drama it can be no other than Mariana Pineda, the figure of a girl who for embroidering the Republican flag dies on the gallows.

His three rural tragedies, *Blood Wedding, Yerma, The House of Bernarda Alba* tie up and twist the strands of a few people's passions so tightly that only the "tiny knife, the tiny golden knife," sometimes real, sometimes symbolical, can probe the center of the tangle, the center of the conflict. Whom is the bride in *Blood Wedding* destined for? For the bridegroom or for Leonard, that other man who attracts her with irresistible fascination? The Bride decides in favor of the latter, elopes with him. But who is she to make the decision? It is Death, disguised as an old beggar woman, who must decide everything. She brings the two men face to face, makes them fight and die; it is death that carries off all sweethearts.

Mortal, too, is the *dénouement* of Yerma. Yerma kills, not only her husband, but in him all her potential children, since she will never belong to any other man.

In *The House of Bernarda Alba* the problem of *Blood Wedding* crops up again. Pepe el Romano, typifying man, the male secretly coveted in the tormented souls of those women, will not give his love to any of the sisters: neither to the one chosen to be his legal spouse, nor to the one who offers to be his mistress in a rapture of passion, and who, seeking to quench her thirst for life in the embrace of a man, falls into the arms of the one who is concealed behind him, death.

A poet's work is not a philosophical system; it is not a philosophy, consciously worked out, and conveyed as such in a discursive form. But in the work of no great poet can one fail to find a conception of man and life, just as in paper one finds a watermark, almost invisible, denoting its distinction, individualizing it. All great poets have, one way or another, tried to decipher some secret of the world. Poetry is always a reply to the eternal interrogation addressed to man by the things that surround him. "Here I am," the world, with apparent simplicity, says to the poet. But underneath its simple affirmation of being, the question pulses: "What am I for you?" That is why a poet, up to the moment when he is asking this question, really is replying to what life, in a hushed voice, confidentially, asks him about—questions that he alone understands. He is a witness who, in the trial to which the world is eternally brought, gives evidence in its defense or in its prosecution.

The vision of life and man that gleams and shines forth in Lorca's work is founded on death. Lorca understands, feels life through death. This idea may seem paradoxical, but only superficially and at first sight. For in reality the religious and moral tradition of the centuries has offered man as his best guide in life meditation on death. Death is the mentor of life, its teacher. But the nineteenth century has prepared that attitude of thought usually called the cult of life, which entails the regarding of death as a kind of adversary and opponent of life. Mechanization and vitalism lead to "an estimation of death as something that should be essentially repressed." Existence is exalted as the mere duration of human life, and man is urged to fill it with his satisfaction, enjoyments, and acquisitions, without thinking of the dimension of morality. Ever since Pasteur, man's existence has been defended by ever improving means. People surround themselves with comfort and precautions, merely in defense of their material being. The formula "Safety First" has become almost sacred. A kind of conspiratorial silence has been created around the mortal destiny of man. Cemeteries look for new euphemisms and circumlocutions so that they may be called by some other name, for example, Memorial Parks. But, despite all this, one detail of utmost importance proves that men are keeping the vision of death in the bottom of their hearts. However much they pride themselves on keeping it out of mind, on pigeon-holing it into oblivion, the institution of life insurance is spreading throughout the world.

If the value of death has been disparaged in the twentieth century, there is no denying that the latest trends of contemporary thought—art, philosophy, poetry, painting—offer evidence of its revaluation. The pontiff of existentialism, Martin Heidegger, has coined his definite expression on man's life: "existence for death" ("Sein zum Tod"). Death is an inseparable element of existence. Another German philosopher of our time, Georg Simmel, speaks of "life's needing death inside," and he says that life would not have, without it, either its specific meaning or its specific form. Applying the idea to Shakespeare's characters, he sees their deaths, not as fatal accidents, but as what he calls life's coming-of-age: "The coming-of-age of their destiny, insofar as their destiny expresses their lives, is in itself the coming-of-age of their death."

A great modern poet, well-known in America, Rainer Maria Rilke, is the best possible example of this tendency converted into poetic experience. His is the distinction between small death and great death; personal death that is proper to an individual, and the death of others, impersonalized and common to all. Hence his famous prayer: "O Lord, grant to each man his own death—a death that proceeds from his life . . . —The great death that each one has inside him—is the fruit around which all evolves." ("O Herr, gib jedem seinen eignen Tod—das Sterben, das aus jenem Leben geht . . . —Der grosse Tod, den jeder in sich hat, das ist die Frucht, um die sich alles dreht.") Death is not a misfortune that assails us from without; it is the companion of our life; it develops inside us and grows as we grow. To deny death would be to deny an indispensable condition of our life, one which slowly models it, setting it on the path to its final fulfillment. I would suggest that the English word *achievement* denotes perfectly this dual meaning of death: to achieve is to finish, to put an end to something, as dying puts an end to material life; but *to achieve* in English is likewise to fulfill, to complete, to realize.

It should not be thought that I am comparing Rilke with Lorca. They are extremely different poets. What I am pointing out is the coincidence of their both seeking in death the center of gravity of their conception of the world and life. But the poet from Prague expresses his obsession with mortality in meditative accents, tinted with hues of melancholy tenderness: Lorca, in violently dramatic shouts and cries, in metaphors flashing with dazzling colors. As an example, one might take the different way they have of rendering objectively an identical thought: the death that lives within us, that we bear inside us. Rilke speaks of a girl's death, and says: "Your death was already old—when your life began." And Lorca, pretending that he has been asked: "What do you feel in your mouth—red and thirsty?" answers "The taste of the bones—of my great skull." ("¿Qué sientes en tu boca—roja y sedienta?—El sabor de los huesos—de mi calavera.") In the German poet, a concept, expressed by the logical contraposition of the youth of life and the old age of death inside a human being; in the Spaniard, metaphors charged with impressive sensuality, in dramatic contrast, a red mouth and the bones of a skull.

For me the difference between the two poets is to be found in the different origin of each one's obsession with the thought of death. In one case, Rilke is slowly evolving in his poetic conscience, through inner experiences that he analyzes, contemplates, and explores, a sort of *Thanatodicea,* or doctrine of death; he can be seen locked up in his solitude like an alchemist in his cave, distilling feeling, refining visions, in his search for the meaning of death. But Lorca, who expresses the same feeling for death with an undoubted originality and personal accent, has not had to search for it through processes of intellectual speculation along the innermost galleries of the soul. He discovers it all around him, in the native air that gives him breath, in the singing of the servants in his house, in books written in his tongue, in the churches of his city; he finds it in all of his individual personality that has to do with people, with the inheritance of the past. Lorca was born in a country that for centuries has been living out a special kind of culture that I call the "culture of death."

Recognition of the importance of death in the life of Spaniards is a common place in many books on travel and the psychology of peoples. We have selected by way of illustration an English writer, Havelock Ellis, who speaks of "the deliberate insistence on the thought of death so congenial to the ethical temper of this people." No superficial or extreme interpretation should be given to this thought of death: it should by no means be regarded as a *Thanatophilia,* or cult of death. Nor should it be construed as indifference to life, or as a denial of life; just the reverse, as Rilke says, since in giving us an awareness of death, it sharpens, intensifies our awareness of life.

What I understand by the "culture of death" is a conception of man and his early existence, in which the awareness of death functions with a positive force, is a stimulus, and not a hindrance, to living and acting, and makes possible an understanding of the full and total meaning of life. Within this conception a human being may affirm himself, not only in the acts of life, but in the very act of death. An existence in which the idea of death is hidden or suppressed is like the representation of action on a movie screen, flat, inapprehensible, and lacking in something essential; it is lacking in the dimension of depth, in the dimension that gives life its tone of intensity and drama. Man can only understand himself, can only be entire, by integrating death into his life; and every attempt to expel death, to take no account of it, in order to live, is a falsification, a fraud perpetrated by man on himself.

Few indeed are the great Spanish writers in whom this fraternal relation of life and death is not confirmed. I select as a very typical example, Quevedo. Quevedo did not reject any of the temptations presented to him by this life. On the contrary, his vital experiences reach out to all phases of existence: he advises great lords in palaces, he enjoys the favor of the king, he is a politician and a powerful minister, he pulls strings of intrigue in Italy, he knows at close quarters the common people, the riff-raff, the underdog; he is an accomplished humanist, and writes both Latin and the slang (or *germanía*) of the underworld with equal ease. Prone to fall in love, a great dueler, a practicing eroticist, a translator both of Anacreon, the poet of sensuality, and of Seneca, the stoic philosopher; no one can fail to see in Quevedo a burning love of life. Now this man is to be seen ever accompanied by the thought of death. "You begin at one and the same time to be born and to die" ("A la par empiezas a nacer y a morir"), he writes on one occasion; and on another, "You were born to die, and you spend your life dying." The hours are spades, he will write in another sonnet, that "dig up my monument out of my life." ("cavan en mi vivir mi monumento.") That is to say, it is out of the very earth of life that the monument, the memorial stone, of death is fashioned.

The Spanish public who attended the performances of morality plays saw in them, before their eyes, the figure of Death, represented in brilliant allegorical costume, going, coming, speaking amidst the other powers of the world. About the same time a character is created—Don Juan, who has come to be universally famous as the hero of life and love. But really, in the intention of his creator and dramatist Tirso de Molina, he is the hero of death. Every year, on the First of November, the drama of the Romantic poet Zorrilla, *Don Juan Tenorio*, is put on in most of the theaters of Spain. What the public witnesses year after year, entranced by it as if it were something new, is a drama that first presents man as the hero of untrammeled life, of feats of love piling up on top of one another; but later, in the final apotheosis, it witnesses, in a spectacular, musical, macabre staging, the death of the seducer. A death that leads to his salvation, despite his many sins. The public admires the hero, and enjoys the play, in the scene of his death as well as in those of his life. They feel that Don Juan knows how to die.

This conception is just as discernible in the arts: architecture, sculpture, painting. The most Spanish of architectural monuments, the monastery of the Escorial, includes a royal residence and the royal mausoleum of the Kings of Spain. It has been called "The Palace of Death." In that monastery is a picture by El Greco, which more, perhaps, than any other work of art exemplifies the "culture of death." It is his *Saint Maurice*. According to the legend, Maurice, the leader of the Theban legion, opposed the Emperor's orders to be converted to paganism; and with all his comrades he suffered decapitation for the sake of his religious belief. The theme is portrayed in a surprising way: the actual scene of the sacrifice, of the decapitation, is relegated to the background of the picture, and is painted in modest proportions. The focus of attention in the foreground is given to four knights in armor, who are talking, or rather listening, to Maurice, who by the expression on his face and by his attitude, seems to be persuading them to let themselves be killed, is urging them to die. None of the faces reveals any anxiety or fear; gravely, seriously, these people are making a decision, of their own free will and pleasure, to die. Saint Maurice is so firm, so upright in figure and bearing, simply because he is affirming himself in death, with all the fullness of his being. He represents to perfection that dying of one's own death, the great death, as Rilke says.

Velazquez did not paint many religious pictures; but the best of them has as its subject Christ in his death agony, Christ crucified. The portrayal of a dying man? No; as Christian doctrine tells us, the portrayal of eternal life, which is fulfilled in a willingness to die. This death is life's triumph.

We could not speak of a "culture of death" as proper to the Spanish people, if we did not find it not only in the creations of learned art, but also rooted in the most expressive declarations of the popular spirit. It can be seen quite clearly in the popular songs, those transmitted by oral tradition. But I propose to observe it in the fiestas. In the spring two fiestas are celebrated in Seville: Holy Week and the Fair. The first is a religious festival of extraordinary pomp and beauty. The images of the saints that are kept in the churches go forth into the city in processions, carried on litters, and at a slow pace they pass through the streets, where they are admired by a large crowd. And one of those images, one of those splendid seventeenth century wood carvings, is of Christ on the cross. It is impressive to see, over the heads of the people, the naked body of the dying Christ, proceeding step by step, in the night. Anyone who might regard this spectacle as indelicate morbidity, as pleasure taken in the funeral symbol of a dying body, would be wrong. No; as far as the people are concerned, in the death of that God-man, everlasting life is actually being achieved.

When the religious festival of Holy Week ends, the Fair starts in Seville. Its most talked-about attraction is the bullfights. Is fighting bulls a fiesta, a game? Many deny it these qualities—and with some reason. But undoubtedly in it is something of a representation and mystery. And what it at once conceals and represents is in my view the popular reaction to this "culture of death." To all who attend a bullfight the ring looks like a pageant of magnificent joy and brilliance. Everything rises up to a joyous vitality, to a pulsation of unrestrained happiness. The passes of the toreadors with their gracefulness have a suggestion of the dance in them. But soon a hint of mystery begins to appear: blood, the two-fold sign of life and death. And the spectators feel, whether they are aware of it or not, that when the bullfighter moves close up to the animal, when the two of them, alone, are engaged in a phase of the fight, another, a third and invisible presence, compels them to look at that game with tremendous emotional tension: it is the presence of death. The bullfighter achieves himself, reaches the full meaning of his existence, so different from that of other men, precisely by revealing to all eyes—even though they may not see it physically—the presence and the danger of Death. In his performance the people feel the twofold existence of man, the constant possibility for him of living and of dying, concentrated dramatically into a single instant. Only a people having in the depths of its spirit that "culture of death" can find a meaning in such a strange fiesta.

Perhaps that is why Lorca attained one of the peaks of his poetry in the *Lament for the Death of a Bullfighter* (*Llanto por Ignacio Sánchez Mejías*). The most modern art of surrealist imagery and the most ancient popular tradition of the "culture of death" converge in the poem. So the poet sees the bullfighter, going out of life, as if walking up the stands of the ring "with all his death upon his shoulders." ("Por las gradas sube Ignacio—con toda su muerte a cuestas.")

It is the bullfighter, man, who carries death, just the opposite of the old macabre conception in which Death carries off, kidnaps, man; an example of personal death, of great death, as Rilke said. A symbol of that conception of living in which the human being advances through time, always the bearer of his death.

Lorca is a modern poet: his sensibility responds to all the tensions of contemporary ways of life; his language illuminates the paths of poetry with a new brilliance. But to me, and this is the point I have tried to emphasize, he cannot be understood in his entirety unless we see him set in that tradition of the "culture of death" that he inherited from great artists of his native land, and that he has passed on to us, made richer with the proud gift of his poetic work.

The Ritual Sacrifice in Lorca's
Poet in New York

by Richard Saez

Lorca's *Poet in New York* has received very little critical attention. The Grove Press edition contains an introduction by Professor Angel del Río in which he suggests that further light might be shed on *Poet in New York* by demonstrating its relation to the works of English poets.[1] He refers to T. S. Eliot's *The Waste Land* peripherally and to the certainty that Lorca was familiar with the poem. Eliot's poetry is one of the major keys I have used to interpret *Poet in New York* as an allegory of death and rebirth, which has a parallel in the Grail Quest legends and in Eliot's *The Waste Land* itself. (In my comparisons with T. S. Eliot's poetry, as well as with the works of other English and continental writers, I am not source hunting. I am merely attempting to demonstrate universal literary archetypal patterns. Eliot's poetry is particularly helpful in this respect, because it is so consciously constructed with archetypal patterns and imagery. Whether Lorca read or was influenced by T. S. Eliot does not interest me. In the end *Poet in New York*, like every work of art, must be understood and judged as a whole and integral structure, and not as the receptacle of sources and influences.) The symbolism based on fertility rituals, in both Eliot and Lorca, is the most important aspect of this parallel, aside from the narrative sequence of the Grail Quest itself. Professor Angel del Río describes Lorca's arrival in New York, his temporary refuge in Newburg, Vermont, his return to the city, and his final departure. These steps are described in this essay allegorically as Lorca's descent (as quester) into

"The Ritual Sacrifice in Lorca's *Poet in New York.*" To appear soon in *Cuadernos Americanos.*

[1] Federico García Lorca, *Poet in New York*, Complete Spanish Text with a New Translation by Ben Belitt (New York: Grove Press, 1955). Copyright © 1955 by Ben Belitt. This bilingual edition of *Poet in New York* is the most convenient available to the reader unfamiliar with Spanish. Mr. Belitt has granted me permission to quote his English translation of Lorca's book. All of my quotations are taken from it. Page references are to this edition. This translation is published in England by Thames and Hudson Ltd.

the abysmal Waste Land, his defeat and temporary flight, and his return and eventual triumph over the Waste Land monsters.

"Blood has no doors in your night," a line from the "King of Harlem" (p. 21) states metaphorically the malady which Lorca discovered in the contemporary Waste Land of New York. It is not that blood is shed or that he encountered human and animal sacrifice. The sickness of New York is that the sacrifice, which the natural cycle of events demands, is not made ritually or ceremonially, or in the metaphoric language of the poet, that it is not given the proper doors through which to flow. The absence of a ceremonial ritual to celebrate the annual sacrifice of nature, results in the diseased congestion of unspilt blood, occasionally bursting cataclysmically, which in turn dictates the disoriented form and night-mare imagery of the poems.

Of the many aspects of *Poet in New York,* the most obvious is the maze of images of decadence, sterility, and perversion, which describe the poet's descent into a psychological limbo. The images of destruction in the volume fall into two major groups: the first, the vomiting and urinating multitudes destroying and perverting life, and the second, those instruments of retribution and purgation which will fall upon the city. The two poems, "Landscape of the Vomiting Multitudes" and "Land-scape of the Urinating Multitudes" (pp. 39 and 43) offer the most con-centrated collection of the former. We see "the fat lady" of the first poem, "pulling up roots and wetting the drumskins," "(turning) the cuttlefish wrong side out and (leaving) them to die," and "(leaving) pigeon-skull trails in the corners." Throughout the volume we are presented with images of violated nature: "crack-brained creatures" ("Back from a Walk," p. 3), "the butterfly drowned in an inkwell" (*Ibid.*), "the lately beheaded seafarer" ("Christmas on the Hudson," p. 49), and "a cat's paw smashed by a motorist" ("Office and Denunciation," p. 101). Among the many threats of retribution throughout the volume, there is the image of "Unsleeping City" (p. 53):

> The living iguanas will arrive and set tooth on the sleepless;
> The heart-stricken one who takes flight will meet on the corners
> the incredible mute crocodile under the timid reproach of the stars.

However, the genuine agony which Lorca expresses in *Poet in New York* is not found in the images of violent and unnatural perversion and slaughter which the city exacts on living things, nor in the night-mare creatures which the inhuman butchery of New York will beget as the only possible retribution for its sin. These are too unnatural to evoke human sympathy. They at most engender a shudder. The true agony of *Poet in New York* is in the *narrative* of Lorca's search for meaning and identity in the concrete jungle: a search which at times takes the shape of a quest for love, at times a quest for the poet's proper self, which he has lost in his inhuman and unidentifiable surroundings, and finally, a search which has as its central expression the attempt to establish a meaningful and ordered sacrifice that will give back to the quester as well as to the city their identity, virility, and place in the cosmic order. It is this pattern which I shall attempt to trace in this essay.

Eyes are a frequent symbol for Lorca's lost identity. There is a striking similarity between T. S. Eliot's use of eyes as a symbol of fertility or salvation or the Holy Grail itself in *The Waste Land* and *The Hollow Men* and the frequent appearance of eyes in *Poet in New York*. In *The Waste Land* the eyes of the Grail quester fail him. This failure, occurring in the hyacinth girl passage, symbolizes his sexual and spiritual impotence:

> "You gave me hyacinths first a year ago;
> "They called me the hyacinth girl."
> —Yet when we came back, late, from the Hyacinth garden,
> Your arms full, and your hair wet, I could not
> Speak, and my eyes failed, I was neither
> Living nor dead, and I knew nothing,
> Looking into the heart of light, the silence.
> *Oed' und leer das Meer.*

Eyes as they appear in *The Hollow Men* are a painful reminder of a lost salvation. However, the state of the hollow men is so fallen that even those reminders appear only in fragments:

> Eyes I dare not meet in dreams
> In death's dream kingdom
> These do not appear:
>
>   .   .   .   .
>
> The eyes are not here
> There are no eyes here
> In this valley of dying stars
> In this hollow valley
> This broken jaw of our lost kingdoms

Lorca's quest for identity begins by an appeal to the eyes of his childhood, in "1910, Interlude" (p. 5). He hopes to transform the Waste Land with the innocent vision of youth, which had not been exposed to its perversions:

> Those eyes of Nineteen-Ten, my very eyes,
> saw no dead man buried,
> no ashen bazaars of dawn's mourners
> nor the heart, in its recess, like sea-horses, wavering.

Immediate failure is met. In the language of T. S. Eliot, the eyes will not appear in death's dream kingdom. All that the poet is able to evoke is a series of incoherent objects of ominous significance. The eyes remain locked in the attic of the memory and all effort to find a significant course out of the Waste Land is renounced:

> Question no further. All things, I have seen,
> that hold to their course find only their vacancy.

In "Your Childhood in Menton" (p. 13) the direction of the poet's search is shifted from his youth to a lost beloved. It begins with a refrain from Jorge Guillén, "Yes, your childhood, a fable for fountains now," which has the effect of a strongly affirmative declaration. The "childhood" of which the poet speaks is that of a girl he once loved. The poem is an attempt to rediscover the positive significance of that lost love. The central movement of the poem lies in that the object of that love ("your childhood") has grown into a mature woman ("the lady"), who retains none of her former meaning for the poet, just as he has fallen into his contemporary situation, i.e., New York, represented as an abyss of trains and lonely hotels. The change from "your childhood" to "the lady" is conditioned by the revolution which the poet's own psyche is experiencing, i.e., as we shall see, the initiation into secret wisdom which Lorca is undergoing.

"The lady" is represented by a mask, which the poet seeks to remove but to no avail, since he cannot discover his identity in the city. Just as the positive significance of her past childhood once broke the sterile symbol of wisdom's spectacles and her innocence defined his virility, now, the woman's leanness, having come from following equivocal, brief dreams and misdirected paths, will cripple the man of Apollonian beauty whom she, in fact, formed. However, he determines to pursue through all corners that spirit which she (or rather he) has lost, and finding it, will smash the mask that now hides the lovers from each other:

> Love's pattern I gave you, Apollonian man,
> the nightingale's rage, in a cry,
> yet, pasture of ruin, you grew lean
> on the brief and equivocal fantasies.
> Yesterday's brightness, antagonist mind,

chance's notations and omens.
Your waist of irresolute sand
heeded only the footpaths that found no way upward.
Mine then to pursue you in corners,
your spirit's lukewarmness, that cannot construe you, still lacking you,
with the grief of a hobbled Apollo
by whose power I shatter the mask that you bear.

And although the spirit being sought is an ineffable object ("The flight of a deer / through an infinite bosom of whiteness"), he is adamant in his right to search for it and denounces those destructive forces that would prevent him. The lost soul can never be found again in the poet, or the lady, or all the corners of the cosmos, but in the song of the poet it remains an inviolable dream of infancy. The attempt to murder the beauty of this memory of childhood's innocence is described through symbols of sterility. Those who would prevent the poet from rediscovering his lost love by singing its beauty are pictured looking for Saturnalian wheat in the snow, and castrating animals in the sky:

> do not stop up my mouth, you who seek
> Saturnalian wheat in the snow,
> or unsex the creatures of heaven,
> anatomy's groves and dispensaries.
> Love! Love! A childhood of ocean!

Thus, we are introduced to the symbol of the poet's verse as the life-giving waters themselves, which ultimately execute and give meaning to, or mythologize, the ritual sacrifice. (The idea that poetry, by its very nature, imposes order on chaos is not unfamiliar to modern criticism and has always been known to great poets. It is very important in *Poet in New York*.) By the sudden shift from the poet's love to his verse, we also encounter the first of the frequent metamorphoses which occur in the volume. The metamorphoses are of themes, symbols, or persons. And it will not be unusual to encounter the poet's love, as well as his verse, as the symbol of a life-regenerating force, or the channel through which to gain identity. In "Nocturne of the Void," for example, love is evoked amid fertility symbols—"Stone among waters, voice on the wind" (p. 83)—as the regenerating force of future generations: "Enough to set hands on the pulse of our manifest love/ for the blossoms to break overhead for love's other children" (*Ibid.*).

The eyes that do not appear in death's dream kingdom continue to elude the poet in "Abandoned Church" (p. 27). Here the personal identity which the poet has been seeking in his childhood and in a lost beloved is represented as the poet's dead son. Within the poem the son undergoes several metamorphoses. He appears as a daughter, a fish, a sea, a giant, a

bear and, indeed, almost every object of mythical proportions in the
poem—the anemones, the worm-eaten fruits, the uplifted ass and ox—
which are encountered in the search for the son, but which are always
in some degree perverted, and may be understood as metamorphoses of
the son, or as symbols of the identity, which is being sought. In short,
the son is a symbol, as were the failure of the eyes in "Interlude" and
"the lady" in "Your Childhood in Menton," for every aspect of perverted,
impeded, or castrated life in the New York Waste Land. The son has
the same significance as the lost daughters of Shakespeare's romances—
Marina, Perdida, Miranda—and Ferdinand in *The Tempest*; ambiguous
symbols of lost salvation, also embodying the mystery of regeneration
and resurrection (as the archetype of the child always does). "The son"
closely relates "Abandoned Church" with "Little Boy Stanton" (p. 73)
and "Little Girl Drowned in the Well" (p. 79). Both Stanton and the
girl drowned in the well are symbols of faith toward which the poet
turns, but which fail him: Stanton dying of cancer and the girl drowned
in "water that never disgorges."

In "Abandoned Church," although the son is invested with all the
symbols of faith (his metamorphosis into a fish, for example, a traditional symbol of the church), he fails as a sufficiently strong symbol for
the poet. Although the ascent is made to ring the bells of the church, the
poet discovers worm-eaten fruits, burnt-out matches, and violated wheat.
A giant is not enough, perhaps if his son had been a bear, the poet would
not have to endure the violation of nature (the sea tied to a tree to be
ravished by a regiment) which now confronts him:

> Had my son been a bear,
> I would never have feared for the crocodile's secret
> nor gazed at a tree-tethered sea
> to be ravished and bled by a rabble of troops.

Before turning to the ritual sacrifice, there is one further direction
toward which Lorca guided his search for identity. It is in the Negro
population of New York City. He felt they were closer, through their
ancestral heritage, to the primal and eternal laws of the universe from
which the metropolitan Waste Land has severed the multitudes and with
which the poet has also lost contact.

In "Pattern and Paradise of Negroes" (p. 17) the spiritual pattern of
the Negroes' soul, particularly as it differentiates itself from the sterility
of the multitudes, is defined. The poem presents, not a physical description of Hell and Paradise, but a definition of a spiritual condition, an
indication that the descriptions of New York in the rest of the book are
objectifications of a spiritual malady, which is Lorca's true concern,
rather than an indictment of a mechanized society. "Pattern and Paradise
of Negroes" is profoundly imbued with negative mysticism. (The term

"negative mysticism," as I use it here, implies a real world of Platonic ideals, but denies any meaning—identity—or reality to the world of experience.)

The protagonist of T. S. Eliot's *Ash-Wednesday* renounces hope in both sexual ("the blessed face") and spiritual regeneration ("the voice"):

> I renounce the blessed face
> And renounce the voice
> Because I cannot hope to turn again

He hopes to find peace in the self-negation of St. John of the Cross, submitting to God's will. The ideal of Lorca's poem is also one of self-negation. The sleepers erase their profiles and all that remains is the void of a dance over ashes. The Negroes hate any conflicts or even shadows over their vast expanse of denial, and their hate extends even to the promise of the word or all abstract hope ("the incorporeal arrow") and to the exactness of measurement, which would be the opposite of Eastern negativism. They prefer the ineffable.

> Here, in insatiable grass, the torsos lie dreaming.
> Here the coral is drenched with an ink's desperation,
> and the sleeper effaces his profile, in the skein of the snail,
> and the waste of the dance on the ultimate cinders, remains.

This last stanza of "Pattern and Paradise of Negroes" introduces two themes which can be understood only in terms of their later development in the volume; the absorbency of coral and the "insatiable grass." In contrast to the absorbent coral of the Negroes' paradise, dry rocks are an important symbol of sterility in both Eliot's *The Waste Land* and *Ash-Wednesday*. In "Heaven Alive" (p. 69), in which the poet makes the choice to renounce the negative mysticism of the Negroes' paradise and to go deliberately in search of the Grail, dry rocks symbolize the place he must leave.

The "insatiable grass" may be interpreted in the light of the poem "Ruin" (p. 91). "The grasses" of "Ruin" have the ambiguous character of being the metamorphosis into Waste Land imagery of both the Furies and the Eumenides. Like the symbol of the moon in the whole of Lorca's work, "the grasses" are destructive, demanding sacrifice.

> I saw that the grasses had come
> and I cast forth a whimpering lamb
> under their lancets and fangs.

But they are also symbols of purgation. The pervading tone of "Ruin" is of resignation to a purgatorial death:

> The grasses! Love, take my hand.
> In a house's smashed windows
> blood lets its long hair.
>
> I and your sole self remain.
> Prepare your skeleton for air.
> You remain and my sole self.
>
> Make ready your skeleton.
> Love, hasten, there is left us to hasten
> the dreamless quest of our profile.

The comparison with the resignation to a purgatorial death in the second section of *Ash-Wednesday,* making an analogy between "the grasses" and the "three white leopards" of Eliot's poem, as well as between Lorca's "skeleton" and the "chirping bones" of *Ash-Wednesday* is very instructive:

> Lady, three white leopards sat under a juniper-tree
> In the cool of the day, having fed to satiety
> On my legs my heart my liver and that which had been contained
> in the hollow round of my skull. And God said
> Shall these bones live? shall these
> bones live? And that which had been contained
> in the bones (which were already dry) said chirping:
> Because of the goodness of this Lady
> And because of her loveliness, and because
> She honours the Virgin in meditation,
> We shine with brightness. And I who am here dissembled
> Proffer my deeds to oblivion, and my love
> To the posterity of the desert and the fruit of the gourd.
> It is this which recovers
> My guts the strings of my eyes and the indigestible portions
> Which the leopards reject.

In "Ruin" the functions of the "juniper-tree" (a rebirth symbol) and the "white leopards" (purgatorial)—and to some extent "the goodness of this lady"—are combined in "the grasses." With the added knowledge that devouring is a variant of the descent pattern (Dante discovers Satan devouring his victims at the bottom of Hell), the significance of "Ruin" in *Poet in New York* becomes quite clear. It is the purgatorial descent to be followed by the resurrection in "Office and Denunciation." The "insatiable grass" also has its place in the vision of the Negroes' paradise. Since the Negroes are both the victims of the multitudes, suffering purgatorial death for the city, and the race on which the hope of resurrection is laid, "the grasses" is properly their symbol.

However, with the pitiful picture in the first stanza of "The King of Harlem" (p. 19) of the Negroes fighting the agents of destruction with a spoon, we realize that the Negroes have failed the poet as did his other symbols of faith. We realize that the Negro, hopelessly enslaved in a lackey's costume by the millionaires of New York, is impotent to respond to the primal calling of his blood, in which Lorca has placed so much faith.

One of the most notable aspects of T. S. Eliot's *The Waste Land* is the metamorphosis of the Grail quester into almost every person in the poem. He is first of all Tiresias, who is also the sterile or ailing king. He then appears in the characters of Tristan, the Phoenician Sailor, the hanged man, Stetson, Anthony, Sweeney, the young man carbuncular, Ferdinand, Parzival, Siegfried, Phlebas, the Fisher King, and St. Augustine. Similar metamorphoses, as I have already indicated, are an important aspect of *Poet in New York*. In "The King of Harlem," the identity between Lorca and the king of Harlem is important (it interprets the lackey's costume in which we see him imprisoned as a symbol of Lorca's loss of faith which is manifested later in the volume), as is his later identity with Walt Whitman. Indeed, the comparison between "the poet" of New York and Tiresias, the blind prophet, who is the Grail quester as well as the Fisher King, who suffers the malady of the Waste Land while being the potential instrument of its salvation, is enlightening to the conception and meaning of Lorca's volume. I have discussed the blindness of the poet in "Interlude" and his sterility in "Your Childhood in Menton." The recognition of the Grail and the successful asking of the question, will be discussed in connection with "Office and Denunciation." And, finally, in "Cry to Rome," the poet assumes completely the mantle of the prophet of doom, enshrined in a tower raising him above humanity, who is unable to prevent the catastrophe, but nevertheless prophesies the forthcoming resurrection.

"The King of Harlem" symbolizes the poet defeated both internally, by his own impotence, and externally, by the corruption of the city. It also contains the prophecy of a new age which is to become dominant in the last two odes of the volume. The king, the instrument of salvation, is for the moment hopelessly lost. Before he can be found the descent must be made to wrestle with the forces of evil which now plague the city. This descent is pictured as the crossing of a bridge (which symbolism is orthodox enough in Dante and Virgil) and the powers to be fought and conquered are, in the particular language of the New York Waste Land, the sellers of whiskey, the rich Jewesses in their bubble baths, etc.

Reinforcing our interpretation of the malady of the city, or the poet, as a spiritual one, the apple of evil and the traditional dragon, in the form of crocodiles, also appear. The visions that will come through the descent —"the perfume we bear in our lungs . . . in its guises of peppery pine" and "the infinite beauty of the dusters, the graters, the kitchenware coppers and casseroles"—are typical of the highly esoteric visions of symbolist poets. The first, with its mixture of visual and scent perceptions, reminds us of the "correspondences" of Baudelaire and the symbolists. The second vision, the infinite beauty of kitchen appliances, borders on the absurd, but so must the frenzied ejaculations of the visionary always seem absurd to the uninitiated, and since at this point in the volume even the king of Harlem, or the poet, has not completed the descent, it is appropriate that his preliminary vision should be cloaked in highly surrealistic abstraction.

The metamorphosis which the king of Harlem is to suffer in the later *Odes* of the volume and in "Office and Denunciation" into the clearer vision of a ritually sacrificed fertility king, is anticipated in the closing stanzas of "The King of Harlem." The mystery of the fertility rituals, in which the souls of the slain divinities were believed not to die but to be freed in order to imbue the year's crops with their life, is indicated by the serpent, zebra, and mule *unpaled* by death, by the clamorous trees which *do not* expire at the moment of being cut down, and by the *vegetable* shadow of the king. The hemlock, thistle, and thorn are all positive symbols of regeneration (Socrates and Christ):

> Never serpent or zebra or mule
> Paled at death's imminence.
> Not even the woodcutter knows
> when the death of the thunderous tree he brings down is accomplished.
> Abide in the vegetal shade of your king
> till the hemlock and thistle and thorn rock the furthermost roofs.

The following last two stanzas celebrate frenziedly a new age, in which Harlem's king appears as Moses, to be ritually slain.

In "Double Poem of Lake Edem" (p. 65), it is again the voice of a past spiritual condition, ignorant of the Waste Land horrors, which appears to the poet in a maze of symbols of fertility and spiritual forces. However, the return of this voice is rendered pitifully fruitless ("I foresaw it, lapping my feet") by Lorca's present spiritual blindness. Despite the attempt to return to a state of innocence ("Let me pass by that gate. . . . to the grove of the loose-limbed and the outleaping happiest") the present condition, represented as innocence ravaged by forbidden knowledge, is too strong. The difficulty is that the descent into the dreadful secrets of the Waste Land has gone too far to permit a return without first fully embracing its dark forces. The initiate would gladly renounce the world ("But I want neither substance nor shadow") to return to his former state of innocence. But the amoral forces of nature, to which he has been introduced, in the particular language of *Poet in New York*, tinsel and talcum, overwhelm him. In the language of Joseph Conrad, another poet of the descent, the only possible answer after the journey has already begun is "in the destructive element, immerse." Indeed, with the pursuit of fogs, dreams, and death, at the end of the poem, there is no choice.

To continue the analogy with Joseph Conrad's *Lord Jim*, it is understood that the descent into the destructive element must be a self-willed choice. It is only then, if the initiate survives all the trials which his descent entails, that it will end in a successful resurrection, lifting him above the conflicts of temporal experience into a realm of transcendent knowledge and perfection. Lord Jim achieves a tragic victory at the end of Conrad's novel by willingly submitting himself to the destructive element from which he had earlier attempted to escape. This decision is implied in the gradual progress which *Poet in New York* makes toward a more ordered view of the malady of the city. It is stated explicitly in "Heaven Alive" (p. 69). In discussing "Pattern and Paradise of Negroes," I mentioned the similarity between the dry rock imagery of "Heaven Alive" and Eliot's *The Waste Land* and *Ash-Wednesday*, as a symbol of sterility. It is a form of sterility, as I said, related to negative mysticism. "Heaven Alive" (p. 69) is a decisive return from the dry rocks to the human condition despite the painful facts it will reveal of the struggle between the forces of nature themselves. ("In the sapless world of the stone and the void of the insect/ I shall not envision the duel of the sun with the creatures of festering flesh.") But the immersion into conflicts also contains the sounds of life, its spiritual fluids, and the child archetype of regeneration:

> I go into genesis' landscape
> of rumblings, collisions, and waters
> that drench all the newly-born,
> and shun all the surfaces,
> to understand rightly my target-convergence in joy
> when passion is mingled with dust and I rise upon the air.

The attempt to establish order through the ritual of sacrificial death becomes increasingly important throughout the volume. However, the loss of identity of the sacrificial victim and his passage at death into nonexistence or complete annihilation rather than ritual burial initially frustrate this attempt. In the opening poem of *Poet in New York*, "Back From a Walk" (p. 3), the poet is assassinated in a maze of nonidentity:

"Stumbling each day with my *different* face?/ Ah, heaven-murdered one!" The death of the three friends, and the poet himself, in "Fable and Round of the Three Friends" (p. 7), further illustrate this frustration. The three are frozen, burned, and buried; however, the means of their death is far from the sacrificial altar: they expire in the worlds of the bed, of the eye and the hand's laceration, of the topless academies, and are buried in a staling jigger of gin and in the vacant eyes of the birds. Obviously, in order for death to have sacrificial significance it must be ritualized. Far from being resurrected or even sharing in the many carefully marked graves of the Egyptian fertility god, Osiris, the remains of the poet cannot even be traced in the last stanzas of the poem:

> They ransacked the cafés, the graveyards, the churches,
> they opened the wine-casks and clothes-presses,
> they ravaged three skeletons to gouge out the gold of their teeth.
> But me, they never encountered.

The last three lines of the poem—"Still, it was known that the sixth moon fled up the torrent,/ and the sea could remember—so suddenly! —/ the rout of its drowners by name."—introduce the symbol of salvation through water into the poem. (The symbol is a variation of the concepts of salvation through love or the poet's own verse which we have already encountered in "Your Childhood in Menton.") The three lines are similar to T. S. Eliot's use of water as a symbol of resurrection in *The Waste Land* and "Marina." The ambiguous symbol of the moon as the destruction and yet salvation of man, i.e., his resurrection through death, is personal to Lorca.[2] In his poem it is the moon that escapes through the torrent into the sea rather than the lost daughter or the Phoenician sailor. However, the image of the names of the drowned ones being remembered suddenly by the sea is strikingly similar to the face of the lost child returning through the action of the sea in "Marina."

In "Little Girl Drowned in the Well" (p. 79) the important difference in the symbol of water is that the well in which the girl drowned is perverted by the Waste Land atmosphere. It is water "that never disgorges." The horror is not that the girl drowned but that the well will never yield her up again. Water as a symbol of a resurrecting power which gives new life, as it is used by T. S. Eliot and as it appears in Shakespeare's *The Tempest*, in which everything "doth suffer a sea-change/ Into something rich and strange," is implicit in this poem. *The Golden Bough* describes primitive tribes throwing straw effigies, representing their fertility gods, into a river from which a new god was to be

[2] See Gustavo Correa's article: "El simbolismo de la luna en García-Lorca," *PMLA*, January, 1958.

born in a few days. In some tribes the effigy was thrown into the river at a point outside of the settlement and it would then be awaited, as it flowed down the river, by the tribe. When it passed the spot in the river at which the tribe was congregated, it would be lifted out of the water as the newly resurrected god. With this implicit meaning of water as a symbol of resurrection, the explicit understanding that this water will not yield up the child becomes extremely powerful.

The rejection of everything temporal by a transcendental negative mysticism is opposed to a belief in the Incarnation, which Lorca's presentation of the ritual sacrifice implies. "Blind Panorama of New York" (p. 57) rejects the possibility of any genuine regeneration in human experience. Women who die giving birth know that all finds its end and beginning in the sterility of dry rocks and hollow air spaces. Even the possibility of genuine suffering, which conditions the inability to regenerate, is rejected: "The kinships of woe and mortality, we know,/ but grief absolute is not given to spirit." However, the particular way in which the nothingness or emptiness of "Blind Panorama of New York" is conceived, as a still point in a turning world, prepares the way for the culmination of the ritual sacrifice embodied in "Office and Denunciation."

The major burden of Frazer's *The Golden Bough* is to demonstrate the universality in primitive cultures of animism. Animism conceives of the essence or spirit of one body as transferable into another and of the life force of a whole community as bound in one man or object, most frequently the totem. The title of his voluminous studies comes from the legend of the King of the Wood at Nemi, who could not be killed in order to be replaced by a younger and more virile king until a golden bough, which was believed to house the king's spirit and therefore his strength, had been plucked. The legend is echoed in the Sixth Book of Virgil's *Aeneid*.

In "Blind Panorama of New York" the golden bough is de-incarnated and placed in a realm which is, in fact, the metaphoric language of a negative mystic. The golden bough, containing the virility or identity of the poet, and also of the whole city, is metamorphosed into "a small, infinite burn in the eyes of other systems," which is nothing and nowhere. We have come, then, to a definition of the malady of Lorca's Waste Land. It is a complete loss of faith in the temporal, in actuality, in the Incarnation, in history, which conditions his inability to act in order to extricate himself from his own psychical abyss:

> Not air, nor our lifetime's duration,
> nor the smoke-laden terrace retains it.
> Grief absolute, grief of the wakened awareness of things,
> is a part of eternity's burning,
> in the eyes of the guilelessly onlooking systems.

Although Lorca has searched for meaning (represented as the totality of humanity's suffering) in actual experience, he has failed to discover it. This interpretation becomes obvious in the last stanza, in which what are usually positive symbols of earthly reality are rejected: "Here *only* our planet persists./ Our earth, with its gates of forever,/ that give on the flush of its fruits."

Lorca feels at this point that he can have faith only in a world of Platonic ideals, but because they are unattainable he is despondent. The faith in his verse, as a possible instrument of salvation, expressed in "Your Childhood in Menton," is lost, because there is "No woe in our voices." Humanity's suffering and salvation is not there either. Even the stage of purgation, which we encountered in "Ruin," has been metaphorically de-incarnated. The purgatorial teeth are silenced in black satin: "Only the teeth, teeth to be stilled in a fold of black satin."

"Office and Denunciation" (p. 99) is, in terms of the power of imagery and symbolic merit as well as the centrality of the intellectual and emotional pattern of the volume, the most impressive poem in *Poet in New York*. In it we have both the culmination of Lorca's apocalyptic vision and the end of his agonizing search for meaning and identity in the city. Meaning and identity are discovered in acting out a willed ritual self-sacrifice. The sacrifice links the poet with the cosmic order, identifying him as the sacrificial victim through whom the universe is also given significance and, indeed, preserved. In gaining his own identity, Lorca is now able to name also his surroundings. He is not in a nightmare Waste Land but in a real city filled with real objects and people:

> This is not hell, but a street.
> Not death, but a fruit-stand.

He is suddenly able to look at his surroundings objectively without having to annihilate his whole past:

> The mountains exist; I know that.
> And the oracles's eye-glasses;
> I know it. But I have not come here to ogle the sky.
> I am here to look upon blood, the silt,
> in the blood that delivers the engines over the waterfalls
> and our souls to the fang of the cobra.

He realizes the necessity for a ritual sacrifice similar to the primitive King-gods of fertility, in order to absolve New York from the sins plaguing it and restore it to new life.

In transposing the ritual slaying of the fertility god from its primitive setting into New York, Lorca accomplishes a subtle reading of what anthropologists have called homoeopathic magic as a belief in the Christian doctrine of the Incarnation, i.e., that God has become man or that man is God. The "capsule of air" of "Blind Panorama of New York," a Platonic and nonincarnate ideal, is in this poem incarnated in the cat's paw and in the person of the poet himself:

> Here is the world of the sundering rivers, the infinite distances
> in a cat's paw smashed by the motorist.

This incarnation, the descent of the ideal into the real or actual, frees the poet from his previous impotence to act. When the poet offers himself to be sacrificed at the end of the poem, to compensate for the millions of creatures of nature which must be sacrificed daily in order to keep a vast metropolis like New York alive, he becomes the "small, infinite burn in the eyes of other systems." As such he bears all the agony of the sacrificed creatures and with his ritual murder the sin of exacting that agony is absolved from New York. Lorca has exposed himself to one of the horrors of life, in watching the train loads of blood pouring into New York daily and the streams of blood which flow under its concrete, but which are hidden to all save the initiate. To renew an already given analogy, like Kurtz in Conrad's *The Heart of Darkness*, he has almost succumbed to the horror of the mystery. However, in realizing that the fertility god himself is slain every year in order that Spring may be reborn and that he himself, like the cat's paw, is a potential god of fertility, he transcends the horror.

If we take the whole of *Poet in New York* as purely the poet's vision, a projection of his own psyche at the time, not having any correspondence to the actual city, which in one sense it certainly is, then we see the malady of the city—the city of the poet's psyche—as a temporary loss of faith. Or rather, the progression from the loss of a childish faith to the attainment of a maturer belief. The loss of faith rejected the truth of the Incarnation, and thus underlined for the poet the inadequacy of his childhood in "Interlude," his love in "Your Childhood in Menton" and his son in "Abandoned Church," to regain spiritual health.

The comparison between a line from T. S. Eliot's *The Waste Land*, "Shall I at least set my lands in order?" and the following lines from 'Office and Denunciation" was made by Angel del Río:[3]

> What shall I do now? Align all the landscapes?
> Muster the lovers who turn into photographs
> and later are splinters of wood, and mouthfuls of blood?

[3] Lorca, *op. cit.*, "Introduction," p. xxxi.

The similarity is striking, and the relationship can hardly be ignored. The protagonist of *The Waste Land*, for the moment in the person of Tiresias or the Fisher King, asks his question after having failed in his quest of the Holy Grail, because of sexual inadequacy (clearly symbolized in the hyacinth girl passage of Part I) and spiritual impotence (symbolized in the reinvocation of the passage to Emmaus). Lorca's quest for the Holy Grail, as I have tried to demonstrate in the earlier poems, has also proved fruitless because of sexual and spiritual impotence. However, in "Office and Denunciation" we have a virile assertion which overcomes the bitter failure of the Fisher King in Eliot's Waste Land. The decision to leave the dry rocks and flee to humid lands and rivers was announced in "Heaven Alive." Here it is accomplished. By sacrificing himself as a propitiatory victim for the murder of life which the multitudes of the city are effecting, the poet vindicates his own virility. He is able to do more than set his lands in order. His act establishes the ritual pattern through which the blood, which has heretofore flown aimlessly, will be given the doors through which to flow fruitfully.

It would be entirely too facile to interpret *Poet in New York* as a Christian allegory. Christianity is certainly a part of its story, but not the whole. The crucifixion and resurrection are seen in universal cyclical terms rather than as a unique event within the history of a people. Christianity is used by Lorca to serve his symbolism rather than his thought. "Crucifixion" (p. 109) may be considered together with "Jewish Cemetery" (p. 105), which refers to Christianity in an extremely obscure way. As with Christianity, Judaism is merely a symbol (of materialism) for Lorca, with no direct or restricted reference. In "Jewish Cemetery" the peaceful slumber of Christ's children and their affirmative dream vision—"a pigeon, a heron, a hummingbird, and even the living asylums of fire were consoled by the leap of the grasshopper"—are contrasted with the frantic searching and preparation of the Jews. "Unsleeping City" (p. 53) helps us to understand the significance of the Christians' sleep. The sleeplessness of the earlier poem, a symbol of the city's fallen state just as it is in Shakespeare's play for Macbeth's fall, results from the absence of the Incarnation and resurrection: "Another day/ we shall see, rearisen, the anatomized butterflies." The peaceful slumber of the Christians is expressed much differently in "Crucifixion." The poem begins with the cessation of movement in the whole universe in order to observe a single action of cosmic proportions, which we know to be the crucifixion:

> The moon could rest, at last, on the whitest curve of a horse.
> A beam of violet light that breaks from a wound
> blazons heaven with the dead child's instant of circumcision.

Though we observe the circumcision of a dead child, it is, nevertheless, a virile act of faith as is symbolized by the ray of light which it projects into the heavens. The symbols which follow in the next twenty-four lines of the poem, until the "But" of the twenty-fifth line, would almost seem to carry us back to the hopeless defeat and anarchy which preceded "Office and Denunciation." The unchaliced blood, the lame dogs, the dry night, the burned phallus of the horses, the tailors who specialize in mourning cloths of purple (placed over the statues of Christ from Good Friday until Easter Sunday), the three Marias locked up and taunted with a skull, and the cross, the nails, and the thorns all seem to betoken a return to the nihilism of the earlier poems. However, although in the poem there is no mention of Christ, he appears metamorphosed in the cow, who effects his role of propitiatory sacrifice. The frightened horror of the Pharisees at the milk-filled dugs of the cow, and the blood, flowing from the mutilated cow, gaining an affirmative significance when it wets the feet of the Pharisees, can be understood as horror at the reality of the Incarnation. The "odour of blood when Christ was slain," is used by the Irish poet W. B. Yeats in his play *Resurrection* to express awe at the reality of the Incarnation. The Greek in Yeats' play represents that same idealism which we encountered in "Blind Panorama of New York." He does not doubt the divinity of Christ, but rather the actuality of his incarnation in human flesh. Like the Pharisees in Lorca's poem he is horrified at the beating heart of Christ, Who is no phantom. The power to believe in the Incarnation is symbolic of the divine grace of the Incarnation itself, and immediately frees the poet from the inadequacies to which his disbelief had bound him. The moment at which the blood of Christ or the sacrificial cow is spilt, is known to be the moment of our salvation. The destructive gestures of the poem, summarized above, are redeemed. The horses' burns are symbolically washed with water and the poem closes with the resurrection of the butterflies which was prophesied in "Unsleeping City": "Another day/ we shall see, rearisen, the anatomized butterflies."

In the last two major poems of *Poet in New York, Two Odes* (pp. 113 and 119), the necessity to completely annihilate the city is reinforced by the knowledge that this apocalypse must occur because the mystery of the ritual sacrifice, revealed in "Office and Denunciation," is ignored. The "Ode to Walt Whitman" redefines the ambiguous nature of sacrifice encountered in "Office and Denunciation" (i.e., the destructive slaughtering of the multitudes and the ordered sacrifice of the poet), in terms of love and perversity. The "Ode to Walt Whitman" presents two distinctly different types of homosexuals; the ostentatious homosexuals, whom Lorca must have seen parading themselves in New York—the Fairies, Pájaros, Jotos, Sarasas, Cancos, Floras, and Adelaidas of the world—and the somehow meaningful agony of those creatures who, as Proust says, are female souls incarnated in male bodies, and who suffer innocently the

agony of the divine purpose which they do not understand. Lorca embodies these latter as majestic towers of virility in the person of Walt
Whitman. On a superficial level, giving the poem little merit, the "Ode
to Walt Whitman" may be read as an evocation of the glorious virility
of figures like Walt Whitman and their dream of a democratic Utopia
and a lamentation of the perversion to which this dream has been sub-
jected. However, it is the silent agony, the other side of the virile figure
of Walt Whitman, that gives the poem its depth and meaning and links
it to the sacrificial theme of the volume, particularly the life-renewing
power of frustrated love. The agony is powerfully evoked in Lorca's
description of a boy writing a girl's name on his pillow, the young man
adorning himself like a bride in a dark closet, and the green stare of
men who love men. Lorca's association of Walt Whitman with these
homosexuals is implied in his repeated insistence throughout the poem
that he is not confusing him with "the perverts." Whitman's own agony
and its sacrificial nature is clearest in the analogy made with a bird who
has had his sex crossed: "you cried like a bird/ whose sex is transfixed
by a needle." Whitman's Apollonian beauty depends upon his figurative
castration. We are reminded of the eunuch priests of Attis. That association leads us to contrast the Apollonian grace of Whitman with the
Dionysiac frenzy of the fairies, whom Lorca describes shivering between
the legs of chauffeurs, rising in clusters out of sewers, and being sadistic-
ally beaten for pleasure. Just as the barbaric multitudes of "Office and
Denunciation" usurp thoughtlessly their daily millions of slaughtered
victims, not realizing—as does the poet—that it is divinity itself which
they are slaying, so the "perverts" of the city are taking their pleasure
careless of the price it is costing. The present erotic joys of the fairies
will be the cause of a future annihilation: "It is fitting that no man
should seek/ in another day's thickets of blood for his pleasure." Just
as the poet discovered a means of ordering and ritualizing the inhumane-
ness of the city, because "Heaven has shores for our flights out of life,"
there is no necessity for eroticizing the agony of the victims of perversion.
Even their desire has its paths of fruitful expression. The homosexuals
may depersonalize their desire into rocks, and their agony can attain the
stillness of a dreaming breeze in the trees:

> Yet we might, if we would, lead our appetite on
> through the vein of the coral or the heaven-sent nude.
> Tomorrow our passion is rock, and Time,
> a wind come to sleep in the branches.

In "Your Childhood in Menton" the poet saw his voice, i.e., his verse,
as the only possible hope through which to regain and preserve his love.
Walt Whitman radiated his agony through poetry into a desire to become a river and clouds and into love of the leaves of grass and the blue

tongue of beaches. It was a way of "evading" life, of ritualitizing necessary sacrifice, of virilizing castration. He expressed no perversity, but
desired only what poetry could give him. Now, as Lorca tells us, that is
over. No one detains himself to dream as Whitman did. New York is in
the hands of a Satanic dark angel, the demonic counterpart to the white
god which Whitman represents, and has forgotten the mystery of the
wheat celebrated in primitive rituals and the anemones, supposed to
have sprung from the pure blood of the slain Adonis, are stained by the
fairies.

With the stanza referring to "the truth of the Wheat" and the "stained
anemones" the poem becomes extraordinarily complex. The contrast between the shameless ostentation of "the perverts" and the silent agony
of Whitman, the white bearded God, is deepened by the association that
is made between Whitman and the mystery of the wheat. He is mytholo-
gized into a fertility god, becoming the American counterpart to the
divine kings, Attis, Osiris, and Adonis. Unlike the fertility gods, who are
slain that their spirits may be reborn in the next year's crop of grain,
Whitman's sleep is without a rebirth or awakening. His purity, which
conditions his resurrection, has been stained by "the perverts," who fall
over his decent and luminous beard. Although "the perverts" are spe-
cifically the fairies of New York, they are but one metamorphosis of
characters who have appeared in many forms throughout the volume;
"the pharisees" of *Crucifixion*, for example, or "the jewesses" in "The
King of Harlem." As such, they represent a spiritual condition into which
the Waste Land inhabitants, or even, for a period of time, the poet himself, have fallen. The poem ends with a cry to an age in which the wheat
will reign again. The kingdom is announced by a small Negro, the race
upon which Lorca had built his hopes. But this is a kingdom in the far
distant future, which will come only after America has completely an-
nihilated itself with its own machines.

"Cry to Rome" presents a summary of the maladies of the New York
Waste Land. It presents them, line by line, as dogmatic statements rather
than in the descriptive manner of the previous poems. The didactic
statements of the poem make it clear, as does Lorca's elevated condition
on top of the Chrysler Building, that Lorca feels he has already assimilated the city and understood and intellectualized its sickness.

The first stanza is a prophetic statement of the ruin which has in
part already descended and will continue to descend upon the city. The
sharks are essentially the same as the serpents, crocodiles, and winged
beasts which we have already met and "the worm-eaten passions" is a
successful surrealistic metaphor for the loves of "the perverts." However,
the tone of the stanza is considerably less frenzied than the previous
descriptions. The next two stanzas are almost a line by line summary
of the spiritual shortcomings of New York:

There is none to apportion the bread and the wine . . .

We are not only reminded of the sacrificial death of Christ, but of the cow's udders filled with bird-shot and the ritual sacrifice of which the poet was himself the victim. In the vast metropolis there are no such doors through which the dead may enter resurrected life.

> [None] to cultivate grass in the mouth of the dead . . .

A reference to primitive rituals, like those described by Frazer, in which the straw effigy representing the Spirit of Vegetation was watered after it had been symbolically murdered, in order that new life spring from the sacrificial victim. We are reminded particularly of Egyptian ceremonies of sowing, in which an effigy of Osiris was buried with the seed of corn, in order that at the time of harvest the seed would seem to be sprouting from the body of Osiris.

> None to turn back the linens of quiet . . .

Again, a symbol of resurrection, associated with Egyptian ceremonies of burial. The unwinding of the linen cloths metaphorically represents the doors opening up into resurrected life.

> [None to] weep for the elephant's wounds . . .

Fertility gods were slain because the mythical consciousness of primitive people regarded everything as divine, or animated, and when the corn or wheat was cut down with the scythe its spirit was rendered homeless and was believed to inhabit some human being or animal. This divine animal or person, here the elephant, henceforth embodied the Spirit of Vegetation and had to be slain to release it for next year's crop.

The blacksmiths making chains, the carpenters constructing coffins unmarked by a cross (the symbolic door through which blood may flow), and the men deprecating swallows are at the same time metaphors of the decadent community and symbolic representations of the impotent and diseased king of the Waste Land. The dove, a potential symbol of the Grail, will not be recognized by the quester until he has been purified by a trial of purgatorial agony. The self-infliction of leprosy may be a sufficient endurance to break down the walls of materialism ("rings and the diamond telephones") which now keep the quester from Grace:

> Whosoever despises the dove must declare himself,
> must cry from the shafts in his nakedness,
> must force in his bloodstream the leper's infection,
> and shed the unspeakable tears
> that melt down his rings and the diamond telephones.

For the present, however, the mystery of the wheat, of rebirth ("the birth-cry") and of the life-giving waters continues to be ignored.

The Holy Grail, metamorphosed during the course of Lorca's search in New York into images of childhood, eyes, redeeming love and ritual sacrifice, appears once more in the next stanza of "Cry to Rome" as a symbol of love:

> The masters reveal to the children
> supernatural light moving out of the mountain;
> but what has remained is a concourse of sewers
> where the black nymphs of cholera cry.
> In their ardor, they point the big cupolas out, fumed by the censers,
> but under the images love has no place,
> under the eyes of definitive crystal, love has no room.
> Love waits in a thirst-broken flesh,
> in the hovel that strives with the deluge,
> in the ditch where the serpents of famine contend,
> on a desolate ocean that dandles a carcass of gulls,
> in the darkest kiss of them all, piercing under the pillow.

The masters pointing to a supernatural light are symbolically parallel to Walt Whitman. Just as his dreams were defiled by "the perverts" so is the Grail toward which the masters point. (The sewers, crystal eyes, fighting serpents, dead gulls, and the piercing kiss underneath the pillow are all images with which we are familiar. However, their nightmare tone has disappeared and they are presented with an intellectual clarity which assures us of the progress the poet has made in the Waste Land.) The stanza closes with the vision of an old man who proclaims the in-evitable triumph of love. If we interpret his translucent hands as the result of purgatorial purification, then we understand that the kingdom of love which he announces will be a phenomenon of the future and that there is a lapse of time between this announcement and its eventua-tion.

The final stanza of "Cry to Rome" announces the trial which must be actively endured before the mystery of the sacrificial ritual and the mysteries alluded to in the second stanza are understood. The Negroes and the whole race of men enslaved by civilization, or by the perversions of their own psyche, must announce their protest. It is to be announced from the stakes of their martyrdom and in the misery of their defilement. It must be understood that the earth gives its life to all, because all participate in the divinity. Then the secrets of Rome, the mystery of the wheat and of communion, will be understood as the continual self-sacrifice of God for the perpetuation of life:

> Meanwhile, and meanwhile, and meanwhile:
> the negro who sets out the cuspidors,

the terrorized boy shaking under the livid director,
women drowning in mineral oil,
the mob of the hammer, the fiddle, the cloud—
let them cry till they splinter their brains on a wall,
cry across cupolas,
fire-maddened,
snow-maddened,
let them cry with a head full of excrement,
cry like all darkness made one,
cry with such ruinous voice
that the cities will tremble like girls
and break open the prisons of music and oil.
Give us that daily bread, for we wish it,
flower of the alder, threshed tenderness, world without end;
earth's will be done, for we wish it,
who offers her harvest to all.

Lyrical Primitivism:
García Lorca's *Romancero gitano*

by Juan López-Morillas

I

There are serious difficulties in the attempt to offer within a brief space an account of even a small segment of the work of a great poet, and particularly of a poet who, like Federico García Lorca, awakens in the receptive reader a rich flow of musings and suggestions. These difficulties are of a twofold nature. In the first place we face the problem of perspective. García Lorca's life is almost contemporaneous with ours; it is part of a human reality which, in a manner of speaking, is also our own. Between him and ourselves there is an historical intimacy. With him we share a span of time or, more precisely, a mass of prejudices, of motivations, and of artistic and ideological objectives; in short, we are coparticipants in a common cultural psychology. But this intimacy, flattering as it may be to us, is the greatest obstacle to genuine understanding. To understand is first of all to become aloof, to establish an ideal distance between the person who seeks to understand and the thing to be understood. To understand García Lorca and not merely to plaster him with sticky epithets involves an act of disconnection. We sever the ties that join us to him, draw away from him, and having regained our freedom of critical action we scrutinize him from various points of view. In other words, we aim to do in regard to time what the painter does in regard to space. Whether or not we succeed is of little consequence. It is enough to remember that such is the only method which may make real comprehension possible.

The second kind of difficulty is even more serious, for it has to do with an illusory transposition of means of expression. The language of the modern poet is characterized by an extreme compression. His figures and images have, when chosen felicitously, the quality of being at once

"Lyrical Primitivism: García Lorca's *Romancero gitano*." Translated by Frances López-Morillas. From *Intelectuales y espirituales* by Juan López-Morillas (Madrid: Editorial Revista de Occidente, 1961), pp. 194-216. Copyright © 1961 by Juan López-Morillas. Reprinted by permission of the author.

terse and diffuse. Taken in isolation, these images may appear at first to possess an innocent and artless simplicity, as if the poet wished to ingratiate himself with us by deliberately selecting words in ordinary currency. But if we look again we are apt to discover that the concrete image, like the famous "canals" of a neighboring planet, grows dim as we focus our attention more sharply on it, and at the same time expands its apparent meaning into a nebula of blurred suggestions and vague allusions. This replacement of *meaning* by *suggestion* is, of course, the relevant feature of most modern poetry, a large body of which shows a remarkable lexical poverty coupled with an incomparable suggestive wealth. And this is as it should be, for we cannot ask the poet to describe or define anything for us. If he did, he would by that very fact cease to be a poet. Whatever poetic language may be, it is certainly not denotative or descriptive.

On the other hand, the language of the critic is eminently logical or, if it is not, ought to be. We who are not poets cannot speak of poetry in poetic language, for that would be a ludicrous intrusion into the poet's function. Our function in speaking of poetry is to see whether it is possible to transmute *poetic suggestion* into *logical precision* without destroying poetry in the process. There are several reasons for doubting that a transmutation of this sort can be effected. And when we are confronted with the study by a great poet, like Jorge Guillén, of another great poet, like Bécquer, we are tempted to conclude that only a poet can understand and explain another poet.

II

Among the numerous studies, commentaries, glosses, and notes which have been centered on García Lorca during these last years we select at random a special issue which the review *Méduse* (Toulouse, France) devoted to him in 1947. We read therein that Lorca's "fantôme n'a cessé de parcourir l'Europe en appelant *camarades* tous les hommes qui devaient mourir comme lui pour la seule cause que défendront toujours les poètes." We are not told what this "only cause" may be for which poets must die, but the context of this *Souvenir de Lorca* makes it possible to guess that it is the struggle against tyranny. It is, of course, a praiseworthy cause, but one in the advancement of which poets do not necessarily occupy the front rank. Nor does the defense of any cause, however meritorious, enhance automatically the worth of a poet as a poet, whatever it may do to his worth as a man. In point of fact, it would not be difficult to postulate the opposite tenet, to wit, that the worth of a poet diminishes in the measure in which his poetry is subordinated to the defense of a cause, in the sense commonly given to this expression. Victor Hugo is not at his best in *Les Châtiments,* an otherwise effective attack against Napoleon III; Alberti's proletarian phase is, in our opinion, distinctly inferior to the rest of his work; and Carducci's political poems gain in useful propaganda precisely what they lose in poetic value. We do not wish, however, to give the impression that the "defense of a cause" has no place in poetry. We merely wish to emphasize that if a poet undertakes to use his poetry as a means of defending a cause he should expect his effort to be judged as poetry, good or bad, and not assume that the merits of the cause will contribute *per se* to the greater merit of his poetry.

The statement quoted from *Méduse* is typical of the false evaluation placed on García Lorca's life and work by some French and American critics. They have stressed his tragic death and, as a consequence, they have wrapped him in a cloud of pathos which threatens to attenuate his vigorous poetic personality. His murder was, undoubtedly, barbarous and stupid, and its recollection continues to fill us with horror; but to place an inordinate stress on the circumstances of the poet's death will impair the understanding of his genuine merits. For it must be remembered, above all, that García Lorca is not an ideological poet, that he shunned the political turbulence of his time, and that nowhere in his work—not even in *Mariana Pineda*—did he unequivocally undertake the defense of any cause, except the only cause of a true poet, the cause of poetry.

III

García Lorca, let us repeat, is not a poet of *ideas;* he is a poet of *myth;* and myth begins just at the point where ideas end. The development of the human intellect is essentially the story of the replacement of myth by objective knowledge. Whole areas of the spirit, whole structures of belief which in primitive man were the province of myth have fallen under the control of reason. Faced with the onslaught of reason, myth has tried to preserve, if not its identity, at least a semblance of it, by entering into art in an auxiliary capacity as an ornamental, formalistic instrument of beauty. Myth has, in this manner, contributed to the creation of such works as Virgil's *Aeneid,* Milton's *Paradise Lost,* and Cervantes' *Don Quixote.* This is not, however, the kind of myth we have in mind when we call Lorca a "poet of myth." Underneath reason, in the subsoil of the irrational, still persist vague and formless beliefs, unsuspected impulses, unfathomable fears, waiting for the moment when, catching reason unawares, they will attempt to supplant it. Myth thus conceived may be regarded as an atavistic force which draws man back to that immemorial past when, reason being still undeveloped, life appeared before him as a powerful, amorphous, and sinister outpouring of energy, a gorgeous display of imagination, checked only by the presence of unknown forces and hostile and capricious gods. We see, then, in myth the original substance which holds men together, all men, for in impelling them back into the remotest past of the race, the *mythical past,* it tries to uncover what is primal and common to them all.

But is there, indeed, anything original and common to all men? Is it possible to discover in human life an irreducible core which acts as a center for man's disparate activities? García Lorca's poetry answers, or so we believe, in the affirmative and his answer appears to tally with the result of recent speculations on the nature of myth. In the words of Susanne K. Langer, "myth . . . is a recognition of natural conflicts, of human desire frustrated by non-human powers, hostile oppression, or contrary desires; it is a story of the birth, passion, and defeat by death which is man's common fate." For Lorca, too, myth is the expression of the radical conflict which we call life, a view of the world as a struggle of the individual for self-assertion against forces as ruthless as they are unconquerable. There is something noble and heroic in the naturalness with which man faces the unequal contest and in his refusal to accept ultimate defeat. Against the array of enemies who confront him he has only himself. And his intrepidity, far from being an impulsive gesture of bravado, springs directly from an awareness of his duty as a human being. Prometheus, chained to his rock, is the archetype of man. Through the lips of Aeschylus he tells us: "I foreknew my fate, and if I erred, I erred with conscious purpose, purchasing man's weal with mine own grief."

One may be inclined to assume that myth is a synonym of irrationality or, further, that it is a term used to clothe in decent attire the basic animality of man, the *bête humaine.* Such an assumption would be far from the truth. Though growing out of irrationality, myth seeks to supersede its source by confining itself within definite boundaries. Each myth is an entity endowed with substance and form. It has an objective validity tacitly granted by the men who come to look on it as something independent of themselves, and bow before it as before something incarnate. We might call it, with an expression dear to Don Quixote, "the reason of the unreason." Whatever a myth may stand for, we may be sure that it is always the delimitation and purification of an irrational impulse. Hence the ritual precision, the exacting formalism which is associated with it. And that blend of myth and ritual called religion affords us an excellent example.

García Lorca would say, and rightly so, that myth should not be sought exclusively in the dawn of mankind, but also in the living present. An ingenuous and imaginative man, his eyes look upon the world as upon a brilliant cascade of unrehearsed forms. He is free from the intellectual compulsion to rearrange reality, to force nature into a preconceived pattern. He is indifferent to what the metaphysician or the scientist would call the "natural order." He has the simplicity and spontaneity of a child, and we should venture to call him *childlike* if it were not for the derogatory connotation often attached to this epithet. A child looks about himself with eyes as devoid of prejudice as they are full of avidity. The world stretches before him like an undifferentiated mass in which color prevails over line, as if the untrained retina had not yet learned to rest caressingly on the contours of things. Awe takes the place of understanding, and impression is a substitute for analysis. Life is a spectacle, the supreme spectacle, and the world of forms dances and capers in feverish contortions. But it is also a fearful world. Each shape, each shadow may, suddenly and unaccountably, take on a lurid and threatening appearance. Ignorant of the law of causality, the child will start at the rustling of a leaf, the creaking of a floor, or the rumble of a summer storm. His is a precarious balance between limitless joy and limitless terror.

This is the primal, elemental world. This is the world which Lorca proposes to rediscover by diving under the surface of contemporary life and reaching those masses of humanity little affected as yet by the complexity and impersonality of a civilization nourished by the intellect. Like Gauguin, the poet is obsessed by the *enfant de la nature,* blissfully forgotten in the nooks and corners of the earth. Unlike Gauguin, he does not confine himself to immortalizing his poetic creatures in a set of artistic forms. Lorca's gypsy is also the *enfant contrarié,* jostled, repressed, and often crushed by the grownups, i.e., by those who act in the name of reason, law, morality, and convention. Properly speaking, García Lorca's poetry dramatizes the conflict between primitive myth and modern ideas.

IV

It is in the gypsy that we must look for the key to decipher our poet's primitivism. He grew up in an environment where the gypsy had somehow become indispensable, no longer the member of a wandering race which had attracted Prosper Mérimée, George Borrow, and Washington Irving, but a sedentary individual whose presence gives the Sacromonte in Granada and the suburb of Triana in Seville their peculiar character. This urban nature of García Lorca's gypsies should not be overlooked. In it lies the source of the conflict apparent in most of the poems of the *Romancero.* The gypsy who dwells in the city has *ipso facto* submitted to a diminution of his freedom of action. We say that he *submits* to it, not that he *accepts* it, just as a child submits to being confined to his room without accepting this form of punishment. No one quite knows the circumstances which led the Spanish gypsy to trade his itinerant ways for a sedentary life, but it is not improbable that social pressures and municipal ordinances had something to do with it. In the roamings of the tribe, in its sudden appearances and disappearances over the horizon, the timid city dweller perhaps saw a threat, often justified, to the security of himself and his property. And gradually perhaps he compelled the vagabond to take root, to settle in the outskirts of the towns where, closely watched ever since, the gypsy has led a marginal life, following with his mind's eye the line of the caravan along the dusty road.

The conflict between the gypsy's determination to live freely and his enforced sedentary existence corresponds on a small scale to the larger conflict between primitivism and civilization. As a symbol it haunts the poems of the *Romancero gitano*. We discover it in the gypsy nun who from behind the lattice of her austere, whitewashed cell follows with her eyes the swift galloping of two horsemen across the sun-drenched plain. We encounter it in Antoñito el Camborio who, sauntering along the road to the Seville bullring, surrenders without a fight to the Civil Guard and thereby disgraces himself in the eyes of his comrades. We feel it in the terrified gypsies who, surprised in the midst of a gay festivity, are attacked with pistol and sword by a detachment of the Civil Guard. Simple and unwary, primitive man sees himself crushed by a vast and inhuman machine in whose construction he has had no part and which he does not understand. All he knows of it is its cold, metallic power to destroy what he holds most dear: his liberty. Law and order appear to him as "a vague astronomy of inconcrete pistols," and social institutions, like the Civil Guard which embodies them, "have skulls of lead."

This, however, is only one side of Lorca's gypsies, the negative side, as it were, since in it are reflected just those factors which tend to hamper what is an essential attribute of primitive man, namely, his freedom of action. On the positive side Lorca emphasizes the rudimentary forces which characterize the psychology of the *enfant de la nature*. These forces, let us remember, are spontaneous and concrete. They have the irrevocable directness which an unshackled will imparts to the simplest action. In his eagerness to reach an objective the gypsy may be said to display the graceful and feral skill with which a tiger leaps upon his prey. But perhaps this comparison is farfetched. The actions of primitive man, though spontaneous and direct, must, however, be ritually performed. He must abide by a minimum of rules on which the stability and welfare of the tribe depend. But in every other respect the world is his.

Violence is the inescapable consequence of willful actions, for will it self is, in a manner of speaking, a form of violence. The function of the will consists in apprehending something outside itself and, with that end in view, it directs and regulates action. To want something is to do violence to it, to draw it from its usual place in the order of things, and to appropriate it as being indispensable to the one who wills. Will has this characteristic of violence even when it does not lead to the actual capture of its object. The biblical lawgiver who included the prohibition to desire the wife of one's neighbor among the Ten Com-

mandments showed a keen psychological insight in addition to a com-
mendable regard for social stability. He was aware of the violence
implicit in merely desiring another man's wife, even if such a desire is
not instrumented by action.

Lorca's poetic world emerges from a foundation of violence, and some
of his most felicitous images embody the willful violence of inanimate
things: "the furious wind bites," "the mountain, a thieving cat, bristles
its prickly cactuses," "the swords of the lilies engage the air in a duel,"
"the fig tree rubs the wind with the sandpaper of its branches," "the
sky slammed its door to the sudden noise of the forest," "the stars drive
spears into the gray water," "in the turns of the sky the brackish dawn
crackles," etc. The world, in short, asserts itself in the spasmodic clash
of its forms. Nature is a wild and merciless genetic force who transmits
to her creatures her own frenzied cruelty. Man, her favorite offspring,
mirrors her riotous example and, accordingly, fashions his life in a continuous stream of acts of violence. But, far from being dismayed by his
stormy existence, he takes it in his stride and seeks in it the full assertion
of his masculinity. The vehemence of Lorca's gypsies is not, as in the
case of more rational men, momentary and explosive. It flows steadily.
Its consequences, however extreme, are regarded as natural and are
readily admitted, without wonder or remorse. No man who is a man
could do otherwise in similar circumstances. The gypsy's sole obsession
is to be himself or, as Lorca puts it, to behave "like a legitimate gypsy,"
in accordance with the basic spontaneity of his nature, the assertion of
which gives substance and meaning to his life. This is why, in the case
of Antoñito el Camborio mentioned above, his not having resisted the
Civil Guard with knife in hand is interpreted as an act of treason against
his essential masculinity—an act which involves not only the man who
commits it but his whole race as well. Antoñito's peers can well say
that he is "nobody's son," that he is not a "legitimate Camborio." And
his rehabilitation does not take place until, much later, he dies under
the knives of the four Heredias whom he is fighting singlehanded. We
might perhaps see something heroic in this unequal contest. The gypsy,
however, feels that Antoñito has done nothing out of the ordinary. He
has simply behaved like a "legitimate gypsy."

V

Will being the substance, and violence the form of a gypsy's life, it
is not strange that all his basic beliefs have purposeful violence as a
substratum. Love, for example, is stripped of its sentimental wrappings
and reduced to the starkness of violent desire. The equipoise between
lover and beloved, so fundamental in our refined notion of this passion,
is quite absent from the gypsies of Lorca's *Romancero,* the beloved
being nothing more than the object on which the sexual violence of the

lover is spent. One might say that even physical gratification plays a
secondary role—as the result, and not the cause, of the sexual urge.
There is something acutely sadistic and impersonal about this primal
impulse which man, in a more advanced stage of development, has
tried to tame or, at least, to divert into more lasting and beneficial
aims. Lorca's primitive man, rectilinear and undifferentiated in his
volition, has as one of his objectives that of imposing his unequivocal
masculinity upon the woman of his choice. It is as if in the midst of
gratification he remained conscious of an exclusive duty to his sexual
capacity within which the woman is no more than the passive instrument of his sexual adequacy. And, indeed, the gypsy's physical love par-
takes of the somber and hieratic quality of a ritual performance. On
returning from the river bank with another man's wife, the gypsy's
terse, unemotional statement is: "I behaved like what I am: a legitimate
gypsy"; and the faithless woman walking by his side is almost forgotten
in the egotistic satisfaction arising from a duty well performed.

Violence and eroticism are so closely intertwined in Lorca's poetry
that a separation of the two is merely a matter of critical expediency
and, if carried too far, is bound to harm the understanding of this facet
of his work. Those poems in the *Romancero gitano* in which violence
is the dominant theme often have a marked sexual quality, while those
with eroticism as their core exude a biting, blood-chilling frenzy. In
the composition entitled "Martyrdom of Saint Olalla," the maiden's
atrocious torture is described by means of frankly sexual images. In the
quivering of her flesh is evinced a monstrous, depraved eroticism, a
mixture of raw pain and mystic exaltation, while the Roman Consul
who presides over the grisly scene displays the indifferent cruelty of the
sadist. In the ballad of "Thamar and Amnon," the theme itself—the
ravishment of a girl by her brother—conjoins sex and violence in a
setting in which a nominal Palestine bears an unmistakable resemblance
to the scorched, harsh, and lascivious landscape of Gypsy Andalusia.
Even when the tone of the composition seems playful, as in the ballad
of "Preciosa and the Wind," the combination of violence and eroticism
is by no means absent. Old Pan, the Greek god of shepherds and flocks
who amused himself by frightening travelers, is transformed by García
Lorca into a searing wind, the wind of desire, pursuing "with a hot
sword" a gypsy girl along what appears to be the Málaga coast. Panic
fear thus becomes identified with fear of sexual violence.

VI

Another prominent theme in García Lorca's poetry, the theme of death,
is, like that of eroticism, a crystallization of willful motive and violent
action, and it would not be exaggerated to say that death, as he understands it lyrically. has the exclusive denotation of "death by violence."

Not only his purely lyrical poetry, however, but also its dramatic projection, the folk tragedy (*Yerma, Blood Wedding*), stresses the willful nature of the deed which leads to death. To primitive man, death from what we call "natural causes" is a baffling, meaningless phenomenon. The steady deterioration of the living organism, when unrelated to a tangible material agent, fills him with awe and terror, and the cold, motionless body bearing no visible marks of violence is an enigma with which his rudimentary reason cannot cope. It is no wonder, then, that he should try to imagine objective, though unperceived, agents of death, endowed with the same attributes of willfulness and mercilessness as the real enemy who attacks him with knife in hand. Disease is looked upon as an evil spirit who, lodged within the human body, sucks away at the very source of life. But there is something insidious, cowardly, and repellent about this sort of enemy. He refuses to materialize, to expose himself to the just revenge of his victim. A man set upon by this indecent foe somehow becomes abhorrent and polluted, an abomination in the eyes of his fellows, who can no longer discriminate between the unseen agent and his victim. The contempt which Lorca's gypsy feels for a "natural death" originates in his irrational conviction that such a manner of dying is impure and cowardly. A truly masculine man may perhaps die of superstitious terror, like the Amargo in the "Ballad of the Summoned Man," victim of a mysterious fate, a strange force which he accepts and to whose superior will he submits. Here we have what may be called a stylized form of death by violence. But this is unusual. The "dark angels" hover only above the man who falls in bloody combat. And, like the wounded horseman in the "Somnambulist Ballad," he will consent to "die decently in [his] bed" only after his blood, gushing forth from his torn flesh, persuades him that he will die a man's death.

Blood, then, is the essence of life and the shedding of it is the essence of death. Man's most meaningful actions are all outlined in blood, since it is the agent which cements will and deed together. The expression "hot blood" is equally applicable to sexual desire and to physical violence. The shedding of blood is concomitant with both rape and death. García Lorca sets up a powerful lyrical structure around the symbol of blood, in which this substance is invested, not merely with biological, but also with aesthetic and metaphysical attributes. At times the use of the blood symbol has a chromatic motivation, as a desire to impart an impressionistic touch to a given image, but even in such cases it is the blood that takes into itself the substance of the image, while the object on which it appears as a color is reduced to a mere accident. For example, in the expression "the Albacete knives beautiful with the opponent's blood," the blood, not the knife, stands for beauty. On other occasions blood represents sexual desire, as when Amnon tells Thamar: "my filaments of blood weave flounces on your skirt." Or it may entail a delicate circumlocution for the loss of virginity: "warm corals sketch rivulets on a blond map." But the usual image instrumentalizes blood as a symbol of death: "the slippery blood moans its silent snake's song," that is, the song of death, the dirge for those fallen in hand-to-hand fight. It is, however, extremely difficult to summarize the use of the blood symbol in García Lorca's poetry. As a relevant aspect of his poetics it still awaits careful analysis.

VII

It has been our intention to bring out a few characteristic aspects of the poetry of García Lorca. By purposely ignoring the formal and technical features of this poetry, we have restricted our comments to what might properly be called the "poetic psychology" of the *Romancero gitano,* in short, to what we regard as the foundation of almost all of Lorca's production. These aspects could, of course, be multiplied and perhaps treated with critical views other than those here presented. The wonder of any great poet lies in this: that as we reach the depths of his lyrical world we are at once struck by numberless possibilities of interpretation, each of which merits careful attention. In exploring just a few of them we admit the limitation of our task.

Lorca's Theater

by Angel del Rio

As is so often the case in Spanish literature, Lorca's dramatic work is inseparable from his poetry and is a natural emanation from it. We have many examples of this: Gil Vicente, Lope de Vega, the Duke of Rivas, Zorrilla; in modern times, Villaespesa, Marquina, Valle-Inclán, Unamuno, and the Machado brothers. In European Romanticism we frequently find the phenomenon of lyrical poetry being turned into dramatic poetry. In this respect, as in so many others, Lorca can be placed within the framework of the Romantic attitude. But let us understand Romanticism not as a school of a certain period, but as a manner of feeling and artistic expression.

Lyricism and Romanticism seem to be fused from the start of his career. His first play, *El maleficio de la mariposa* (*The Spell of the Butterfly*) was written at the same time as his Symbolistic early verse and was animated by the same inspiration as his poems about insects and animals.

Leaving aside the dramatic intensity of his poetry, especially that of the *Gypsy Ballads,* his dramatic work developed side by side with his poetic work, both oscillating between the two magnetic poles of his inspiration and his style, the poles of the select and the popular, the capricious and the tragic, the stylized grace whose art was close to the art of the miniature painter, and the anguished passion within a whirlwind of sensuality.

Mariana Pineda

In 1927, several years after the premature *Spell of the Butterfly,* Lorca really began his dramatic career with *Mariana Pineda.* Conceived in the popular vein, the work suggests a childhood ballad: "Oh, what a sad day in Granada." It follows a technique similar to that of many of his

"Lorca's Theater." Translated by Gloria Bradley. From *Federico Garcia Lorca: Vida y obra* by Angel del Rio (New York, 1941), pp. 50-62. Copyright 1941 by the Hispanic Institute in the United States. Reprinted by permission of the author.

first poems and songs. We see here the attempt, probably intuitive, to fuse elements of the classical and Romantic theater and to do so with a modern flair. From the classical tradition he takes the essential spirit, the dramatization of a popular ballad in whose verses the drama is suggested. On the other hand, from the Romantic era he takes the historic theme, the feeling of background, and above all the character of the heroine, an angel sacrificed on the altar of love. Judged on its own merit, the work lacks true dramatic dimensions. It is a static picture. Only in one or two dialogues between Pedrosa or Fernando and Mariana can we catch a glimpse of the clash of wills without which there can be no drama. As for the intimate conflict of the heroine, Marianita, it is barely sketched. From the very beginning she seems predestined to her end; she is the embodiment of sacrifice: neither the hope of saving herself, nor the certainty of Don Pedro's love for her can change her tone of resignation:

> Through this love true
> that devours my simple soul
> I am turning marigold
> through suffering for you

She is revealed to us not through action nor in intimate dramatic soliloquies but in lyrical fugues, as in the beautiful ballad that begins with the lines, "With what an effort/ the light leaves Granada!" In the rest of the play the same thing happens. The best moments are due to the presence of lyrical elements, either directly, separated from the action, as in the ballads describing the bullfight in Ronda and the arrest of Torrijos, or as a lyrical motif in contrast to the dramatic action. The latter we find in the ballad of Clavela and the children or the song in the garden, "Beside the water." In many scenes there is a pathetic, almost musical atmosphere. On the whole we detect throughout the play the lack of maturity of an author who is experimenting with a new technique. Even his verse has a naïve and occasionally clumsy cadence. Though doubtless inferior to the poetry of these years, in which Lorca had already written many of his *Gypsy Ballads, Mariana Pineda* is not without interest. In more than one way we can catch a glimpse in it of the great merit which the best dramatic work of Lorca was to exhibit. There is a clear feeling for the tragic and a faultless good taste: aesthetic dignity saves the most dangerously poor passages, those on the border of immature and trite melodrama, like the scene of the conspirators, the seduction attempt on the part of Pedrosa, and the chorus of novices. Above all, there is a conscious effort of innovation in his intention to synthesize in the theater the plastic, lyrical, dramatic, and musical arts into a superior unity. For this reason Lorca took great pains to "tune up" each scene within a stylized atmosphere of colors, lights, allusions, and constant musical interludes and backgrounds, until at the end of the play a sort of operatic and symbolic apotheosis is achieved.

At its premiere during the period of Primo de Rivera's dictatorship many people saw in the main theme a political intention which was completely alien to its spirit. Such eminent critics as Enrique Díez Canedo, however, pointed out the mistake of interpreting the principal character as a revolutionary symbol. Mariana Pineda as Lorca conceived her was, he wrote, "a ghost who embroiders her flag, not as a symbol of liberty, but as a lover's gift. And only when she understands that in the soul of her beloved the love for freedom is stronger than the love for herself, does she become transfigured and convert herself into a symbol of that very liberty" (*El Sol*, Madrid, Oct. 13, 1927). This meaning is clear throughout the play and is explicitly stated in the final words of the heroine:

> I am Liberty because love willed it so.
> Pedro: the Liberty for which you left me.
> I am the Liberty wounded by mankind.
> Love, love, love, and eternal solitude.

Only in a few words by Don Pedro, in scene 2, can we possibly see a direct allusion to politics:

> It is not the time to think of fancies, it is time
> to open the breast to beautiful realities at hand,
> of a Spain covered with wheat and flocks of sheep,
> where people eat their bread with joy,
> in these wide eternities of ours
> and this keen passion for breadth and silence.
> Spain buries and treads on her old heart,
> her wounded heart of an errant peninsula
> and we must save her soon with our hands and our teeth.

Outside of these lines, the play develops through exclusively artistic channels, within a typically Lorcan world in which social preoccupations seldom exist, except as a projection of deeper human problems.

Short Plays, Farces

Far better constructed, although of less emotional intensity, are the works which followed *Mariana Pineda*. We find in them again the same qualities—expertness, self-confidence, stylization—as in his *Book of Songs*, but here enriched by a well-defined and conscious ironic grace.

Three farces in prose, written between 1929 and 1931, make up this phase of his work and constitute at the same time a group by themselves within his theatrical writings. The first is *Amor de Don Perlimplin con Belisa en su jardin* (*The Love of Don Perlimplín for Belisa, in His Garden*), not produced until 1933 but written long before then. Then came *La zapatera prodigiosa* (*The Shoemaker's Prodigious Wife*), first presented in the *Teatro Español* of Madrid in 1930 and later in an enlarged version in the Coliseum Theater in 1935; and finally the delightful *Retablillo de Don Cristóbal* (*In the Frame of Don Cristóbal*), a farce for puppets dated 1931 in the Losada edition of Lorca's complete works.

They have in common the same stylized popular background and a similar theatrical technique which results from the combination of elements taken from the courtly comedies at the end of the seventeenth and the beginning of the eighteenth centuries, from the Italian stage, from the puppet theater, and from the modern ballet. Each one, depending on which element predominates, has its particular character.

The Love of Don Perlimplin is the most cultivated of the group in technique and the most lyrical in spirit. Although not distinguished by the careful technique or the lively movement of *The Shoemaker's Prodigious Wife,* it is nevertheless superior in its poetic qualities. Always within the framework of irony, we can detect passages of beautiful lyricism, as in Perlimplín's lament: "Love, love, wounded love," and in Belisa's song: "Along the banks of the river." In the third scene—Perlimplín's suicide—buffoonery is raised to an atmosphere of delicate melancholy. The playfulness of the farce becomes impregnated by a pathetic aura, diffused in soft tones like the sonatas of Scarlatti, which were used by Lorca as melodic interludes, or like the poetic theater of Musset, which Lorca had read with great interest. We find ourselves at the limit of pantomime where an intentional dehumanization of characters takes place, and nevertheless we perceive in the comic profile of Don Perlimplín his sentimental anguish, caused by a love which is at the same time pure and grotesque.

The Shoemaker's Prodigious Wife is a stylization of pure folk charm, the most complete and successful work of this group. Directly inspired by folklore, the shoemaker and his wife, the chorus of neighbors, the dialogue and the action are conceived with a picaresque, old Spanish flavor, which reminds us of certain short plays of the Golden Age. The popular ballad of the shoemaker preserves the common and clumsy flavor of the ballads commonly recited by blind men, refined through touches of the best poetic quality. The play is an exercise in wit: the few dramatic scenes are expressed in a knowing gradation through the contradictory feelings of the shoemaker's wife toward her husband. Throughout she is bad-tempered and tender, piquant and impudent. The farce is resolved in the triumph of love, when the shoemaker and the shoemaker's wife are reunited. Even within the framework of comedy Lorca places a trace of bittersweetness, when after the reconciliation of the couple the work closes with the half serious, half ironic lamentations and insults of the shoemaker's wife: "How unfortunate I am with this man that God has given me!" We should take notice of this ending, basically a happy one, because it is the only time that it occurs in Lorca's dramatic works, which are primarily concerned with frustrated love. As in his other plays, the music—song, rhythm, background—has an essential role, producing an effect of unreality and giving the play the subtlety, grace, and movement of a ballet.

In the Frame of Don Cristóbal, like Los títeres de Cachiporra (Cachiporra's Puppets), comes from the period of the first youthful experiments and was inspired directly by the puppet theater. It is not much more than a game, a folk Andalusian divertissement; it is important only as an example of Lorca's versatility, that constant search for a better integration of the arts which characterizes his theatrical writings as much as his poetry. It also reveals the piquant background of malicious country wit which was part of his mental makeup and added spice to his conversation. In the Frame of Don Cristóbal, full of naïve fantasy, is a magnificent example of "naughtiness" and spontaneity.

These short unpretentious plays illustrate typical aspects of Lorca's artistic personality; his more profound self we find in his treatment of anguish and tragedy, but even here we shall continue to find a counterweight of light and joyfulness, of pleasure generated by wit and innocent irony.

Experiments in Surrealistic Theater

Así que pasen cinco años (If Five Years Pass) and some scenes from the drama El público (The Public), written between 1929 and 1930, belong to the period in which he was interested in Surrealism. This work comes a little after or at the same time as his poems about New York City. They coincide with the climax of Surrealism in France and its reflection in Spain, with Alberti in poetry and Gómez de la Serna and Azorín on the stage. Lorca never made up his mind to stage them, and it is possible that once the vogue for this kind of art had passed, he did not pay much attention to them.

The fragments that we know from El público do not give us an accurate idea of the total work.[1] It seems to have been inspired by the problem of reality and poetic "super-reality" on the stage and in real life.

---

[1] The play was completely finished by Lorca, but in the Losada edition of his complete works only a few scenes appear, not enough to judge the whole. We know that Lorca himself and his friends who knew the play attached a great deal of importance to it.

Besides, we can detect in several episodes a vein of perverse and abnormal sensuality corresponding to the preoccupations which must have tormented him during those years. The characters are beings of fantasy and beings taken from real life, without any distinction between them. All act and speak with the same incoherent automatism. The play is full of bloody and violent images mixed with humor. In the first extant scene he formulates the poetic idea of the metamorphosis of forms, which constitutes the basis of all Surrealistic aesthetics:

> *Figure covered with little bells:*
> If I should change into a cloud . . .
> *Figure covered with tendrils:*
> Then I would change myself into an eye.

This is an idea which inspired some of the poems of *Poet in New York*. It reminds us especially of "Death": "What an effort,/ what an effort of the horse/ to become a dog," etc.

If Five Years Pass ("a legend about time in three acts and five scenes") is of greater interest than *El público*. Here the theme is a combination of two typically Lorcan preoccupations: the passing of time and the frustrations of love. The central characters, the young man and the fiancée, are new versions of Marfisa and Don Perlimplín and the waiting for a wedding which never takes place is almost a foretaste of *Doña Rosita la soltera* (*Doña Rosita the Spinster*). The technique and the atmosphere are, however, completely Surrealistic. It is an atmosphere of dreams, with masks, mannequins, clowns, or real people like the rugby player or the card players dehumanized in the manner of the characters of Gómez de la Serna, to whose influence this work is largely indebted. Lorca manages to sustain an unreal atmosphere suspended somewhere between humor and drama and with an undercurrent of mysterious sensuality. As in the best of his plays, the lyric elements are ever present. The scene of the dead child and the cat in the first act has all the characteristics of his poems about children, including the use of images, the "white handkerchief," "the roses that wounded my throat," the "voice of silver," the "fish through the water," and so forth. Many other poetic fragments of this play bear the imprint of the best of Lorca, as this delightful song of the rain:

> I return for my wings,
> let me return.
> I want to die being dawn,
> I want to die being
> yesterday.
> I return for my wings,
> let me return.

> I want to die being a spring.
> I want to die away from the sea . . .

The dialogue, whether in prose or in verse, almost always shows a growing mastery of the theatrical technique which the poet was slowly acquiring through his various experiments. Lorca never confined himself to a definite type of poetry or of drama nor to the inflexible formula of any fixed school. Thus, having learned all he could from it, he soon abandoned Surrealism and returned for inspiration to the feelings and themes of Spanish reality where his art finally found its focal point.

Doña Rosita the Spinster

Leaving aside till later the analysis of *Blood Wedding* and *Yerma*, which in our opinion occupy a unique place in the dramatic works of Lorca, we now come to examine the last play staged during the poet's life, in which the sentimental attitude of his first years reappears, but enriched by all the experiences of his artistic development.

Doña Rosita the Spinster, or The Language of Flowers, was produced in Barcelona by Margarita Xirgu the thirteenth of December, 1955. It had enormous success and the critics saw in the play a new trend of Lorca's already many-sided dramatic art. If his tragedies represent a balance between lyricism and drama, *Doña Rosita* is the fusion of poetry and comedy, with subtle historical overtones.

The author describes the work as "a poem of Granada in 1900 divided into various 'gardens' with scenes of singing and dancing." Like *Mariana Pineda,* to which it bears a strong resemblance in technique and mood, it deals with the evocation of a period. But the shading of the poetic, plastic and emotional elements of the play is better achieved. The direct romanticism of the earlier work now becomes soft irony. The intense drama of love becomes diluted and is dissolved into lyrical fragrances. The somewhat artificial pathos of *Mariana Pineda* is replaced by a sweet melancholy, a pure and intense emotion. Doña Rosita, a woman (the most important characters in Lorca's plays are always women), is not a heroine but rather a symbol of womanhood in the Spanish provinces at the end of the century. Thus we have a lack of real dramatic intensity. In order to become a deep psychological play it would have had to delve into the individual soul of the characters. This is precisely one of the main shortcomings in all of Lorca's plays, including his tragedies, where passion never quite acquires full psychological embodiment and always remains skin deep, with no motivation other than a kind of tragic destiny before which the characters submit with hardly a struggle. What happens in *Doña Rosita* is that the poet turns this limitation into his main creative force. The drama of resigned love incarnated in Doña Rosita, the endless waiting for the sweetheart who will not return, is consciously subordinated to a more impersonal anguish: what moves the spectator is neither the passion nor the suffering of the protagonist but the bodiless presence of time itself hovering over the stage and the life of every character. Lorca is a master of creating a lyrical atmosphere, and in this play he succeeds completely. The evocation of those quiet years from 1890 to 1910 in which Spanish life seemed to be at a standstill as if it had lost all its vital springs gives us a perfect picture of both reality and trite pathos, touching in its irony. All the sentimental mood of the play, all its lyrical quality find their maximum expression in the "language of flowers," a symbol of existence without desires and without ambitions, and a symbol at the same time of the slow withering of Doña Rosita:

> The rose? It was still open
> but night was coming fast
> and the thud of sad snow
> was weighing on its branch;
> when the shadows returned
> the nightingale still sang,
> but she, with deathly pallor
> into the darkness shrank,
> and when a metal horn
> sent shivers through the night
> and the wind embraced the mountain
> falling asleep on its lap
> she lost her petals and died
> while dawn gathered her last sigh.

Some critics have mentioned the influence of Chekhov. There seems to be a definite similarity between both writers. The end of the play, when the mother, the governess, and Rosita leave the house, taking with them all their memories, while the wind softly moves the curtains and the stage is engulfed by the weight of loneliness, cannot but remind us of the almost identical end of *The Cherry Orchard*. Other points of coincidence with Chekhov, whose works Lorca doubtlessly knew, could be found. There is the fact that both turn to nature when looking for a symbol of action and a lyrical background. The atmosphere in *Doña Rosita* reminds us in many ways of the melancholic atmosphere in *Three Sisters*. But the parallels seem to end there. There can be no similarity between Lorca's characters, as simple as shadows, and the characters created by the Russian playwright, who are at the brink of desperation, and struggle tragically while looking for a justification of their existence.

Chekhov's lyricism is the result of a delving into the deepest layers of human feelings and human anguish; in Lorca lyricism is a poetic fact alien to every intellectual and psychological motivation.

Neither in *Doña Rosita* nor in his dramas can Lorca's art be characterized by its intellectual strength. Its essence is rather an instinctive intuitive penetration and an extraordinary gift for poetical expression.

Mature Works

Born during a period of permanent crisis in art and in society, Lorca was bound to reflect in every facet of his work the varied experiments of the new aesthetics, struggling to find a firm basis and solid ground. This variety of styles can be explained by the influx of new literary movements, the new "isms" that have dominated the arts since the First World War. It differs nevertheless from the variety and the changes in style to be found in the works of many poets or artists of our time, inasmuch as throughout Lorca's works a personal accent and the expression of a personality basically impervious to outside influences can be detected. The development of his different facets was carried through a long process of growing simplicity and integration. The abundant and sometimes confusing themes and feelings of his youthful poetry became increasingly pure and simple; the experiences and artistic forms suggested by the changes in modern sensitivity and the restlessness of his own moods became increasingly better integrated. This phenomenon need not be ascribed only to Lorca; it can be observed in every true artist, in almost any period. What seems to be characteristic of Lorca is its pervasive importance and at the same time its fruitfulness. Without sacrificing any essential element in his inspiration, he managed to create a synthesis which finally became stabilized around certain folk themes. These folk themes were "popular" in the best sense of the word, because of the essentially traditional nature of style and form and because of the spiritual and poetic contents. In *Blood Wedding, Yerma, Lament for the Death of a Bullfighter,* we find the same human, elementary, passionate mood of the *Poem of the Cante Jondo* and the *Gypsy Ballads.* The poet comes back to the Andalusian world, but now, in a splendid artistic plenitude, all that was marginal or merely picturesque disappears, only essences remain.

Poetic Tragedies

In *Blood Wedding* (another English title for the same work is *Bitter Oleander*), which had its premiere in the Beatriz Theater in Madrid in 1933, Lorca for the first time finds the right expression for the passionate intensity vibrating in the inner recesses of his best poetry: a peasant tragedy. At times the dehumanized, stylized art of his songs and stage artifices make us forget the frantic trembling of life and nature which the voice of this dark and passionate poet brought to us from the time of his earliest creations. This constantly present trembling of life can be found in the dramatic quality of his lyrical poetry as well as in his tragedies, where it comes to be felt with all its violence, subordinating the lyrical content to the dramatic tone in a perfect fusion which Lorca had to achieve if he wished to express fully his most complete self.

"I was," the Fiancée says, "a burnt woman, full of sores outside and within. And your son was a drop of water from whom I expected children, earth, health." Here is the essential element of tragedy: beings who are scorched by a deep passion against which it is futile to struggle. The situation is a simple one and an old one: the rivalry within a family, and the rivalry of two men for a woman who struggles between the attraction of a fiancé, who offers her peace of mind, and the more powerful attraction of her lover. However, having been abandoned by her lover, Leonardo, who, in the meantime, has killed off many relatives of her prospective bridegroom's family, the Fiancée finally decides to get married. The preparations for the wedding are clouded by premonitions. The wedding takes place in an atmosphere full of bad omens; there is the presence of Leonardo, now married to another woman, the flight of the lovers, and the death of the rivals after a pursuit and a frantic struggle in the forest. At the end we find the three women, the Fiancée, the Mother, and Leonardo's Widow, expressing their hatred, their sorrow, and their loneliness when confronted by death, among the lamenting chorus of the neighbors.

Using this basic and timeless plot,[2] Lorca creates a drama in which the dark and somber passion of tragedy becomes stylized within a lyrical and musical framework, but without losing any of its intensity. Straightforward to the point of being schematic in the exposition and development of dramatic conflict, he makes use with admirable economy of all the known devices of his art. Music has a role, together with folk poetry, in the lullabies and wedding songs, and in the rhythm which envelops the action (especially noticeable in the psalmodic tone of the concluding lamentations). Lyricism has its role in the characteristic themes of Lorca's Andalusian vision: the horse, the knife, the rider, the flowers, or in the nocturnal symbolism of the scene with the woodcutters and the moon. The tiniest slip in the handling of any of these elements of

[2] On the other hand the play was inspired by newspaper accounts of a real event that had taken place in the province of Almería. Lorca had read about it many years before and remembered it. His posthumous play *The House of Bernarda Alba* was also inspired by real life events, as one of Lorca's friends has pointed out. This is important because it underlines the fact that Lorca's inspiration both as playwright and poet accepted concrete reality as a point of departure.

the play would have reduced it to a melodrama of local color and have destroyed the nobility of its inspiration by scenes of facile and mannered lyricism.

Blood Wedding is saved from these dangers through its balance and precision. Although some of its musical interludes or lyrical fugues might better have been eliminated, they nevertheless do not break the classical structure of the plot, nor do they destroy the cold and objective pathos of the forces which move the characters and even give them a universal meaning.

Sensuality, hatred, love, and tragic destiny bringing with it a bloody and violent death are the central themes of this play. Underneath them as the source of all these human and elemental events, raising tragedy to the level of inescapable fatality, is the earth, the land, which possesses and inspires all the characters. Leonardo will say as his only justification for his criminal love:

> For the guilt cannot be mine,
> for the guilt is in the land
> and this fragrance that arises
> from your breasts and from your hands.

The woodcutters in their symbolic commentary during the scene of the crime will explain the earth's power as a fate, an end, a goal which gives birth to human desires, the desires of the two lovers, and also provides an end to them:

First Woodcutter:
They were deceiving each other and finally blood was more powerful than either one of them.
Third Woodcutter:
Blood.
First Woodcutter:
We must follow the blood's path.
Second Woodcutter:
But blood that sees light the earth drinks up again.

The earth is above all the wet clay which nourishes the roots of grief and the hatred of the Mother, the true incarnation of the moving pathos of tragedy. In the final scene she says to the Neighbors,

Your tears are tears only of the eyes. And my tears will come when I am alone; they will come up from the soles of my feet, from my roots, and they will burn more than blood.

The earth is the only companion of her solitude, because in it there lie the beings born from her womb:

I will make out of my dream a cold dove of ivory which will carry camellias of frost to the churchyard. But no, not a churchyard: a bed of earth . . . I do not wish to see anyone. The earth and I . . .

The earth is the only consolation, because it changes the blood of the dead into a new fountain of life, and so when the Fiancée appears before the Mother asking to be sacrificed in atonement for her guilt, she controls her impulse toward vengeance and hardly looks at her:

But, what do I care for your honor? Why do I care for your death? What do I care for anything? Blessed be the wheat, because my sons are beneath it; blessed be the rain, because it moistens the face of the dead; blessed be God, who lays us out to rest.

The play should have ended here. Lorca fell into the temptation of closing upon a lyrical-musical-symbolic scene and added a chorus where there are allusions to sunflowers, bitter oleanders, sweet nails, and small knives and which spoils to some degree the tragic tone of the final scene.[3]

Blood Wedding is a work of the highest artistic rank. In it we can detect the breath of classical influence, a touch of Mediterranean tragedy and even a certain Shakespearian quality. The sources are many. From the Spanish traditional comedy it has borrowed the peasant touches and the technique of fusing music and action. The whole atmosphere of the wedding scene is reminiscent of Lope de Vega. Modern touches can be found in the symbolism of death, which seems inspired by Maeterlinck, and in the Andalusian folk background accompanied by realistic details that suggest the Machado brothers. The poet's use of naked tragedy also brings to mind D'Annunzio or Valle-Inclán, but it is without the literary affectation of D'Annunzio or the purely verbal charm and the archaic atmosphere of Valle-Inclán. When we mention these influences, we are not speaking about direct and literal influences but rather of vague subconscious memories (with a possible exception to be made in the case of Lope). Essentially Lorca does not abandon for even one second his own peculiar poetic world and his usual method of composition, with all its limitations and all its genius. A typically Lorcan play with its mixture of different elements, *Blood Wedding* does not have a clear precedent or source. It may very well miss becoming a world classic because of its local color and the fact that its action seems limited and appears to lack real spiritual content. The lukewarm reception by the public of its English and French versions shows that many of its values are lost in translation and that a great deal of its atmosphere can be communicated only to a Spanish-speaking public steeped in Spanish artistic traditions.

[3] After writing this essay we have learned that Lorca actually did finish his play with the lines quoted, but because of certain pressures felt compelled to add the final chorus later.

But even with all these reservations, it is impossible to doubt the exceptional value of this play. The unity of its poetic elements, the moving clarity of its drama, and the breath of folk life that animates it make it the most complete and beautiful masterpiece of Lorca's theater and place it well above the mediocre productions of today's Spanish dramatic literature.

Yerma, written two years later, is similar in its main idea and its technique to *Blood Wedding.* In many ways it is a more finished product. The subject is a more ambitious one. Lorca had been elaborating it for many years. It deals with a love frustrated because of man's powerlessness to respond to woman's passion. The subject appears in some of Lorca's earliest poems and reappears later as an obsession in *Mariana Pineda,* in some of the *Gypsy Ballads,* in *Don Perlimplin,* in *If Five Years Pass,* in *Doña Rosita.* Sometimes he deals with spiritual love, sometimes with sensuous lubricity. In *Yerma* the situation develops within the framework of frustrated motherhood, and the passion becomes intimate and spiritualized. The play's structure follows an order in which dramatic elements predominate. The lyrical elements—songs, washerwomen's chorus—are less important. The tragic conflict acquires greater density because within a primary climate of passion surrounding the characters there is a more complex hierarchy of forces. As in *Blood Wedding,* there is a suggestion of pagan forces struggling in Yerma's soul against her moral sense of duty, until she is incapable of giving in to either of the two forces and decides to kill her husband.

In spite of all this and perhaps because of its ambitious scope, *Yerma* does not quite reach the artistic level of *Blood Wedding.* It does not have the same artistic unity; the dramatic motivation is less clear. In *Blood Wedding* everything is concrete and basic, earthy, within a folk poetic atmosphere. In *Yerma* at bottom every element strains toward abstraction. We could well suspect that Unamuno's presence hovered around Lorca's subconscious while he was writing *Yerma.* The very character of the heroine reminds us of Unamuno's literary creations. Her last words, after killing her husband, seem inspired by the author of *The Tragic Sense of Life:*

Do not come near me for I have killed my son. I myself have killed my son!

Doubtlessly Lorca wanted to go beyond Unamuno's disembodied approach to tragedy; he wanted to add to it life, blood, individuality. He managed to do so up to a point, but in order to give to Yerma's intimate anguish all its pathos and its universal meaning he needed instruments for abstract reasoning and at the same time for subtle psychological penetration. These Unamuno possessed abundantly but Lorca lacked, being an intuitive spontaneous artist. Lorca's domain extended from

direct speech to symbols, from folk elements to styli'
the reading of *Yerma* is somewhat disappointing. \
the lyrical pathos or the burning dialogue of *Blood*
stage the effect would be more positive. Lorca's the
a spectacular theater and words lose a great part ot ..
read outside a total atmosphere that was posited at the
the work was written. Lorca was a past master in the renou.
dramatic elements in terms of visual details, rhythm, and lyrıc..
symbols.

Yerma is one more step toward the intensification of tragedy. This
purpose seems also to inspire Lorca's last tragedy, *The House of Bernarda
Alba,* which according to his friends he finished a short time before his
death. This last play was, with *Yerma,* part of a trilogy on the theme of
sexual obsession and unfulfilled love, a theme, as we have pointed out
previously, that is one of Lorca's most characteristic and permanent,
since it is at bottom a projection of the conflict between pagan and
Christian attitudes which is ever present in the Andalusian soul and
basic for the psychology and the artistic temperament of Lorca.

Adolfo Salazar, one of the poet's friends who had heard Lorca's reading of the play, has published the following synopsis of it:

> Seven women, without a man, in a country house, closed down by a recent
> mourning, within the calcinated atmosphere of an Andalusian August.
> Bernarda Alba is a character that seems to come out of the classical Greek
> stage, as does Yerma, as does the Mother in *Blood Wedding*; a crazy old
> woman, long time a widow; an old servant; and the four daughters of
> Bernarda Alba. Seven women without a man who try to catch a glimpse of
> Pepe el Romano's warm shadow. Three anguished, dry, laconic acts. Words
> of ice beneath which beats rancor; the hatred of one woman toward an-
> other in whom she suspects a possible rival. Because Pepe el Romano, who
> is never seen on the stage, is constantly present and his corduroy trousers
> dance before the eyes of the seven women tortured by sex. A brutal episode:
> the distant beating, of which only the rumor is heard, of the woman who
> committed adultery . . . Pepe el Romano succeeds in evading the hundred
> eyes of Bernarda—Argus and Medusa under the guise of a vestal virgin
> watching over the chastity of her daughters. The adulteress . . . Pepe el
> Romano's portrait under the pillow . . . The youngest daughter, the one
> who was not yet bitter. A noise in the barn. A woman hung from a rope
> . . . Bernarda's form grows larger. She ascends a mythological peak. Silence!
> Not a word of this outside of this house! Silence! Let no one suspect any-
> thing. The hatred of the rejected ones is the only responsory for the dead
> girl.

Salazar adds that every time Lorca finished reading a scene he exclaimed
with enthusiasm: "Not a drop of poetry! Reality! Realism!" This seemed
to be his goal and aspiration: to reach cold, objective, essential tragedy,
tragedy without any lyrical addition. He was reaching a serene maturity

t having lost any of his fresh creative genius. It is therefore not
rising that in the *House of Bernarda Alba* he may have achieved a
plete and inspired masterpiece, anticipated by *Blood Wedding* and
repared by *Yerma*, which, although less accomplished as works of art,
had already given him a first classical pattern.

Humor in the Plays
of Federico García Lorca

by Susan Smith Blackburn

The Theater is a school of pain and laughter.[1]

If in certain scenes the audience does not know what to do, whether to laugh or to cry, this will be a success for me.[2]

Is there humor in the plays of Federico García Lorca? Certainly the writer's most famous plays are tragedies. Lorca has never been called a humorist. When a reader or student of Lorca thinks of him, it is as a lyric poet or a tragedian. Yet, in truth, he could be called a master in the creation of humor.

Federico García Lorca's life was an intimate part of his artistic creation. He believed that the world was a great stage; life, a dramatic game. His brother Francisco has written, "It is rare that the dualism of art and of life (in the works of Federico) has been integrated in such a simple, spontaneous and, at the same time, profound way. Art was a consequence of his life." Therefore, in an analysis of Lorca's work one must know something of his life and his character. Was there humor in his life? in his personality?

A glance at his childhood gives us the first key to the answer. During his earliest years he already had an extraordinary affinity for the theater and often staged small plays, imitating the people around him, reciting masses, or presenting caricatures of his friends. The talents of observation

"Humor in the Plays of Federico García Lorca." Originally published in Spanish in *Letras*, Spring, 1953, pp. 21-36.

[1] Federico García Lorca, "Charla sobre teatro" *Obras Completas*, Madrid, 1954, p. 34.
[2] Federico García Lorca. Cited by Francisco García Lorca in the prologue of *Three Tragedies of Federico García Lorca*, New York, 1947, p. 16.

and imitation are indispensable to the artist, be he painter, novelist, poet, tragedian, or humorist. A small theater was his first game.[3] The plays could not be bought with the theater; Federico had to write them. It was then he began to look at the world as a game of drama. Life became for him a great world-wide stage. When only a year old, Federico could follow the rhythm of a song.[4] Music was an integral part of Federico's art: it runs through all his creation, and surely his understanding of rhythm and measure helped develop his sense of humor.

During the years that Lorca studied at the University of Granada we know by reflections in his poetry that he absorbed all the enchantment of Andalusia: the color, mystery, and romance of the Arabs and the gypsies. And one has yet to find an Andalusian who does not enjoy laughter. Mixed with the romantic, the melancholy, the dramatic, there is in each the joy of life, the hearty laugh, the wide smile. And Lorca? From the University he wrote in a letter, "I have gained enormous popularity giving everyone silly nicknames." [5]

At the age of twenty-one Federico arrived in Madrid, an animated young man full of life, interested in everything, a friend of everyone. Pedro Salinas described him, "We all followed him, because he was the fiesta, the joy that would suddenly fill us, and there was nothing to do but to follow him." [6] An aura of happiness always surrounded the poet. At a reunion or party he would sit at a piano, recite poems and satirize in caricature the pedantic arrogance of so many Spanish intellectuals.[7] He would improvise or recite with a light ironic touch some scene from *Don Juan Tenorio*. He could tell anecdotes and imitate to perfection comic types of provincial life—the humor of the *pueblo* or the conversation of a Madrid tavern—yet always with an understanding for the problems and sadnesses of each person. He lived in laughter, as he lived in tears. He lived dramatically.

During the years in Madrid Lorca wrote the major part of his poetry, including his *Romancero gitano* in 1927. Following these years he entered a period of depression and despair. One cause of this state was the discovery that the success he had wished for and attained gave him neither satisfaction nor happiness. Also it is rumored that he had certain unhappy personal relationships. Whatever the causes, the poet entered a phase of sadness, loneliness, and restlessness. He left Spain for New York. Even in this deeply unhappy condition there flickered a light of laughter and fun. He is remembered in New York as the life of the party. He en-

---

[3] Angel del Rio, *Vida y obra de Federico García Lorca* (Ebro: Zaragoza, 1952), p. 11.

[4] *Three Tragedies of Federico García Lorca.* (New York: New Directions, 1947). Prologue by Francisco García Lorca.

[5] A. del Rio, *op. cit.*, p. 13.

[6] Lorca, *Obras completas,* with a preface by Jorge Guillén (Madrid: Aguilar, 1954), p. xxiv.

[7] A. del Rio, *op. cit.*, pp. 12-24.

chanted everyone—even those who spoke no Spanish—with his songs and jokes, his imitations and anecdotes. Little by little joy seemed (at least superficially) to obliterate his despair, and in the last years of his life in Latin America and later in Spain he seemed to feel a greater optimism for life than during any other period of his life. It is interesting to note that in these years he wrote his greatest plays—his tragedies.

What, then, can one deduce about the humor of Federico? He was gifted with humor; and he used it not only to amuse and entertain his friends, but also as a counterbalance or even a disguise for the passionate longings and deep insecurities of a sensitive poetic soul. Since humor was a large part of his uniqueness as a person, it is only natural that it be reflected in his creation.

Word Humor

Shaw has said, "There is no literary symptom more dangerous than a temptation to write about humor. It shows a complete loss of humor." There is some truth in this. If one reads or hears a joke or humorous story many times it suddenly ceases to be amusing. This is the first danger in a study of this kind. The second is that fragments of humor lose a great deal when taken out of context. One must, then, imagine each example in its context and presented on a stage in a theater with an audience. The success of theatrical humor (especially that of situation or character) depends on its circumstance, and loud laughter is a social reaction. As Henri Bergson has pointed out, one rarely laughs aloud alone.

We shall begin with the *pun*. The pun is the wit of the sophisticate. Lorca uses it infrequently; he had more interest in simple and pure humor than in that which is over-refined.

In the fifth scene of his *El Maleficio de la Mariposa* (The Spell of the Butterfly), Alacranito, the drunk, refers to the poets and philosophers of the world as members of the "alistogracia." His pun is three-fold: these men are clever (*listos*), are amusing or gracious (*gracia*) and form an aristocracy (*aristocracia*).

In *Los títeres de Cachiporra* (The Puppets of Cachiporra) there is a different kind of play on words. It occurs in the fifth scene between Don Cristobita and Fígaro, the barber, and must be quoted in Spanish.

Cristobita: Yo no convido a nadie, porque sois unos ladrones todos. (I invite no one because you are all thieves.)
Fígaro: Son. (They all are.)
Cristobita: ¡Sois! (You all are.)
Fígaro: Son . . . las diez. (It is ten o'clock.)

The barber who has begun to fear the fury of Cristobita abandons his argument and pretends, suddenly, to have been talking of something else.

So far we have seen examples of puns used descriptively and as an escape hatch. In Act II of *The Shoemaker's Prodigious Wife* (*La zapatera prodigiosa*) Lorca enjoys humor of this kind for its own sake. The shoemaker's wife pretends to offer a refreshment to the Mozo de la Faja:

Zapatera: What will you take?
Mozo: Whatever you wish.
Zapatera: Well, the door.

In the first act of *Así que pasen cinco años* (*If Five Years Pass*) the Amigo describes a woman as "a *morena* of the type one desires at noon on a summer day." The word *morena* has two meanings: a brunette, and the darkness or shade which one misses on a hot summer day.

In *El público* (*The Public*) one finds a different kind of humor with words. The Centurion announces, "The Emperor is looking for one." Pámpano and Cascabel both answer, "I am one."

Centurion: Which of the two?
Pámpano: I.
Cascabel: I.
Centurion: The Emperor will decide which of the two is one.

Here, besides the obvious pun in "which of the two is one," Lorca has Centurion suggest that perhaps one of the two is the first or number *one;* or *one* (as is often true in Spanish) could mean *someone*. Lorca is ridiculing the use of the undefined word *one* and amusing himself with its possible interpretations and misinterpretations.

The pun is not the only word humor that Lorca enjoys. He often misuses a word or invents a word for comic effect. In the *Retablildo de Don Cristóbal* (The Frame of Don Cristóbal) a sick man cries: "Ay! Ay! how my carotid (artery) is paining me. I have carotiditis." The dramatist invents a word and jests at the pedantic terminology of the medical profession.

Lorca achieves humorous effects often by repeating a word or phrase, or by exaggerating a conversation or manner of speaking. The best example of the former is a scene from Act II of *Doña Rosita la soltera* (Doña Rosita the Spinster). This conversation begins when Rosita's Uncle says "Thank you" to Señor X for a gift he brought to Rosita. It continues:

Señor X: I am delighted at your favorable reception.
Uncle: Thank you.

Señor X: Remember me to your wife.
   (Literal translation: "Place me at the feet of your wife.")
Uncle: Thank you very much.
Señor X: Remember me to your enchanting niece, for whom I wish good
   fortune in her celebrated undertaking.
Uncle: A thousand thanks.
Señor X: Consider me your devoted servant.
Uncle: A million thanks.
Señor X: I repeat. . . .
Uncle: Thank you, thank you, thank you.
Señor X: As always. . . .
Uncle: Thank you, thank you, thank you.

It is difficult to classify this scene under one kind of humor. Part of the humor is in the repeated thanks of the Uncle. There is also humor in the exaggerated and ridiculous language of Señor X. Of course it is used to satirize the overeducated Spanish gentleman, courteous to an absurd degree.

Splendid examples of humor in exaggeration abound in Lorca's plays. In the second scene of *Maleficio de la Mariposa*, Doña Curiana (her name itself is a satire on her desire to find a cure for everything) sings a recipe for curing love given her by a magician.

> Just give to all the lovers
> a couple of blows on the head
> and never never allow them
> to stretch out on the grass as in bed.

Another example of the exaggerated idea or phrase is found in the fifth scene of *Los títeres de Cachiporra*. Fígaro is speaking:

> News comes to the world after having passed through the classification of the barbershop. . . . Naturally! We are the mayors of the heads, and in our manner of opening little paths among the forests of hair we find out what is being thought within.

We know that by cutting or parting hair one does not see into the cerebrum, but it is also common knowledge that everyone discusses his problems with his barber. Lorca mocks society's custom of gossiping, and at the same time amusingly reveals a truth.

Another example of absurd exaggeration is found in *La doncella, el marinero y el estudiante* (The Maiden, the Sailor, and the Student). Two women are talking of embroidering.

> Doncella: On my clothes I am embroidering the whole alphabet.
> Vieja: For what reason?
> Doncella: So that the man who is with me may call me any name he likes.

In the farces of Lorca humor abounds in exaggeration of insults. In *The Shoemaker's Prodigious Wife* the shoemaker's wife uses all the pungent expressions of the Spanish *pueblo*. She calls her husband, "long-tongued, little bird proud of the tuft on your head, powdered little viper," "kitchen pothook," "old wine-skin, rascal, urchin, rake and scoundrel." (The English translation refines many of these expressions.) Here neighbors are "wine gourds," "zeros to the left," "affected puppets." As a youth Lorca had lived very close to the "people," and retained always an understanding of the absurd and genial humor of its characteristic types.

Before entering the discussion of other types of humor (of character and situation) I would like to mention briefly the delightful little humorous songs found in many of Lorca's plays. These verses, in rhyme and slang, defy a just translation. The reader with a fair knowledge of Spanish will find great diversion in the Enfermo's song of "Veinte Duros" in the *Retablillo de Don Cristóbal*, in Doña Rosita's mother's song in the same play, and especially in Rosita's little verses about her lovers.

Humor Based on Character

We turn now to humor found in character or situation. In the first example Lorca creates humor through two extremely naïve characters. The play is *Los titeres de Cachiporra,* the conversation between Cocoliche and Rosita has just told Cocoliche that she will marry him at last. Cocoliche answers, "I am going to write a letter to Paris immediately asking for a baby . . .

> Rosita: To Paris? Don't be absurd! I don't want one who resembles the French with their "chau, chau, chau."

The naïveté of the two is ridiculous. The humor is enhanced by a seeming conflict of rational and irrational. Cocoliche believes in the old wives' tale that babies come from Paris. Suddenly the audience is led to believe that Rosita will save his ignorance when she shouts, "To Paris! Don't be absurd!" But we are fooled. Rosita carries this naïveté to an even more ridiculous extreme: If babies come from Paris they will necessarily be French and speak French.

There is a similar example in Act II of *Doña Rosita la soltera*. The nurse wants to take revenge on the nephew who is engaged to Rosita because of his absence. She asks, "Señora, couldn't we send a poisoned letter to him, so that he would die suddenly on receiving it?" Here the conflict of incongruity is achieved by injecting an antique idea (poisoned books did exist in the fifteenth century) into a modern situation.

A related type of humor is that of the *non sequitur*—an answer, action, or explanation having no logical relation whatsoever to that which preceded it. In *Los títeres*, sixth scene, Cristobita asks, "You haven't seen me kill anyone with the cudgel? No? . . . Well now you will see me. I go pun! pun! pun! . . . and into the ravine." Rosita answers, "Yes; it's very pretty." Such contrast is essential in comic theater.

There are many examples of *non sequitur* in *El Paseo de Buster Keaton* (The Walk of Buster Keaton). Keaton announces, "I should like to be a swan. But I can't be even though I'd like it. Because where would I leave my hat? And where my elegant collar and my moire necktie? How unfortunate." His explanation for the impossibility of becoming a swan is neither rational nor natural. It is absurd and incongruous.

In *The Shoemaker's Prodigious Wife*, first scene, the shoemaker's wife shouts that she is enraged, because her neighbor's child has told her that the whole town is saying that she will never have children. The child then says, "Don't get mad at me, I am not to blame and every day I study my grammar very hard." No allusion to study has been made in the play at this point. The child's exclamation of his innocence in this way is a delightful example of the *non sequitur*.

Closely related to the humor of the *non sequitur* is that of the paradox. In the second scene of Act I of *El maleficio de la mariposa* Lorca describes one of the characters. "Silvia, in her class of repulsive insects, was enchanting." Later Silvia herself describes her fiancé, saying, "and yellow are the divine tips of his antennae." In the first case the paradox is formed by the ridiculous juxtaposition of the words *repulsive* and *enchanting*. In the second the paradox is found in the contrast of our concept of an insect's antennae with Silvia's concept.

Often the paradox exists in the opposition of two parts of the same expression, as in Act I of *The Shoemaker's Wife* when the shoemaker's wife shouts, "May lightning strike my brother, may he rest in peace!" She insults her brother in one breath, and then, remembering him dead, mechanically blesses him.

There is another humorous device involving contradiction. This is achieved by a sudden change in the character himself. A perfect Lorcan example of this conversion of character is found in the second scene of Act I of *El maleficio*. Doña Curiana has been talking with Silvia: talking in a normal tone of voice as any woman might. Then she discovers that Silvia, who is very rich, has fallen in love with Doña Curiana's own son. What follows? A sudden change from the normal woman to one of sweetness and concern who treats Silvia as one would a precious jewel. The change has a comic effect, and moreover a satirical one as Lorca amuses himself laughing at the hypocrisy of women who hope to make a good match.

In *Los títeres* the character of Don Cristobita undergoes a change in

the second half of the play. Throughout the first Act Cristobita hopes
to marry Rosita. Shortly before the speech below, Cristobita is en-
thusiastically describing how beautiful and desirable the sixteen-year-
old Rosita is. Then the father decides to work out a marriage contract
with Cristobita. But now Cristobita says, "I will give you 500 pesetas to
free yourself from debt, and you give me your daughter Rosita. You
should be very content, for after all she is . . . somewhat over-ripe."
The enthusiastic lover becomes the wary miser and Lorca points out the
hypocrisy of a man where money is concerned.

In the fifth scene of the same play, Fígaro, the barber, is heard con-
versing passionately with Don Cristobita as with an equal. Suddenly
Don Cristobita shouts, "come on!" and Fígaro must quickly adjust himself to a servant-master relationship. He says, "What a beautiful head
you have! But how magnificent! A perfect model!" Again Lorca's genius
not only for humor but for understanding people of every walk of life
is demonstrated.

In the third scene of *Mariana Pineda* a group of nuns is gathered outside Mariana's room in the convent. They take turns spying at her
through the keyhole, for she is a woman of the world. Then the Mother
Superior approaches and discovers them huddled there. She shouts,
"Aren't you ashamed of yourselves?" and the frightened, guilty nuns
quickly run away. The Mother Superior waits a few moments, looks from
left to right, and silently puts her own eye to the keyhole.

Sometimes such a change in character is not abrupt. In a farce it can
occur after the circumstances have changed. Then the character, in order
to adapt to the new situation, is forced to change. In *The Shoemaker's
Wife*, first scene, the shoemaker's wife is continually annoyed with her
husband. She remembers nostalgically her other beaux—one in particular,
who had a beautiful pony, and a blue velvet cape. Her husband interrupts, saying proudly, "Yes, I, too, had one of those . . . they are
beautiful capes." The wife shouts, "You? When would you ever have
one of these? . . . But why must you invent such illusions? A shoemaker
never in his life wore a cape of that kind." In the second Act the shoemaker has deserted his wife. The abandoned wife now paints a new
picture of her husband. In reminiscing with the neighbor's child she
describes him in glowing admiration.

> When first I saw him he was mounted on a beautiful white pony.
> Child: Ha, Ha, Ha. You're teasing me. The shoemaker never had a horse.
> Shoemaker's Wife: Child, show more respect. He did have a pony, of course
>   he did, but . . . well, you weren't born then.

Having shouted in Act I "get out" to her husband, in Act II we hear
the shoemaker's wife say, "I married my husband. Well, so be it till
death!" In Act I she has ridiculed her husband's work and lamented her

social position. In Act II when he has left her she refuses jewels and presents offered by the Mayor and vows, "I will never be anything but a shoemaker's wife." In the beginning of the play she called her husband an "old leather bag" and said to him, "You, you were NEVER eighteen." Later she calls his fifty years "blessed" and says that even at that age he is to her more virile and masculine than all the men in the world.

García Lorca has again revealed his understanding of female psychology. Yet Lorca does not leave his theme with "woman always wanting what is not." The delightful farce continues: the husband returns, disguised. His wife, believing him to be a stranger, tells him of her good and intelligent husband. With assurance of her love the good man unmasks himself, ready for her embrace. Instead, the wife sees him and shouts, "Rascal, rogue, rake, scoundrel! Vagabond! Oh, how happy I am that you've come back! What a life I am going to give you! Not even the Inquisition! Not even the Roman templars!" The change is complete, and forms a perfect circle. Lorca reveals great artistry in the symmetrical construction of his farce.

Another method of creating humor is the use of the surprise: when we are certain something will happen in a certain way—and it does not; or when we are absorbed in a scene and suddenly something totally unexpected occurs.

The Shoemaker's Wife begins with a prologue in the form of a speech by the play's author. A prologue is not uncommon as a curtain raiser, but while the author is speaking, a shout interrupts him. It is the shoemaker's wife saying, "I want to come out." The author stops his speech and answers, "I'm coming! Don't be so impatient to come out . . ." The surprise is the audacious interchange of reality; the author recognizes the reality of one of his creations. Fantasy and reality are intertwined. The amusing scene is not unlike many of Pirandello's.

In a later work, *Retablildo de Don Cristóbal,* Lorca repeats this device. Here, too, there is a prologue by the Poet. He begins by preparing the public. He asks for silence, explains a little about the play, and announces that now he is going to iron the costumes of the company. Suddenly he looks off-stage to see if he is being observed and says, "I want to tell you that I know how roses are born and how the stars of the sea are made but . . ." The voice of the Director interrupts, "Please be quiet . . . the prologue ends where it says, 'I am going to iron the costumes of the company.' " Again the actor has stepped outside of his role, into a new reality.

Often extreme candidness or sudden loss of decorum or reserve causes hilarity. Although considered a lower form of humor, one must remember that it was also employed by Shakespeare. In the same play the Director shouts to Don Cristóbal, telling him to come out, that the play is beginning. The voice of Cristóbal is heard off-stage, "I'm coming, Director. I am just going to the bathroom."

In Act II of *Doña Rosita* the nurse is talking with her employers about the employer's nephew. She begins, "In your family there are no hand-some men." The Señora rather disconcerted, thanks her sarcastically. The nurse does not stop there. "They are all short and a little fallen in the shoulders." The audacity of the servant to a Spanish audience is hilarious. In the same play there is a similar conversation. Rosita has decided to be married by proxy.

Nurse: Well, and "proxy," what is that?
Rosita: Nothing. A person represents the groom in the ceremony.
Nurse: And what else?
Rosita: Well, one is then married.
Nurse: And the wedding night? What then?

In these two illustrations the humor also consists in the discrepancy of the character type with respect to our concept of how he or she should behave.

Exaggeration, we have seen, is a comic element in both plays-on-words and in the manner in which characters speak. Lorca also uses exaggeration for humor in situations and even in the inner life of his characters. In *Los títeres* scene 6, when Rosita and Cocoliche believe they cannot wed, they weep, and should (according to the author's stage directions) weep on and on and on. Both lovers of Rosita weep and shout together in this play, leading it well into the realm of total farce.

A play based totally on exaggeration and incongruity is *El Paseo de Buster Keaton*. As the play opens Keaton comes on stage with his five children. He kills them, then says, "My poor little children!", hops on a bicycle, and is off. At the end of the play a young girl comes on stage. She asks the name of the man who was there. When she learns it was Buster Keaton, she faints. Of course, the entire play is a satire on Keaton and the Hollywood comedy.

The exaggerated character is exemplified by the mayor in *The Shoe-maker's Wife*. The Mayor in advising the shoemaker says, "At your age you should already be a widower . . . of one, at least. . . . I am of four." The character exaggerated to the point of eccentricity is seen in the Uncle in *Doña Rosita*. The Uncle takes care of his flowers through-out the entire play. One of his typical speeches is the following.

Yesterday I found dahlia seeds scattered and crushed on the ground. Don't you understand the importance of my greenhouse; since the year 807, in which the Countess of Wandes obtained the moss rose, no one else in Granada has achieved it except me, not even the University's Department of Botany. It is necessary that you have more respect for my plants.

Eccentricity, if it does not become madness or insanity, is very funny. It is achieved by overplaying one facet of a character's personality to such a degree as to make him ridiculous.

Almost eccentrically shy is Don Perlimplín who in *The Love of Don Perlimplín* is discovered on his wedding night with Belisa:

> Don Perlimplín: May I have your permission to take off my frock coat?
> Belisa: Of course, dear husband. And turn out the light if you'd like.

Many more instances of Lorca's delightful exaggeration can be cited. In the prologue of *Don Cristóbal* he requests a silence so that "if a little ant moves his foot we shall hear him." Or in *Doña Rosita* the mother describes her economic plight with three unmarried daughters. She says when she asks them "What would you like my darlings? Egg at lunch or a chair for the paseo?" all three answer simultaneously, "chairs."

Humor Found in Situation

Situation comedy reached its peak in the seventeenth century Restoration plays. Lorca proves himself a master, too, of this technique. Scene 1 of *Los títeres* is a perfect example of comedy situation. Rosita and her father are happily discussing her coming marriage. Rosita believes that her father has finally decided to let her marry Cocoliche, while the father assumes that Rosita has decided to give in to his own wishes and marry a very rich, very ugly old man. The public, of course, knows the viewpoint of each and can thoroughly enjoy the misinterpretation of the two. In the sixth scene Currito, Rosita's ex-fiancé, disguised as a shoemaker, comes to her house on the day set for her wedding to the rich old Cristobita. Rosita sees through the disguise and is on the point of voicing her fury when her father comes in. Currito hastily adapts himself to the role of shoemaker and begins fitting a pair of shoes on Rosita. The following dialogue ensues:

> Currito: (whispers) Oh beautiful lily-white leg!
> Rosita: Scoundrel!
> Currito: (aloud) Please raise your skirt a little.
> Rosita: It already is.
> Currito: Let's see. A little bit more?
> Rosita: More!
> Father: (from his chair) Do what the shoemaker says, child; more!

A few moments later Rosita is discovered dressing for her wedding. Her two ex-fiancés have been hidden in two closets. The old Don Cristobita enters and kisses Rosita. Each time the old man comes near her the two hidden ones peek out from the closets and shout. Rosita has to invent a series of ridiculous lies to explain away their noise.

The same type of broad situation farce permeates *The Shoemaker's Prodigious Wife*. The scene between the shoemaker disguised as a puppeteer and his wife could be a scene from a Restoration comedy. The wife invents stories saying her husband told them to her, and quotes his terms of endearment. The shoemaker is forced to make constant adjustments from accusing her of lying to realizing that he must carry on his disguise.

Briefly, we can find a thread of humor in almost all of Lorca's plays. In some it is the central thread; in others it serves to hide a more somber theme; in many it is used for relief from an emotionally taut scene, serving only for momentary diversion. But humor there is. It is another facet of the dualism of Lorca and his creation. Both his life and his art are shaped by the contrast of the tragic and intense with the humorous and light. It is often the saddest, most melancholy and most deeply troubled of men who assumes the role of the clown.

Don Perlimplín:
Lorca's Theater-Poetry

by Francis Fergusson

For something like forty years poets in English-speaking countries have been trying to write poetic drama for the modern stage. This movement, if something so scattered and diverse may be called a movement, stems largely from Yeats and Eliot. Their plays are still the best modern poetic drama we have, and their theories still define the prevailing conception of poetic drama. But no one is quite satisfied with the results. We still lack a poetic theater-form comparable to those of more fortunate ages, or to the "unpoetic" convention of modern realism. Poetic drama in English remains unsure of itself, highbrow and cultish —unless *Elizabeth the Queen*, *Venus Observed*, and *The Cocktail Party*, which are fairly well accepted in the show shops, are to be called poetic drama.

Federico García Lorca also wrote poetic drama, very much as Yeats and Eliot have taught us to understand it, yet his plays are neither cultish nor middlebrow-ersatz: they are theater-poetry which lives naturally on the modern stage. Lorca did very little theorizing, but he found, at a very early age, in pre-Franco Spain, singularly direct ways to use the stage for the purposes of poetry. It is true that he is not a creature of the commercial theater. Madrid in his time had a theater corresponding to Broadway, but Lorca was always in more or less hidden opposition to it. He was the director of *La Barraca*, a group of University players which was subsidized by the government and toured the provincial towns and cities of Spain with a repertory of classics. It is evident that his own plays owe a great deal to this experience. *La Barraca* found an "off-Broadway" audience in Spain, and since then Lorca's plays have found audiences in France, Switzerland, Germany, Mexico, South America, and college towns all over this country. No one has succeeded in producing him successfully on Broadway, but in being rejected by the timid snobbery of Times

Square he is in excellent company. And there is no doubt that he can bypass the taboos of the market, and reach a wide contemporary audience in free Europe and the Americas.

Lorca's theater-poetry fulfills many of the prescriptions of Yeats and Eliot, but it is strongly marked by his unique genius, his rare combination of talents. And it is nourished by the Spanish tradition, which was showing new vitality just before Franco put out the light. These matters are already clear in his early play, *The Love of Don Perlimplín for Belisa, in His Garden. Don Perlimplín* is a romantic farce, slighter and lighter than his most famous pieces, *Blood Wedding* and *The House of Bernarda Alba*, but it is a small masterpiece. When he wrote it he was already in control of his difficult art.

The story is old, lewd, and rather savage: that of the old man married to a lusty young wife, one of the standard situations of neoclassic farce. But Lorca, without losing sight of the farce, lifts it to poetry also, and poetry of power and freshness. This he accomplishes in four swift scenes; and to understand his art it is necessary to think over this sequence in some detail.

In the first scene we see Don Perlimplín, a studious type on the dark side of middle age, dressed in a white wig and dressing gown, in his study. His old servant Marcolfa is telling him that it is time he got married, so that when she dies he will have a wife to take care of him. Marriage, says Marcolfa, has great charm, hidden delights; and at that moment we hear Belisa offstage singing a song of shameless childish eroticism. Marcolfa leads Don Perlimplín upstage to the window; we look out with him, and see Belisa on her balcony across the way, very lightly clad. Don Perlimplín gets the point of this vision: Belisa is white inside, like sugar, he says; would she strangle me? Belisa's mother appears, and between her and Marcolfa Don Perlimplín finds himself betrothed to Belisa. The mother is one of those terrible, cold-hearted eighteenth century duennas; she reminds her daughter with speed and clarity that money is the foundation of happiness, and Don Perlimplín has money. The scene ends with Don Perlimplín firmly committed, and trembling with a mixture of terror and delight, like a boy when the possibilities of sex first touch him.

The second scene shows Don Perlimplín's bedroom on the wedding night. In the middle of the stage is a huge ornate bed, and there are six doors, one to the rest of the house, the others giving on to five balconies. First we see Don Perlimplín, magnificently dressed, receiving final instructions from Marcolfa. They disappear and Belisa enters in ruffled negligee, singing to offstage guitar music. After a brief scene between her and Don Perlimplín—who says that she is like a wave of the sea—two sprites draw a gray curtain across the stage, concealing Don Perlimplín, Belisa, and the bed. These sprites giggle and chatter with the inhuman

merriment of little girls of twelve or thirteen—say, bright-eyed, heart-
less, knowing little creatures, as children are when they are full of shrewd
curiosity but not yet seasoned by any human experience. Presently they
open the curtain and depart. Stage and bed are flooded with bright
sunlight coming through the five opened doors to the balconies, the iron
church bells of the city are banging for matins, and Don Perlimplín is
sitting up in bed beside the sleeping Belisa, with a great pair of horns
on his head, decorated with flowers. Belisa, when she lazily wakes, admits
nothing, but Don Perlimplín sees five hats under the five balconies which
show that five men have visited her during the night. Lorca has thus
exaggerated the farcical situation of the old man and his young wife; but
the combination of bright light, loud iron bells, and big ornate horns
adds pity and terror to the scene. When Belisa wanders off to get dressed,
Don Perlimplín is left sitting alone on the edge of the bed, and he sings
a beautiful lyric on the theme that love has mortally wounded him.

The third scene shows Don Perlimplín and Marcolfa. Marcolfa is
deeply ashamed for her master, and moreover she reports that Belisa has
already become infatuated with a sixth man. Don Perlimplín is delighted
to hear it. He tells the weeping Marcolfa that she understands nothing,
and brusquely sends her away. Belisa enters dreamily, mulling over the
new young man, whom she has seen, from whom she has received letters,
but whom she has never talked to. Don Perlimplín catches her in this
daydreaming, tells her that he understands everything, that (being old)
he is beyond mortal life and its ridiculous customs, and that he will
sacrifice himself for her and her new love.

The final scene is Belisa's rendezvous with the young man, in the
garden, at night. First we see Don Perlimplín and Marcolfa, she more
grieved than ever, Don Perlimplín more crazily inspired. He tells Marcolfa
that tomorrow she will be free, and that then she will understand everything; this bit feels like a farewell. When they go we hear offstage singing,
and Belisa enters in her most glamorous finery. She sings a serenade in
alternation with the offstage voices. Don Perlimplín meets her, and
assures himself that she loves the young man better than she has ever
loved before, better than her own body. He tells her that in order that
she may have the young man forever, he will kill him—and he runs off,
drawing his dagger. Belisa yells for a sword to kill Don Perlimplín: but
at that moment the young man, his head wrapped in a scarlet cape, a
dagger in his breast, staggers in mortally wounded. Belisa pulls off the
cape, revealing Don Perlimplín, who dies. He has just time to explain
that this was the triumph of his imagination; he had made Belisa fall in
love with the lover he invented. So he gave her a new and deeper knowledge of love, made a new woman of her, as Marcolfa explains at the
end: gave a human soul, at last, to the beautiful body. It is Belisa's initia-

tion into love's mystery, corresponding to Don Perlimplín's initiation in the first scene.

The poetic effect of this sequence is intense and direct, but Lorca gets it out of a combination of very old and traditional elements.

Thus there is the basic situation of the old man and the young wife, which in baroque Continental comedy, or on the Restoration stage in England, is usually treated in the hearty, simple-minded mode of broad farce. Cervantes wrote a brilliant interlude of this kind called *The Jealous Old Man*, in which the fun is based on the disharmonies of human physiology, and the audience is expected to sympathize solely with the triumphant wife. Lorca expects us to remember that worldly old theme, and he emphasizes both its theatricality and its ancient, classic quality in the characters, their language, and their costumes. Don Perlimplín in his white wig and scholarly dressing gown; Marcolfa in the striped dress of the stage servant; Belisa's mother with her great wig full of beads and ribbons and stuffed birds; and Belisa herself, the sharp essence of the amoral female: this cast of characters is made to seem as old as nightmare, almost eternal.

But just because the farce and its people seem so ancient, it strikes us as not only farcical but also sinister. Lorca, while keeping the cynical old tale, with its neoclassic stagy glitter, also views it in the perspective of a later, gloomier, and more romantic age; he transposes it to bring out also the love-death theme. That theme also is traditional in European literature, as Denis de Rougemont explained in his book, *Love in the Western World*. He traces the terrible aspiration beyond physical love to some of the Provençal poets, and he thinks that the love-death theme which re-echoes through the nineteenth century literature obscurely revives the heretical cult of the Cathari. Lorca certainly seems to echo the theme here with a full sense of its deep roots, especially in Don Perlimplín's lyric on the mortal wound of love, and in the final scene in the garden, which has the ceremoniousness of the dark old erotic rite.

It is an extravagant notion to combine farce and *Liebestod*, but Lorca knew that it was extravagant. It is by means of the *style* of the piece that he makes an acceptable fusion of such disparate elements; for a knowing style implies the limitations of mood and viewpoint which the author has accepted in advance, and thus makes them acceptable and comprehensible to the audience. Lorca indicates the style of his play in its subtitle: "An Erotic Alleluya." An alleluya is something like a valentine: a love poem decorated with pictures, gilt cutouts, lace paper, and the like; something heroic, overdone, absurd: an *extravagant* offering to the beloved. All the elements of the production, music, sets, costumes, acting, should obey the requirements of this style. And one must remember that it is a Spanish style, akin perhaps to those drawings and paintings of Goya's—wounded cavaliers, frightening mustachioed old women, greedy young women in discreet mantillas—in which the remains of eighteenth century elegance are seen in a somber light.

Though this play is so unlike anything in English, it is a species of poetic drama. And it achieves much that Yeats and Eliot sought with only partial success. They were both lyric poets first and dramatists second; and both tended in their early efforts to approach poetic drama as though it were an overgrown type of lyric. Yeats's early plays have the Yeatsian lyric melody, but lack the tensions, the contrasts, and the varied movement of drama. Eliot's *Murder in the Cathedral* and *Family Reunion* sound like his lyrics considerably diluted. Eliot felt that himself, as he has explained; but his usual diagnosis of the trouble is that he has not discovered the right verse form for the stage. He proposes to solve the problem by working out the proper versification. To Eliot's experiments, and to his immense authority, we owe the notion that the problem of poetic drama in our time is simply that of finding a type of verse which will work onstage. And many young poets proceed as though drama could somehow be deduced from the lyric by further exploration of the properties of verse.

Lorca also was a lyric poet before he succeeded on the stage, and his lyric verse shows (like that of Yeats and Eliot) the all-pervasive *symboliste* influence. He is an authentic poet, even by the exigent standards of our masters. But from the first he drew also upon the resources of the old and popular Spanish tradition of balladry: his first collection is entitled *Romancero gitano, Gypsy Ballads*. And the ballad is a far more promising clue to drama than the "pure" *symboliste* lyric, precisely because it typically suggests a story: a situation, contrasted characters, a significant event. The *symboliste* lyric, on the other hand, owes its purity to its source in the single feeling of the isolated poet. It is very difficult to derive from it the sense of separate but interacting lives; the movement of real change; the significance of a deed or an event: in short, the objectivity of drama, which is founded (however indirectly) upon sympathy and perception. We must simply recognize, I think, that the inspiration, the poetic point, of the *symboliste* lyric is not dramatic, while that of the ballad is.

It is clear that the whole conception of *Don Perlimplín*—the gentle, absurd, heroic old man; the animal-beauty and her mother; the weepy servant, the struggle with love's cruelty—struck Lorca as poetic. The narrative sequence is itself poetic, like that of the ballads we know. One can conceive a ballad version of *Don Perlimplín*, but not a *symboliste* lyric which would really capture the theme. Thus in trying to get the poetry of the play one must consider not only the passages in verse, beautiful though they are, but the movement of the play as a whole. The poetry is in the characters and their relationships, in the conception of each of the four scenes, and especially in the sharp but quickly resolved contrasts between them. Cocteau's formula applies exactly to *Don Perlimplín*:

> The action of my play is in images, while the text is not: I attempt to substitute a "poetry of the theater" for "poetry in the theater." Poetry in the theater is a piece of lace which it is impossible to see at a distance. Poetry of the theater would be coarse lace; a lace of ropes, a ship at sea. . . . The scenes are integrated like the words of a poem.

Thus the poetic effect of *Don Perlimplín* strikes us most sharply in the transitions from one scene to another: from Don Perlimplín's study to the glamor and music of the wedding night; from the childish chatter of the sprites to Don Perlimplín's humiliation in the morning. And as soon as we feel the poetry in the whole sequence, Lorca's prose has its poetic effect as well as his music and his visual scheme. Lorca is such a virtuoso of the theater that he can use and control all of its resources to present his poetic vision.

Yeats and Eliot began with verse rather than with the theater, but both of them felt the need of a story and a form which should make the play itself (as distinguished from the language) poetic. And both sought these elements in myth and ritual. Yeats proceeded from Irish myths, to an English version of *Oedipus*, to forms based on the *No* play; Eliot experimented with Greek myths and with adaptations of Christian ritual forms. These experiments have proved to be extremely suggestive, and it may well be that they still have much to teach us. But they seem to show, among other things, that it is very difficult to reincarnate a myth in our time. Myths as we read them in learned collections tempt us with their suggestion of deep poetic insights; but the crucial labor of the dramatic poet, faced with the modern stage and the modern crowd, only begins at that point. So many have failed—either relapsing into cultishness or antiquarianism, or reducing the myth to an abstract and pseudo-philosophical scheme—that the very word "myth" has ceased to be respectable. Yet the problem remains; and in its most general form it is probably the heart of our difficulty with poetic drama.

It is this problem which *Don Perlimplín* solves quite naturally and directly. If the story is not strictly a myth, it has the qualities our poets seek in myth: it seems much older and much more generally significant than any history which is literally true; yet Lorca does not seem to have thought it up, but rather to have perceived it, or heard it, in the most intimate chamber of his sensibility. In embodying it on the stage he is careful to preserve this oft-told feeling, like a song, or a tale told by a grandmother. This he does with the utmost confidence and simplicity. He is sustained by the knowledge that he is talking about things which other artists have seen before in his Spanish tradition; for Don Perlimplín seems to come from the same world—which we now see is still alive—as Don Quixote and Goya's frightening people.

Because the story has this "mythic" quality, its basic form is quite naturally that of ritual or traditional ceremony. The first scene is a betrothal, and we are made to feel that it has been celebrated countless times before, and will be endlessly again: it is the first stage of the initiation into love's cruel mystery; for the old man is as virginal as a boy. The second scene (a kind of interlude in the movement of the piece) is not a ritual; but the third scene, a wedding night with all the pomp of music and costume, is conceived as a sinister epithalamion, moving with decorum toward its predestined pathos. The final scene in the garden, with its serenade in antiphonal form, its symbolic suicide, its cult of love as death, is the place where Lorca's feeling for the ancient heretical love rites that De Rougemont studies is most unmistakable. It is there that Belisa, in her turn, is "initiated." I do not know how consciously Lorca worked all this out; he has the authentic artist's sophistication of feeling combined with philosophical reticence. But I am sure that the ceremonious quality of these scenes (like a duel or a bullfight) must be carefully observed in production, for it is their decorum which gives the underlying passion its cutting edge.

It has been said (notably by Mr. Roberto Sánchez in his valuable book on Lorca) that Lorca is a theatrical rather than a truly dramatic talent. He does not, for example, have Ibsen's moral and intellectual drive, and he rarely deals directly with contemporary scenes or contemporary issues. He usually finds the clue to a play in painting, or music, or poetry, or even in the theater itself. In all his work (as in *Don Perlimplín*) he relies on stage effects to carry much of the burden. And in these respects his art is akin to that of some modern masters of theatrical style, directors and designers, who do not so much create drama as interpret it in the theater. Mr. Sánchez has a point, but I think he somewhat misinterprets the evidence.

He is thinking of men of the theater like Reinhardt or Copeau, who seem to have had some more or less direct influence upon Lorca. Reinhardt was famous for his allusive and learned experiments with style— doing *Midsummer Night's Dream* as romantic music, playing about with expressionism, or the baroque, or the commedia dell'arte. And it is true that each of Lorca's plays is, among other things, a self-conscious period piece. *Doña Rosita* is founded upon the sweet, faded conventions of the turn of the century. It is like a delicately tinted family picture in a velvet frame, a provincial keepsake smelling of lavender and Spanish Victorianism. Even *Blood Wedding* and *Yerma*, for all their power and violence, owe something to painting or balladry. This habit of starting with art may seem perilously close to orchestrating Bach, a substitute for real creation —or even to the next step: the ads for diamonds or perfume, in which certain tricks of French painting are used to produce snob appeal. Lorca in fact does have a fondness for play, self-conscious virtuosity, even chic; but this does not bother me as much as it does Mr. Sánchez. The theater, when it has the proper gusto, often feeds upon itself and the other arts in this way, but without sacrifice of original dramatic content. Lorca's theater accomplished this, I think. The limitations which Mr. Sánchez feels in his art are not those of the merely clever, arty theatrical inter- preter, but those of an artist who, in our fragmented and polyglot cul- ture, stays within the idioms of one national culture. When a national culture revives, its art forms seem significant, filled with immediately relevant moral and spiritual content; and that seems to have occurred in Lorca's Spain. When that happens, the theater, in its play with images from art, may be allusive without being merely arty.

   The House of Bernarda Alba, the play which Mr. Sánchez regards as the best dramatically, is interesting in this connection. Mr. Sánchez thinks it a powerful picture of contemporary Spanish provincial life, with the qualities of the best modern realistic drama. Lorca himself calls it a photograph; and according to people who know the country, he has achieved a surface accuracy comparable to Ibsen's or Chekhov's. But it would be a mistake to take its realism too straight: the label "photo- graph," like the label "alleluya" on *Don Perlimplín,* indicates the very self-conscious style, which alludes to a whole context of meaning. *Ber- narda Alba* is a period piece like the others; it utilizes the conventions of nineteenth century realism with the same kind of sophisticated inten- tion as that with which *Don Perlimplín* utilizes its more ancient con- ventions. The blankness of the photograph is part of the composition which includes the severe character of Bernarda herself, and the deathly white walls within which she strives to hold her myopic vision steady.

   In this problem of Lorca's restaging of Spanish art we must remember the analogies between forms of art and forms of human life. They are most evident in old countries with whose art and literature we are famil- iar. One may feel it even on revisiting New England: the white clap- boards, the old ladies, the slender elms still seem to be "right out of the pages" of Whittier or Hawthorne. The Paris taxi drivers still argue à la Molière; the hard-bitten concierges in cheap hotels are still imitating Balzac. And the Spanish mark on art and character is one of the deepest. I have never been to Spain, but I have seen Sancho Panza and his burro in northern New Mexico, and the faces of old people reflecting (even at a distance of thousands of miles and many generations) the subtle faces in Spanish painting. Perhaps the natural role of the artist in a living culture is to make these forms, with the changes which time brings, visible and significant again.

   But Lorca was unusually fortunate in being able to work with such fertility within his native culture; it is a commentary on our rootless state, in which all the familiar forms of life and art begin to seem vague and irrelevant, that his riches should seem somehow against the rules. It is growing harder and harder in our time for a writer to stay within one traditional culture. Yeats was hardly content with his Irish revival beyond youth. Our own Southern writers hesitate painfully between the South, where their roots are, and the national scene in which they are obliged to live, almost as ill-defined as the rest of us.

The deeply Spanish nature of Lorca's art does not prevent it from speaking to us. His sense of history—"the masquerades which time resumes"—is very modern; in his ability to mingle the most contradictory perspectives in one composition, and to shift with sureness from the pathetic to the farcical-frightening, he is in the class of our favorite poets. And he writes poetry of the theater as our poets would like to do. We cannot use his Spanish language, or the symbolic language of the moral and aesthetic forms of his tradition. But we can learn to read it, and to discover thereby an authentic modern poetic drama.

Chronology of Important Dates

1898	Born at Fuente-Vaqueros near Granada on June 11, the son of a landowner and an ex-schoolteacher.
1914	Enters the University of Granada, where he studies law.
1919	Leaves the province for Madrid.
1921	Publishes his *Libro de poemas* (Book of Poems)
1924-28	Frequent trips to Barcelona. Friendship with Dalí, Alberti, Jorge Guillén, Pedro Salinas. Draws, paints.
1927	Takes part in the Góngora celebrations organized by Dámaso Alonso, Guillén, Salinas, and Gerardo Diego. Holds a successful show of sketches.
1928	First edition of the *Gypsy Ballads*. Edits the magazine *Gallo*.
1929-30	Trip to the United States. Returns via Cuba.
1931	Organizes his theater group, *La Barraca*.
1933	Premiere of *Blood Wedding*.
1934	Premiere of *Yerma*.
1936	Lorca reads *The House of Bernarda Alba* to a group of friends, then leaves for Granada. He is arrested and murdered on August 19.

Notes on the Editor and Authors

Manuel Duran, editor of this volume, is both poet and critic. He has published several volumes of verse in Spanish and numerous articles on contemporary Spanish literature, including a book on Surrealism and its influence on modern Spanish poetry. He is an Associate Professor of Romance Languages at Yale University.

William Carlos Williams, the well-known poet and essayist, needs no introduction to an American audience. His familiarity with and perfect understanding of the Spanish poetic tradition will be apparent to the readers of his essay, which he wrote in 1939 for the *Kenyon Review.*

John Brande Trend (1897–1959) was a distinguished English hispanist, Fellow of Christ's College, Cambridge, and teacher at the same university. He was a correspondent in Spain in 1919 when he met Lorca for the first time. A musicologist, he has written extensively on Spanish music and folklore, as well as on Juan Ramón Jiménez, Santillana, Calderón, and Unamuno.

Dámaso Alonso is the dean of Spanish critics of poetry and a first-rank poet himself. His study on Góngora has not been surpassed. He was a member of Lorca's group. Professor of philology at the University of Madrid, he has taught at Oxford, Yale, and several American universities.

Louis Parrot, French poet and essayist, is a long-time student of Spanish culture. For the Pierre Seghers series on poetry, *Les Poètes d'aujourd'hui,* he prepared Lorca's anthology, preceded by a long study on the poet's works. Alongside Jean Cassou, Jean Camp, and J.-L. Schonberg, he is perhaps the Frenchman who knows Lorca best.

Roy Campbell, South African poet and essayist (1901-1957) lived in Spain and Portugal for many years, and has written a book on Lorca. "He himself has so many of the qualities that he finds, or imagines he finds, in Federico García Lorca—the dash, the gallantry, the Andalusian mixture of raw living and mysticism, and above all, the poetry—that one could scarcely imagine a happier coincidence of author and subject," wrote Dudley Fitts.

Edwin Honig studied at the University of Wisconsin, has taught at Purdue, New Mexico, Harvard, and is now teaching at Brown University. He has written many articles and essays and is the author of a book on Lorca.

Pedro Salinas (1892-1951) was a friend of Lorca and a distinguished member of his generation. Poet, essayist, professor, he has taught at Cambridge, Madrid, Puerto Rico, and Johns Hopkins universities. His *Reality and the Poet in Spanish Poetry* appeared in 1940.

Richard Saez was a brilliant undergraduate student at Yale and is now a graduate student in the department of comparative literature at the same university.

Juan López-Morillas, Professor of Spanish at Brown University, combines solid learning with elegance of expression. He is the author of books and articles on nineteenth century Spanish philosophy and on contemporary essayists and poets.

Angel del Rio (1901-1962) was Professor of Spanish at Columbia University, Director of the Hispanic Institute and of the *Revista Hispánica Moderna,* an excellent scholarly magazine. He wrote extensively on Lope de Vega, Lorca, and many periods of Spanish literature, and also published authoritative anthologies, as well as a widely used history of Spanish literature.

Susan Smith Blackburn was a Spanish major at Smith College and has lived in Spain for many years. Long a student of Spanish culture, she was a most impressive "Shoemaker's Wife" on the stage.

Francis Fergusson is a well-known essayist, critic, and historian of drama. His books include *The Idea of a Theater, Dante's Drama of the Mind, The Human Image in Dramatic Literature.* He has taught at Bennington and Princeton, and at present is teaching at Rutgers University.

Selected Bibliography

Works by Lorca

IN SPANISH

Obras completas. Prólogo y selección de Guillermo de Torre. 7 vols. Buenos Aires: Losada Edition, 1938-42.

Obras completas. Recopilación y notas de Arturo del Hoyo; prólogo de Jorge Guillén; epílogo de Vicente Aleixandre. Madrid: Aguilar, S.A., 1954. (Contains a bibliography, pages 1577-1609.)

IN ENGLISH

Lament for the Death of a Bullfighter. Translated by A. L. Lloyd. London: William Heinemann, Ltd., 1937.

Three Tragedies: Blood Wedding, Yerma, Bernarda Alba. Authorized translation by R. L. O'Connell and James Graham-Luján with an introduction by the poet's brother, Francisco García Lorca. New York: New Directions, 1947.

Selected Poems. Edited by Francisco García Lorca and Donald M. Allen. Norfolk, Conn.: New Directions, 1955.

Works about Lorca

Barea, Arturo. *Lorca, the Poet and His People.* London: Faber & Faber, Ltd., 1944.

Bonet, Ofelia Machado. *Federico García Lorca. Su producción dramática.* Montevideo: Rosgal, 1951.

Campbell, Roy. *Lorca; An Appreciation of His Poetry.* New Haven: Yale University Press, 1952.

Carisomo, Arturo Berenguer. *Las máscaras de Federico García Lorca.* Buenos Aires: Talleres gráficos de Ruiz Hermanos, 1941.

Correa, Gustavo. *La Poesía mítica de Federico García Lorca.* Eugene: University of Oregon Press, 1958.

Crow, James. *Federico García Lorca.* Los Angeles, 1947.

Díaz-Plaja, Guillermo. *Federico García Lorca. Estudio crítico.* Buenos Aires: Kraft, 1948.

Flecniakoska, Jean L. *L'Univers poétique de Federico García Lorca.* Bordeaux: Bière, 1952.

Fletcher, John Gould. "Lorca in English," *Poetry*, LVI (1940), 343-47.

García Lorca, Francisco. "Córdoba, lejana y sola," *Cuadernos Americanos* (Mexico City), XXXIV, 4 (July-August 1947).

Honig, Edwin. *Federico García Lorca.* Norfolk, Conn.: New Directions, 1944.

La Guardia, Alfredo de. *García Lorca: Persona y creación.* Buenos Aires: Sur, 1941.

Pérez-Marchand, Monelisa. "La inquietud existencial en la poesía de García Lorca," *Asomante* (Puerto Rico), 3 (1949).

Schonberg, Jean-Louis. *Federico García Lorca. L'Homme—l'oeuvre.* Paris: Plon ed., 1956.

Zardoya, Concha. "La técnica metafórica de Federico García Lorca," *Poesía española contemporánea.* Madrid: Editorial Gredos, 1962.

TWENTIETH CENTURY VIEWS

S-TC-1   CAMUS, edited by Germaine Brée
S-TC-2   T. S. ELIOT, edited by Hugh Kenner
S-TC-3   ROBERT FROST, edited by James M. Cox
S-TC-4   PROUST, edited by René Girard
S-TC-5   WHITMAN, edited by Roy Harvey Pearce
S-TC-6   SINCLAIR LEWIS, edited by Mark Schorer
S-TC-7   STENDHAL, edited by Victor Brombert
S-TC-8   HEMINGWAY, edited by Robert P. Weeks
S-TC-9   FIELDING, edited by Ronald Paulson
S-TC-10   THOREAU, edited by Sherman Paul
S-TC-11   BRECHT, edited by Peter Demetz
S-TC-12   EMERSON, edited by Milton R. Konvitz
     and Stephen E. Whicher
S-TC-13   MELVILLE, edited by Richard Chase
S-TC-14   LORCA, edited by Manuel Duran
S-TC-15   HOMER, edited by George Steiner and
     Robert Fagles
S-TC-16   DOSTOEVSKY, edited by René Wellek
S-TC-17   KAFKA, edited by Ronald Gray
S-TC-18   BAUDELAIRE, edited by Henri Peyre
S-TC-19   JOHN DONNE, edited by Helen Gardner
S-TC-20   EDITH WHARTON, edited by Irving Howe
S-TC-21   SARTRE, edited by Edith Kern
S-TC-22   BEN JONSON, edited by Jonas A. Barish
S-TC-23   YEATS, edited by John Unterecker
S-TC-24   D. H. LAWRENCE, edited by Mark Spilka
S-TC-25   HARDY, edited by Albert Guerard
S-TC-26   JANE AUSTEN, edited by Ian Watt
S-TC-27   F. SCOTT FITZGERALD, edited by Arthur Mizener
S-TC-28   EMILY DICKINSON, edited by Richard B. Sewall
S-TC-29   EZRA POUND, edited by Walter Sutton
S-TC-30   MARK TWAIN, edited by Henry Nash Smith
S-TC-31   BYRON, edited by Paul West
S-TC-32   DRYDEN, edited by Bernard N. Schilling
S-TC-33   WALLACE STEVENS, edited by Marie Borroff
S-TC-34   HENRY JAMES, edited by Leon Edel
S-TC-35   SWIFT, edited by Ernest Tuveson
S-TC-36   THOMAS MANN, edited by Henry Hatfield
S-TC-37   MALRAUX, edited by R. W. B. Lewis

S-TC-38   AUDEN, edited by Monroe K. Spears
S-TC-39   O'NEILL, edited by John Gassner
S-TC-40   SHAKESPEARE: THE TRAGEDIES, edited by
         Alfred Harbage
S-TC-41   MOLIÈRE, edited by Jacques Guicharnaud
S-TC-42   FLAUBERT, edited by Raymond Giraud
S-TC-43   KEATS, edited by Walter Jackson Bate
S-TC-44   MARLOWE, edited by Clifford Leech
S-TC-45   SHAKESPEARE: THE HISTORIES, edited by
         Eugene M. Waith
S-TC-46   DANTE, edited by John Freccero
S-TC-47   SHAKESPEARE: THE COMEDIES, edited by Kenneth Muir
S-TC-48   SAMUEL JOHNSON, edited by Donald J. Greene
S-TC-49   SHELLEY, edited by George Ridenour
S-TC-50   G. B. SHAW, edited by R. J. Kaufman

Forthcoming Titles

BECKETT, edited by Martin Esslin
BLAKE, edited by Northrop Frye
CERVANTES, edited by Lowry Nelson
CHEKHOV, edited by Robert L. Jackson
COLERIDGE, edited by Kathleen Coburn
CONRAD, edited by Marvin Mudrick
DICKENS, edited by Martin Price
FAULKNER, edited by Robert Penn Warren
E. M. FORSTER, edited by Malcolm Bradbury
GOETHE, edited by Victor Lange
HAWTHORNE, edited by Norman Pearson
HOPKINS, edited by A. N. Kaul
IBSEN, edited by Rolf Fjelde
JOYCE, edited by Cleanth Brooks
MILTON, edited by Louis Martz
POE, edited by Robert Regan
SOPHOCLES, edited by Thomas Woodard
TENNYSON, edited by Marguerite M. Sussman
DYLAN THOMAS, edited by Charles B. Cox
TOLSTOY, edited by Ralph E. Matlaw
VIRGIL, edited by Steele Commager
VOLTAIRE, edited by William L. Bottiglia
W. C. WILLIAMS, edited by J. Hillis Miller
WORDSWORTH, edited by M. H. Abrams